The Moulin Rouge

*A la Cancaneuse
anonyme
qui a fait sa gloire,
le Moulin-Rouge
reconnaissant*

To the nameless cancan
dancer who
raised it to its glory
– the ever-grateful
Moulin Rouge

To Pierre Dac,
who taught me about life
and who staunched its wounds.

J.P.

To Charles Trenet,
the authentic voice of France.

J.C.

To André Hornez,
composer and poet,
loved and admired more
every day.

J.P. – J.C.

The Moulin Rouge

Jacques Pessis · Jacques Crépineau

Editor of the English Edition
Andrew Lamb

ALAN SUTTON

ST. MARTIN'S PRESS

First published in the United States of America in 1990
All rights reserved. For information write:
Scholarly and Reference Books Division,
St. Martin's Press, 175 Fifth Avenue,
New York, NY 10010.

Library of Congress Cataloging-in-Publication Data

Pessis, Jacques.
  [Moulin Rouge. English]
  The Moulin Rouge / Jacques Pessis, Jacques Crepineau.
    p.   cm.
  Translation of: Le Moulin Rouge.
  ISBN 0–312–04566–2
  1. Moulin Rouge (Night club : Paris, France) – – History. 2. Music
-halls (Variety-theaters, cabarets, etc.) – – France – – Paris – –History.
I. Crépineau, Jacques. II. Title.
PN1968.F8P4713   1990
792',09443'61 – – dc20   90–37044
                                                              CIP

First published in Great Britain in 1990 by
Alan Sutton Publishing Limited
Phoenix Mill · Far Thrupp · Stroud · Gloucestershire GL5 2BU

British Library Cataloguing in Publication Data

Pessis, Jacques
  The Moulin Rouge
  1. France. Paris. Music Halls: Moulin Rouge
  I. Title II. Crepineau, Jacques
  792. 7094436

ISBN 0–86299–753–4

Printed in Italy
by S.p.A. New Interlitho, Milan

CONTENTS

FOREWORD

'*Moi, j'aime le music hall*' ('I love music-hall') is a phrase straight from the heart of Charles Trenet and one often taken up by millions of Frenchmen in chorus.

Several generations of lovers of true entertainment look back with nostalgia to those years when the joys of life could be invoked by simple melodies – the 'good old days', when entertainment did not symbolise tawdriness, artists did not represent artificiality, and a singer's talents did not consist of playing an electric guitar in front of a dummy microphone. At the end of the nineteenth and the beginning of the twentieth centuries, years which were not so extravagant as is claimed, the Goulues, the Yvette Guilberts and the Mistinguetts were the queens of Paris, indeed of the world. We feel no sadness or bitterness in acknowledging that they have never been replaced.

It is the unique adventure of these giants, immortalised by an enthusiastic public, which we propose to relive in the following pages. Through documents, most of which have lain forgotten for nearly a century, and many others which have never been published, along with items from our own personal collections, you will discover an era when there were two hundred people on the stage and many more in the audience. Stars of yesteryear, perhaps, but more in tune with the present day than ever. A period whose interpreters, gifted originally with eternal youth, have ended by becoming immortal. .

J.P. – J.C.

ACKNOWLEDGEMENTS

Our thanks to Jacki Clérico, without whose confidence we should never have been able to carry our exploration of this fabulous kingdom of the music-hall to its full conclusion; to Roland Léonar and Jean Miguel, for their unfailingly friendly assistance; to Juliette Bémachévitch and Véronique Marie, who joined the dance with enthusiasm; to Guy des Cars and L.-R. Dauven, for the illumination of their glowing memories; to Gilbert Moreau, for his somewhat suggestive shots; to Jacques Blottière and Dominique Carlin, for their very imaginative page-setting; to Euresys, who was so well able to reproduce the testimonies of an era

Extract on page 206 reprinted by permission of J.M. Dent, and those on page 207 by permission of Methuen London.

English translation by Malcolm Hall, Dursley, Gloucestershire.

Photographic credits are due for pictures on the following pages: 41: Paul Boyer; 74, 75, 79, 96: Paul Darby; 83: A. Bert; 105 – 107: Walery; 156: Harcourt; 178 – 191: Daniel Frasnay, Walter Carone, Guy Champenal and Spina, Press Villard/Barthélémy; 204, 205: R. Capa; 206, 207: Catherine Ashmore.

INTRODUCTION TO THE
ENGLISH EDITION

There is, surely, no other night spot in the world quite like it. For anyone who has visited the Moulin Rouge, it perhaps still carries a – much exaggerated – image of Parisian naughtiness. For those who have actually been fortunate enough to spend an evening there, the memory will be of a place of an exceptionally high standard of entertainment. Whichever category one belongs to, the Moulin Rouge represents as much a part of the image of Paris as Notre Dame, the Champs Élysées, the Eiffel Tower, Sacré Coeur or the Place du Tertre.

It is far from simply that image of Parisian naughtiness or the high standard of entertainment, though, that gives the Moulin Rouge its special place in popular consciousness. There are certainly other Parisian night spots – the Folies Bergère especially – that are able to compete in terms of entertainment value and have a more consistently distinguished entertainment history. What those others most obviously lack is, perhaps, threefold. Firstly there is the Moulin Rouge's location – strategically placed on the fascinating Butte Montmartre (the hill of Montmartre) at the busy Place Blanche, on the broad Boulevard de Clichy, a convenient halting point on the way up to the Place du Tertre and the Sacré Coeur. Secondly there is the quite unique image created by the revolving sails of its famous red mill – a trade mark *par excellence*, and one that other impresarios would have given their right arms to have conceived. Together the location and visual image create a photogenic quality that is quite unique.

Thirdly there is the special place that has been etched indelibly in popular consciousness by the Moulin Rouge, firstly as the home of the cancan, and secondly for the association of Henri de Toulouse-Lautrec. One can only reflect on the stroke of fate that decreed that the unique place Lautrec occupies in popular consciousness is due not simply to his paintings but – perversely – to his physical appearance. Again one wonders what better publicity any promoter could have wished than that created by his association.

The Moulin Rouge was established just over a hundred years ago now – in October 1889 – and this book is just one of the celebrations of its centenary. It records in glorious pictorial detail the triumphs and the disasters of its hundred years. The translated French text and illustrations have been retained virtually complete, but with additional material designed to make the book more accessible to an English-language readership. Alongside the triumphs, the book records also the disasters there have certainly been in its hundred-year history. Difficult though it may now be to believe, the continuity of the Moulin Rouge as a place of entertainment has by no means been assured.

Its history divides into several well-defined periods. It was opened originally as a combined dance hall and pleasure garden. It was in the dance hall – the Bal du Moulin Rouge – that the celebrated performances of the *chahut* or cancan, immortalised by Toulouse-Lautrec, took place. In the adjoining pleasure garden were various amusements and a covered stage on which music-hall turns could be watched. In this form the Moulin Rouge closed in 1902, reopening the following year as a variety theatre where operettas and revues were performed. In 1915 it was burnt down, after which it stood empty for almost ten years before again being rebuilt and reopened. A stylised version of the cancan could then once more be enjoyed in the dance hall in the basement while, in the variety theatre above, spectacular revues were staged.

This phase, too, was to be short-lived. In 1929 the theatre was given over to films, with just an occasional live show of no particular distinction. During the Second World War it struggled through with entertainment provided – mostly for soldiers – in the dance hall below. During the 1950s cabaret performances were given with distinguished international performers. However, it was only during the 1960s that it embarked upon the glamorous, high quality dinner and cabaret for which it is celebrated by visitors to Paris today.

Yet this intermittent entertainment history has been sufficient to leave an eternal mark. The cancan may not have been originated by the Moulin Rouge, but it is the form that crystallised there that has had the major effect on popular impressions. The Moulin's subsequent phase as a home of spectacular revue also made its indelible mark. It was the Moulin Rouge that, in 1908, first staged the *Valse chaloupée* or Apache Dance – the dance of two Parisian street urchins, in which the helpless woman is thrown across the stage by her partner. A generation later, it was the Moulin Rouge revues that launched such songs as *Valencia* and *Ça . . . c'est Paris*, the latter becoming one of the anthems of Paris. These Parisian songs found a ready home in the spectacular revues that were at the same time to be found elsewhere in the world – most notably on Broadway in the *Ziegfeld Follies*, the *George White Scandals* and the revues of the Shuberts, and in London's West End in the spectacular revues of C.B. Cochran. It would be wrong, though, to suggest that the Moulin Rouge was in any way an originator of the international spectacular revue style. That distinction belongs very much more to the Folies Bergère. The role of the Moulin Rouge as an innovator lay in an earlier age.

In its time the Moulin Rouge has nurtured many artists who have gone on to achieve world renown. Yvette Guilbert in its earliest days, Mistinguett in the 1900s and 1920s, Yves Montand during the 1940s are some major examples. In return it has welcomed entertainers from other countries, especially during the cabaret years of the 1950s, when performers such as Bing Crosby and Elvis Presley were to be seen there. Parisian taste has not always concurred with that elsewhere, though, as entertainers such as Johnnie Ray found to their cost.

The name 'The Moulin Rouge' has itself inspired its imitators. The traveller seeking night-time entertainment is still likely to come across Moulins, Molinos or Windmills of one colour or another around the world. New York had its own Moulin Rouge Theatre for a while – a short-lived venture just before the First World War at the theatre built by Oscar Hammerstein I on Broadway, between 44th and 45th Streets – originally opened as the Olympia Music Hall and known for most of its life as the New York Theatre. It should be remembered, though, that the word 'Moulin' did not originate with the Moulin Rouge. The Parisian Moulin Rouge itself came into being in the shadow of the Moulin de la Galette dance hall – immortalised in Renoir's painting and still to be seen on the Butte Montmartre today. Likewise, the name of London's Windmill Theatre, opened in 1931, owed nothing to Paris and everything to local history, though associations with the Moulin Rouge cannot have hindered its conversion to non-stop variety in 1932.

Stage shows and films, too, have used the Moulin Rouge, Toulouse-Lautrec and the place's early entertainers as the basis for new entertainments – most memorably, perhaps, in John Huston's 1953 film *Moulin Rouge*. At other times, as in Cole Porter's *Can-Can*, the Moulin Rouge has been only thinly disguised under other names. Over the years, indeed, the idea of a young lady of sheltered existence getting mixed up in the 'naughtiness' of Montmartre as exemplified by the Moulin Rouge has been something of a staple idea for the entertainment industry. One way and another there is a great variety of shows that have sought to evoke, honour, or simply capitalise upon the place's reputation. The works listed towards the end of this book can represent only a sample.

Reference to the landmarks that create the present-day popular image of Paris inspires the observation that, when the Moulin Rouge was created, the city was inevitably very different from today. The Eiffel Tower was opened in the very same year as the Moulin Rouge, having been constructed for the Universal Exhibition of 1889. The Basilica of the Sacré Coeur was still in course of construction – not to be consecrated until 1919. In those days Montmartre was still developing from being simply an outpost of Paris, frequented by artists and performers, and was still considered less a part of Paris than a village outside it.

Central to Parisian entertainment in 1889 was the tradition of the *café-concert*, or *caf'conc'* for short. Some of these were simply cellar drinking places with a small platform on which a performer did his turn, but others involved a specially built hall with a stage, in front of which were tables around which the clientele sat, talked, ate and drank. Others were now resembling full-scale variety theatres. The Folies Bergère in the Rue Richer had been the home of grand revues since 1886, while the Casino de Paris was to open in the Rue de Clichy in 1890, followed in 1893 by the Olympia, built in the Boulevard des Capucines on the site of a recently demolished switchback railway – the Montagnes Russes. Besides these, there were the dance halls, such as Bullier's in the Latin quarter and, in Montmartre, the Moulin de la Galette and the Élysée-Montmartre. It was on the site of another former Montmartre dance hall – the Reine Blanche – that the Moulin Rouge was built. That original Moulin Rouge, it is perhaps worth saying again, combined something of all these various types of entertainment – predominantly a dance hall, but also a pleasure garden with amusements and variety shows.

So the scene is set . . . The sails of the mill are starting to turn . . . Let the show commence!

ANDREW LAMB

I
THE ERA OF THE CANCAN

Sunday 6 October 1889. The date marks a revolution which will not be found in any school books. It concerns a subject which is very seldom studied in schools: the history of the French music-hall.

There was nothing particularly unusual in the establishment which opened its doors that evening in the Place Blanche. It had been given the name of the Moulin Rouge, and its founders, Joseph Oller and Charles Zidler, had apparently conceived it as just one more entertainment spot in the district of Montmartre. The reality was quite different. The two partners, formidable businessmen with a deep knowledge of the tastes of a well-heeled public, had prepared the ground well. Firstly they chose the ideal site, in the vicinity of the Butte Montmartre, a fashionable area where the lifestyle was not quite that found in Paris. One went there to fill one's lungs with fresh air, to saunter along its sloping streets, to pause for a drink in the shadow of the Moulin de la Galette or on the terraces of picturesque pleasure gardens, rubbing shoulders with dubious characters and their girls, arriving in groups from districts of ill repute. Brawls would break

out, sometimes ending with the flash of knives. It was around the Place Blanche in particular that the first artistic dance halls and bars blossomed. For a long time one of the most oft frequented was the Reine Blanche, where Nini-la-Belle-en-Cuisse (Nini-of-the-Beautiful-Thighs) enjoyed her greatest triumphs. This Nini was an acrobatic cancan dancer, who one evening walked on her hands, thereby displaying that she was wearing no bloomers. Far from preferring a charge against her, the policeman on duty was so stunned by what he saw that he simply exclaimed *'Cré Dieu! Les belles cuisses!'* ('God! What beautiful thighs!'). Beset by debauchery, the Reine Blanche finally closed.

Four years later there opened in the same spot, beneath a sign announcing 'Dancing, entertainment, variety', the Moulin Rouge. The name was borrowed from an old dance hall and restaurant on the Avenue d'Antin (today renamed the Avenue Franklin D. Roosevelt), and the decor was designed by Willette, one of the most noted painters of the day. The design was that of a mill, painted red, its sails revolving, with the miller's wife looking out of one window, while the miller leans out of another. It was so designed that, as the illuminated sails began to turn, the two exchanged gestures of affection. Inside, an ingenious combination of lighting and decoration evoked Spain, Normandy, Holland and other settings.

Success was immediate. From the very first evening, fashionable society and the world of writers and painters discovered the *quadrille naturaliste*, or *quadrille réaliste*, later to be immortalised as the French cancan. La Goulue (The Glutton), Valentin le Désossé (Valentin the Boneless) and other dancers, with names both vulgar and provocative, entered immediately into the legend. 'It's a great life, here comes the quadrille!' shouted one member of the audience, who was none other than Henri de Toulouse-Lautrec. As time passed, entertainments of all kinds appeared on stage in the garden. On 19 April 1890 the public gave an ovation to a collection of dances, songs and mime entitled *Circassiens et Circassiennes*; on 3 May the first spectacular took place, *Les Belles Orientales*. Early in the programme, Le Pétomane (The Farter) was a success, while a certain Nurse Valérie, doing her best to parody an English nanny, received only a few handclaps: no one then dreamed of the success which Yvette Guilbert was later to achieve.

The split between Joseph Oller and Charles Zidler, the departure of La Goulue and the ever-increasing competition from the Casino de Paris sounded the death knell for the great years of the cancan. On 13 December 1894 Paul-Louis Flers put on scenes of Montmartre, *A la pointe du pied* (On Tiptoe). The following Saturday saw the first of the weekly gala evenings. New and varied entertainments made their appearance as the months went by: a grand cycling evening on 7 February 1895, a meeting-point for poets and songwriters from 20 February onwards, children's matinées from 26 February, the famous Bal des Quat'z' Arts on 5 April, a classical concert on 13 April, a celebration in honour of the Grand Prix meeting at Longchamp on 6 October . . . On 18 May 1897, the programmes of the Jardin de Paris, temporarily moved from the Champs-Elysées on account of the Universal Exhibition, found shelter at the Moulin Rouge. It became the fashion – a night in Paris was no longer complete without a visit to the Place Blanche. The success was enormous, but short-lived. As soon as the last of the Universal Exhibition's illuminations were extinguished, the vogue for the Moulin Rouge, too, fizzled out, along with the last hopes of La Goulue . . .

The MOULIN ROUGE of 1889

Imagine a huge dance hall, at the far end of which a tiny stage has been

installed. The scenery consists of flags and bunting; on important evenings, these are supplemented by simply adding another fifty or so. In order to reach the stage, one first crosses an immense garden, laid out in summer with chairs and tables. In the midst of trees there stands an enormous stucco elephant, made for the occasion of the Universal Exhibition of 1889. By ascending a spiral staircase in one of the feet, you enter the animal's hollow belly, there to be entertained by a belly-dance. The visit costs one franc and is reserved exclusively for the gentlemen.

As for the architecture, this is revolutionary. Up to now it has always been assumed that, for this type of dance hall, the entrances are formal arcaded affairs, with porticoes possessing pilasters and balustrades, and flights of steps as if up to a temple. Willette, the architect chosen by Joseph Oller, is changing all that; you find yourself standing before the most extravagant mixture of forms and colours imaginable. In a few seconds you pass from the bullring in Granada to a thatched cottage in Normandy and then on to the windmills of Holland . . .

GALA NIGHTS

6 October 1889: the opening

The Moulin Rouge. Remember the name of this new dance hall in the Place Blanche – you've not heard the last of it. Last night the whole of Paris was there to celebrate the opening, and the show was not only on the stage, but also in the audience. On view were Their Highnesses Prince Stanislas de Poniatowski and Prince Troubetzkoi, the Comte de la Rochefoucauld, Messieurs Elie de Talleyrand and Alexandre Duval, the creator of the famous clear soups, together with the flower of literature and the arts, having the time of their lives. Picture carriage parties arriving from the chic districts of Neuilly and Passy, hobnobbing happily with natives from lower Montmartre and Rochechouart, cloth-capped roughs and young women with unkempt hair, knotted in a bun . . . Picture also the universal smiles, conspiratorial even, during the donkey rides in the Jardins de Paris, or the performance of the belly dancers inside an extraordinary giant elephant. Picture above all the collective rapture when the moment arrived for the dance called the *'quadrille naturaliste'* by some, or *'quadrille réaliste'* by others. An extravaganza worthy of Mabille, Chicart, Rigolboche, Céleste Mogador or Rose Pompon. Never have we seen an audience enjoy itself so much. The scene was indescribable: you had to be there to believe it! When, supported by the brass section, the dancers invaded the hall, whirling and kicking their legs up to a frenzied rhythm, a thrill of pleasure ran through the company. When they created what they called 'the first Palace of Woman', Messieurs Oller and Zidler were playing for high stakes. Yesterday afternoon they promised their associates that this establishment was going to become the most magnificent of all the temples of dancing and music. Already it seems to us that their gamble has succeeded. The *cafés-concerts* will not survive this hurricane, and the other dance halls will from now on seem somewhat dull. La Goulue and Valentin le Désossé, whose performance at the Élysée-Montmartre we have already reported, will find here true scope for their talents. They are gaiety personified and unfold their act well! In the wings, before coming on the stage, the former, with her bust hidden rather than displayed and her coiled-up hair topped by a kind of clover-leaf orchid, hardly inspired any sense of gaiety. As for the latter – the 'Boneless One' – his ugliness was equalled only by his agility. Monsieur Zidler had clearly chosen this item in memory of the days when he followed his trade of butcher, practising daily the art of dismemberment.

This morning the Archbishop of Paris is understood to be concerned, and one can picture the family discussions: good ladies threatening their husbands with divorce if they refuse to take them to the Place Blanche, to introduce them to Le Désossé . . .

In the coming weeks everyone will undoubtedly be hastening in that direction. But what then? For how long will this state of grace continue? That is the question being asked by all observers. Will the Moulin Rouge be a flash in the pan, or will it live on?

Place Blanche

JARDIN de PARIS
et
MOULIN ROUGE
Réunis

Saison 1897

Tous les Soirs à 8ʰ¼

SPECTACLE-CONCERT-PROMENADE

Dimanches et Fêtes à 2ʰ

MATINÉES DANSANTES

The Jardin de Paris, where today's Moulin Rouge now stands

French Cancan

Poster by Roubille

The cancan at the Moulin Rouge evolved from forty years of choreographic activity in the dance halls and *cafés-concerts* of Paris. Céleste Mogador, leading dancer of the Bal Mabille and queen of the polka, devised the first quadrille in about 1850. Its success was immediate and it was copied by Rose Pompon, a pretty, roguish-looking blonde, celebrated particularly for her claim that her father was the illegitimate son of Charles X. In London, in 1861, Charles Morton, the inventor of the modern music-hall, presented it on the stage of the Oxford Theatre, renaming it *French Cancan* (French tittle-tattle), since it came from France and was causing a stir. For the Goulue of the day, a certain Aniola Kiralfy, it was a triumph, but only short-lived. It was considered too daring, and its performance on British stages was forbidden. In Paris, on the other hand, the popularity of the rhythm was increasing. In the dance halls of Montmartre it brought pleasure to humble factory girls, seamstresses and dressmaker's apprentices, seeking to forget their arduous day's work. Little by little it emerged in its definitive form.

To the furious rhythms of Offenbach it takes eight minutes to dance the authentic quadrille, demanding of its performers great qualities of balance, suppleness, acrobatics and rhythm. The dancers refuse to perform to the music of certain quadrille bands, which they do not consider to be in perfect harmony. The average cancan dancer is some five and a half feet tall. The black stockings, the suspenders and the rustle of the skirt are *de rigueur*, and tradition demands that a few inches of flesh be allowed to appear below a mass of lace.

The first souvenir postcards of the Moulin Rouge: the principal steps of the cancan

BAL DU

MOULIN ROUGE

TOUS LES SOIRS à 9 hres

The leg behind the shoulder. One of the concluding steps of the cancan, and also a picture from 1898, signed by Louis Legrand, a contemporary and disciple of Toulouse-Lautrec

The cancan rapidly became a ritual dance, a vaguely erotic ceremony. That the priestesses were young and pretty was of less importance than that they could demonstrate their ability to do the splits. The stronger sex thus found itself excluded from the quadrilles, with the exception of the character portrayed by Valentin le Désossé. It was the feminists' first victory . . .

Every evening at about ten o'clock, at a signal from the orchestra directed by Mabille, the spectators would gather around three dancers and a gentleman. With exemplary grace, the girls grasped the edges of their skirts and began to tap their feet in a pizzicato rhythm, before raising the leg, in a great flight of lace. Guided by the gentleman, each girl in turn moved in a circle, before subsiding to the floor in the splits.

As for the solo routine, which was originally performed by men, at the Moulin Rouge this was to take on its definitive form. Each dancer in her turn was allowed to give free expression to her own imagination, while however observing one ritual: to divest a chosen spectator of his hat, by a nimble and adroit sweep of the foot, to great hilarity among the audience. An ovation would be reserved for the most unexpected hat dislodgement.

TOULOUSE LAUTREC
The Commemoration of Montmartre

Henri de Toulouse-Lautrec, La Goulue and Montmartre are indissolubly linked in history. Without the painter, the notoriety of the dancer would never have crossed the oceans or survived the years. Without her, his pictures and his posters would perhaps never have become immortal. Without the two of them, the fame of the Butte would doubtless never have spread beyond the limits of Paris. It was in 1887, two years before the Moulin Rouge opened its doors, that the paths of these two exceptional creatures crossed for the first time. The young artist had taken to

Yvette Guilbert

frequenting the *cafés-concerts* of Montmartre as a way of forgetting the ailments and the pain from which he had suffered since his childhood. The ambiance of the district and its pervading laughter constituted for him the best of remedies. Several times a week he would climb the Rue Lepic and settle himself beneath the trees, a bowl of mulled wine before him. One day, at the Moulin de la Galette, his gaze fell upon a young girl with blonde hair, who was whirling among the dancers.

She was called La Goulue, and the spectator was destined to be there for the next eight years, at the Elysée-Montmartre where she earned her first wages, and then at the Moulin Rouge. In the Place Blanche, he was present every night in the front row, perched on a stool near the bar, his moustache perpetually dipped in a glass of spirits, ecstatic whenever the frothy skirts swept across his face. The *quadrille naturaliste* became the principal preoccupation of his existence and of his canvasses. This was a world which he valued more than any other, but he was not deceived by it. He knew that, behind the façade of revelry, the pretty dresses, the colours and the *joie de vivre*, there lay hidden vice, evil and death. Through his paintings this milieu, previously considered of little account, was gradually to find favour with art lovers whose first appreciative discoveries were the posters which appeared on the walls of Paris in 1891.

It was the start of his notoriety, the sweetest of revenge on life itself. The dancers became his friends; they called him 'Monsieur Lautrec', or 'Toulouse'. As they passed, he would climb on to a chair to receive a kiss, which he would return noisily with 'lips like the rim of a bath', as Yvette Guilbert put it.

La Goulue did not conceal her appreciation of the work of the artist with the stunted body whom she called affectionately 'the hairy little man' or 'my nice little man'. 'He makes me feel tall,' she would say maliciously. 'When I see my backside in his paintings, it looks so beautiful.' Such was their alliance that, each Friday, she was admitted to the studio in the Rue Tourlaque, where he entertained his friends.

Toulouse-Lautrec soon discovered a nearly equal passion for Jane Avril. When she displaced La Goulue on the stage of the Moulin Rouge, she too found a place in his heart. Accustomed to frequenting literary circles, she appreciated the artist's sense of humour and knew how to demonstrate her affection and admiration for him. For his part, he found this girl with 'the face of a gloomy little rat . . . extremely disturbing'. She, in her turn, was rapidly supplanted by Yvette Guilbert, whom he had known at the Chat Noir. In the Place Blanche, he soon succumbed in his usual manner.

Toulouse-Lautrec also produced many drawings for the magazines of the

period. His work appeared in *Le Figaro Illustré* and in *Rire*. Gradually he drifted away from the Moulin Rouge, which became of diminishing importance both to his artistic nature and to his thirst for life. He certainly continued to drink to excess, against the advice of Joseph Oller and some of his close friends. He discovered other places of amusement, though he did not forget the past, and particularly La Goulue. Thus his door was readily opened to her when, on 6 April 1895, she sent him the following letter:

'My dear friend, I shall be calling by on 8 April at two o'clock in the afternoon. I

The artist in his Montmartre studio, painting 'The dance at the Moulin Rouge' (1890)

should be very grateful if you would find the time to paint something for my booth. It is at the Trône, I'm on the left as you go in – I've got a very good position. If you tell me where I am to buy the canvasses, I will let you have them the same day.'

Thus it was that, in memory of the 'good old days', he produced two immense advertisement panels which became very famous.

In September 1900 fate ordained that the painter should encounter his goddess for the last time. At the Foire du Trône he glimpsed her in her booth, living between a stray dog and a tame swallow; the odour of the menagerie turned his stomach. He did not even feel any urge to greet the ruin which she had become. The decay of the figure on which his imagination had feasted induced him, however, to make a further pilgrimage to the Moulin Rouge. There he found only the shadow of the dance hall of former days, and a few dancers whose ungainly steps gave the impression that they were in the last stages of tuberculosis. He no longer saw anything with which he could identify; the Montmartre that he had known and loved was no more. He knew that it was the end of a world. He was not to know that it was also the beginning of a legend.

18

The works of Toulouse-Lautrec based on the Moulin Rouge

The Rider:
Canvas by Toulouse-Lautrec, purchased from the artist by Joseph Oller and Charles Zidler, and displayed at the entrance to the establishment on the night it first opened.

The Dance (1890):
A canvas on which appears Valentin le Désossé, one dancer who seems to be La Goulue, another who can only be Jane Avril, together with Varney, Maurice Guibert, Paul Sescau, François Gauzi and Marcellin Desboutins.

Exhibited in 1890 at the Salon des Indépendents, and then hung at the Moulin Rouge until 1893.

La Goulue and Valentin le Désossé:
Studies for the poster of the Moulin Rouge.

The Promenade (1891):
In the background, La Goulue and Jane Avril.

La Goulue (1891):
This is considered to be the first genuine poster by Toulouse-Lautrec. In the foreground, Valentin le Désossé; in the centre, La Goulue. The wording can take two forms: 'Bal/tous les soirs/La Goulue' ('Dancing/every evening/La Goulue') and 'Tous les soirs/Moulin Rouge/les mercredis et samedis bal masqué' ('Every evening/Moulin Rouge/masked ball Wednesdays and Saturdays').

The Englishman at the Moulin Rouge (1892)

The Two Waltzers (1892):
With Mlle Cha-Hu-Ka-o and Jane Avril. Seated, the painter Charles Conder and François Ganzi.

La Goulue and her Sister (1892):
With, in the middle ground, the back view of the theatre critic Francisque Sarcey, talking to the impresario Warner.

La Goulue entering the Moulin Rouge (1892):
She is shown accompanied by two women – on her right La Môme Fromage, merged with her sister because of the crowded scene, and on her left Nini Patte en l'Air.

The Start of the Quadrille (1892):
The moment when the well-dressed spectators take their places at the tables, leaving the floor free for the professional dancers of the cancan.

At the Moulin Rouge (1892):
Seated around the table, from left to right: Edouard Dujardin, la Macarona, Paul Sescau and Maurice Gulbert. In the foreground, on the right, facing: Nelly C. In the background, La Goulue arranging her hat, and the silhouettes of Doctor G. Tapie de Celeyran and of Toulouse-Lautrec in bowler hats.

Jane Avril dancing (1892):
Monsieur Warner seated in the background.

Jane Avril entering the Moulin Rouge (1892):
This picture was the inspiration for Jacques Emile-Blanche's description of Rosemary, the heroine of his novel *Aymeris*.

Jane Avril leaving the Moulin Rouge (1892):
On the left, the back view of the painter Charles Conder.

At the Moulin Rouge (1893):
This was used to illustrate the articles by Geffroy in *Le Figaro Illustré* of July 1893 and February 1894.

The Female Clown Cha-Hu-Ka-o (1895):
This was an illustration for 'Carnivals' by René Maizeray in *Le Figaro Illustré* of July 1901. The clown is arm-in-arm with Gabrielle la Danseuse. Behind them is Tristan Bernard wearing a bowler hat. King Milan of Serbia was the original owner of this painting, having paid, at that time, an exorbitant price for it. It escaped without damage from the massacre and looting of Belgrade by Kovak, in the course of which King Alexander and his queen were assassinated.

The Dance at the Moulin Rouge (1895):
The famous advertisement panels in La Goulue's booth at the Foire du Trône. One shows La Goulue and Valentin le Désossé on the dance floor; in the other, Toulouse-Lautrec pays tribute to the former queen of the quadrille, become belly dancer. The dimensions of these works and their original purpose make them exceptional. In 1904 they were exhibited at the Salon d'Automne, in 1910 they were to be seen in the Musée des Arts Décoratifs, and in 1926 they finished up in the hands of the well-known dealers Barbazangues et Hodeberg, and are now cut up into eight separate pieces, not counting wastage.

The sole reason for this last operation was, of course, the profit motive. The smaller pictures thus created could be acquired by philistines eager to hang them on the walls of their suburban living rooms. The scandal was enormous. Georges Duthuit, a prominent critic of the day, and Robert Rey, a conservationist, were incensed at the treatment to which the pictures had been subjected. Four years later, after intervention by the national museums, the two paintings were restored to their original condition and became the property of the State. They were then valued at four hundred thousand francs. Thirty years earlier, La Goulue had sold them for eight hundred francs. . .

Jane Avril

The female clown Cha-Hu-Ka-o at the Moulin Rouge (1895)

La Goulue and her sister at the Moulin Rouge (1892)

La Goulue

AMBASSADRESS OF PLEASURE

Her name was Louise Weber, but she was called La Goulue (The Glutton) because, ever since her adolescence, she had been in the habit of draining the glasses dry in bars. The story of her life echoes the classic French cancan: a reckless pace, with high points and low ones, and plenty of splits. Her character was such as could have inspired Émile Zola to write a new version of *Nana*. Born in Clichy around 1865, she was brought up by her laundress mother and taught

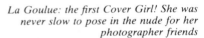
La Goulue: the first Cover Girl! She was never slow to pose in the nude for her photographer friends

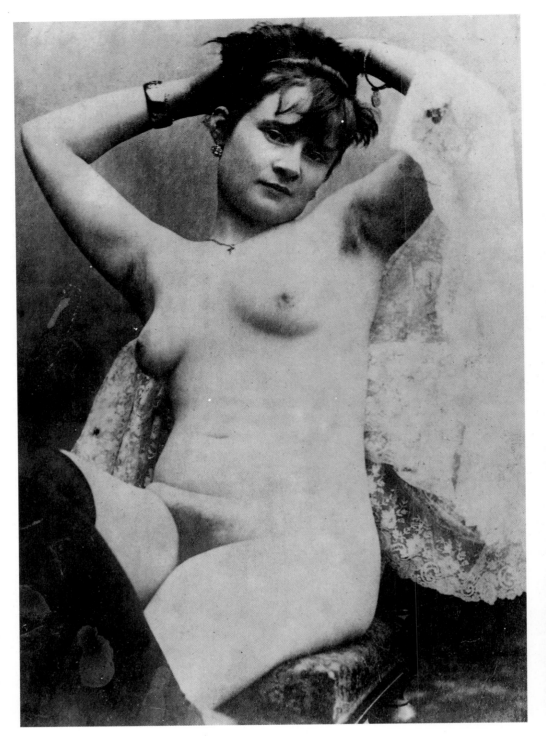

to read by the nuns. At that time, her greatest pleasure consisted of trying on the fine linen left by the customers. Having to wash it – that was quite another matter . . . Her family environment and the opportunities life seemed to offer were clearly not to her taste. Her mind was fixed solely on dancing. On the day of her first communion, she wore dancing shoes which had been stolen from a trapeze artist, a customer of her mother's who had left them for cleaning. At sixteen, in order to earn her living, she took a job in a laundry, in the Rue de la Goutte d'Or, the wash-house described by Zola in *L'Assommoir*. Between one load of washing and the next, she earned a little money selling flowers in the passages. Every evening, unbeknown to her mother, she would deck herself in garments borrowed from the

customers and take herself off to the local dance hall. At a late hour she would return to the inevitable parental displeasure. Greeted by her mother with: 'Think of your reputation, you wretched girl', she could not resist the retort: 'My reputation? If you go to the Île Saint-Ouen, you'll find it there, provided it has shown a little patience!'

She had her first amorous adventure in that same district, at the age of thirteen, on a fine summer's evening. For years afterwards she would remember the young artilleryman with affection: 'Well, soldiers – they bring you luck, you know.'

On the Rue Chaplat, the Rue du Sabot, the Boulevard de la Chapelle, she acquired a reputation as an extrovert, laughing girl who, better than any, was versed in the art and manner of conversing with men.

She met first of all Auguste Renoir, with whom she fell in love and for whom she agreed to pose. He carried her off to the Place Pigalle, where she fell in with 'la louée', a set, as popular as it was select, of models who posed nude solely for the love of art. The rate charged was one hundred sous per sitting, or ten times the wages of a humble factory-girl!

One evening two of her dancing partners, Charlot the removal man and Charles Destauques, nicknamed the intrepid Bottle-Drainer, took her to the Grand Véfour, a fashionable dance hall where gentlemen in evening-dress, with side-whiskers and monocles, were captivated by this young girl in milkmaid's dress who kicked her legs so high and so agreeably. They invited her to dance, bought her glasses of champagne and threw gold coins in her hair and in her slippers. Her first triumph showed unquestionably where her future lay. A little while after, she started to frequent the Élysée-Montmartre, where she encountered the same enthusiasm. The management of this establishment was well aware of the advantages offered by such an attraction, and procured her participation at minimal cost, simply by according her free entry. This dance hall became the rendezvous for fashionable Paris, and Joseph Oller, who was looking for dancers for the Moulin Rouge, succumbed to her charm. He engaged her immediately for the *grand quadrille*. Thus it was that this unknown girl of the streets, who lacked any glamour-girl 'sexiness', became overnight the queen of Parisian sensuality. With an instinctive understanding of how to exploit to her own advantage the atmosphere, the lights, the music, the flags, the intoxication and the unexpected, she chose to push eccentricity to the limit. She was the only woman who went bare-headed (for the rest a hat was obligatory) and she could dance on the tables as no one else could. Saluting the audience with a disrespectful bow, she would display, to those who wished to see, the heart which she had had embroidered on the back of her drawers. Her admirers, men above all suspicion, dressed in black and wearing top hats, would shout with exultation when, at the end of the *galop*, she succeeded in removing their headgear with the toe of her shoe. Other cancan dancers were to try it with less dexterity, and more than one nose would suffer in consequence! She was earning eight hundred francs per month, without counting tours abroad and fees which she collected for performances for visiting princes.

She took up residence in Montmartre, in a little house in the Rue Norvins with a garden where the flowers were carefully tended by her friend Valentin le Désossé. In public she seemed capricious, not to say insufferable. She displayed an appalling character and, when she was in a bad mood, no one dared to speak to her. She thought herself the queen of Paris, went about in her own carriage (the height of fashion at that time), arrived for rehearsals leading a little goat, and agreed to pose for photographs which were regarded as shocking. She was seen flaunting a low neckline, a diadem in her hair, a glass of champagne in her hand and legs apart, one foot on the floor, the other carelessly supported on the arm of a chair. People disapproved of her vocabulary, capable, it was said, of making a squadron of the municipal guard blush. At the Moulin Rouge she took part in processions, gala nights and parades, her breasts outside her bodice, surveying with disdain those she called 'the crowd of little tarts'.

La Goulue at the age of sixteen, during her early days at the Elysée-Montmartre and the Moulin de la Galette

Where her private life was concerned, rumours proceeded apace. Great interest was taken in her obvious amorous interest in La Môme Fromage (The Cheese Kid). She showed respect only for the Church, and regularly exchanged flowers, fruit and jam-making recipes with its representatives.

In the Place Blanche, on 6 April 1895, La Goulue created a sensation. Bored with the cancan and at the height of her glory, she announced that she was leaving the Moulin Rouge to set up her own show. She was at that time very rich, and had decided to invest today's equivalent of three hundred thousand francs (£30,000) in a fairground booth. Abandoning the *galop*, she specialised now in the belly-dance. By this time her conceit bordered on obsession: she believed that, at the mention of her name, the crowds would roll up *en masse*.

Wearing a clinging, flesh-coloured costume, much less becoming than her petticoats of earlier days, shod in ankle-boots and cracking a whip, her voice perpetually hoarse, she tried to achieve the impossible in order to attract the public. The response did not measure up to her expectations. La Goulue without the Moulin Rouge was clearly of no interest to anyone. From the Foire du Trône to the festival at Neu-Neu, with the bearded lady on one side and some dwarfs on the other, she slowly came to realize that she had made a gigantic mistake. Alas, too late. Her fall was to be as sudden as her rise. Rather than attempting to return to her former heights, she chose to sink further. She began by dissipating what remained of her savings in high living and the bottle. Like Nana, she began to frequent women's bars; a friend ruined himself for her; she sold all her jewellery.

In June 1899 she went into partnership with Pezon, the animal-tamer and star of the fair at Neuilly. The entry of La Goulue into the lions' cage was announced as the attraction of the menagerie and was one of history's first examples of misleading publicity. The wild beasts were not as dangerous as some of the audience in the Place Blanche, and the entertainment verged on the ridiculous. Carrying a sort of cauliflower-green net, the female tamer of somewhat monstrous form tried, in vain, to awaken four animals of interest only to a taxidermist. Paranoid, she proclaimed that the whole world was against her and that, out of jealousy, someone had poisoned her favourite panther, which she loved above all else and who loved her in return. In 1903 she was back at Saint-Ouen. She, who could have become one of the richest women of her age, was nothing more than human flotsam. Her home was in a disreputable apartment building without windows, her companion an individual with a pock-marked face. They were drunk from morning till evening; the rows and the threats were so frequent that in the end they were evicted. Around 1910, Francis Carco came across her at the encampment of a fair, and the portrait he paints of her demonstrates the extent of her decay:

'When I met La Goulue at the fair, she was an old woman. For all that, her age was scarcely important. Her pale complexion, her warm pupils dilated with pleasure, her splendid legs, her carriage, her attitude, her avid and lewd expression haunted me, despite myself. The light, the smell of the acetylene lamps, the wind vibrating the canvas painted by Lautrec . . . As if by a spell, the pitiful booth on its trestles where this heavily-built, tired, painted, hoarse gossip put on her show was transformed into a kind of palace, an extravagant Olympus.'

*Top left, Rayon d'Or. On the right, La Goulue and L'Elancé.
Bottom, Margot, Églantine and La Goulue*

Her decline continued during the war. Her last lion died of hunger, she sold off her booth and found herself on the street. In about 1925 a writer, Sylvain Bonmariage, discovered her in Neuilly-sur-Marne. Her hair was white and she was toothless.

'She was a stout old woman, completely lacking in intellect, and we had the utmost difficulty in getting her to say a few words. She understood nothing of what we wanted from her. Now and again, a flash of light would gleam from the darkness. We started her off:

"Monsieur de Lautrec? Oh yes, sir, I knew him. That's a long time ago, Monsieur de Lautrec. . . A small coffee and rum please. I had plenty of fun in those days . . . It's seven years now since I was last in Montmartre. It must have changed a lot . . . Poor Monsieur de Lautrec. Do you think I could have another little coffee and rum?"'

La Goulue and Grille d'Égout in the cancan

In 1928 she returned to Montmartre, selling peanuts, matches and cigarettes on the pavements from the Moulin Rouge to the Cigale. No one recognised her of course. Her thoughts, as she watched the crowd arriving to applaud Mistinguett, may be imagined. Legend has it that she managed to get into Aristide Bruant's former Mirliton cabaret, which had been converted into a poor-house. She was ready to take on any job, from cashier to housekeeper. On 21 January 1929, as she lay dying, she asked for a priest.

'Father,' she managed to murmur with what strength remained, 'will the Good Lord pardon me? Will there be a small place for me in heaven? You see, I'm La Goulue . . .'

The Good Lord has surely not refused her this corner in paradise. It would be the smallest of compensations when all her earthly life, both on the stage and off it, was spent in the underworld.

La Goulue at home . . .

*The finale of the cancan: a rare colour photo-
graph of the period*

The celebrated splits of La Goulue

WHAT THEY SAID ABOUT LA GOULUE

'There is about her a faith which nobody else possesses; sometimes smiling, sometimes shy, bold or feline, as supple as a glove.'

(Toulouse-Lautrec)

'With her firm chin, her halo of red hair and the very distinctive carriage of her head, she has that innate nobility which belongs to the women of a people of ancient lineage.'

(Jacques Lassaigne)

'In her, one notices the grasping face, the greedy profile, the grim mouth, the hard eyes. To put it plainly, she dances with jerky movements. She is of low intelligence, coarse, irritable and shrewish with her companions.'

(Gustave Coquiot)

'A great fishwife, a repugnant mound of fat.'

(Jean Lorrain)

'A superb girl, with an insolent beauty, bursting with freshness and health, so desirable, yet extremely vulgar in her language and her bearing. One of the "delights of the flesh" kind.'

(Jane Avril)

'Pretty, elegant in a vulgar kind of way, blonde, with a fringe level with the eyebrows. She wore her long hair coiled up so that it did not get in the way while she was dancing.'

(Yvette Guilbert)

'For some she epitomises drunkenness. For me she represents excess, seizure of possession, the release of the passions, savagery. She has the blood of a revolutionary. A sort of unconscious animal caught in lassos of sound, beat, rhythm and brass, one who leaps, who gnaws the atmosphere. She is both indiscipline and beauty.'

(Edmond Heuzé, dancer at the Moulin Rouge and, much later on, a member of the Institut de France)

'She was not at all pretty. She differed from her partner, Jane Avril, by satisfying the rather vulgar taste of that period, when the dancers' nicknames suggested drains, bar fittings and artillery equipment.'

(Pierre Mac Orlan)

JANE AVRIL

MAD ON DANCING

S he was the soloist of the quadrille. She was blonde, and they called her 'Jeanne la Folle' (Mad Jeanne), because she was mad on dancing, or 'Mélinite' (a type of explosive), because she had an explosive appearance: both nicknames she detested, with good reason. Her exuberance was only a façade, for her true personality had nothing in common with the back-chat and the provocativeness of a Goulue. Distinguished and refined, she was, they said, 'a governess who had fallen in with the rabble of the *chahut*'. When not dancing the quadrille, she moved in literary circles and among the regulars at the

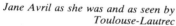

Jane Avril as she was and as seen by Toulouse-Lautrec

Chat Noir. She was nevertheless not as virginal as she appeared. She displayed an imagination which verged on instability. She was a *demi-ingénue* lost in a world of beauties wearing price-tags. The English writer Arthur Symons summed up her personality when he said that she 'had about her an air of depraved virginity', and that she was 'the more provocative because she played as a prude, with an assumed modesty, *décolletée* nearly to the waist'. He referred to 'her morbid, vague, ambiguous grace'. She presented a madness of the body joined to that of the soul.

She was born in Paris in 1868, of a frivolous Parisienne and an Italian Marquis, Luigi de Font. Red-haired at birth,

her adolescence was traumatic. Beaten by her mother, she ran away from home and, at the age of sixteen, found herself in a lunatic asylum under the direction of Professor Charcot at the Salpêtrière. Whether it was a miracle or her destiny, she had landed in an environment to which, in the circumstances, she could hardly have aspired. The sisters adored her, treated her as the child of the house and spoiled her. A feast was even arranged in her honour, followed by a masked ball in a marquee. Intoxicated by the atmosphere, she sprang up like a young deer and whirled round and round before the doctors. It was her first flirtation with music and dancing, and

The Moulin Rouge as seen by Willette

more than that ... Her sudden *joie de vivre* made the specialists aware that she was perhaps not as mad as her family contended. After several examinations, they declared her cured. Her mother prepared to receive her with open arms, but Jane went in the opposite direction and made her home with certain ladies of the town. She began to frequent the Bullier dance hall, at the top of the Boulevard Saint-Michel, where all doubt about her love of dancing was eliminated. Her slim figure resulted in her first nickname: 'Silk Thread'. At the Closerie des Lilas, she got to know the individuals who formed the basis of her real intellectual family: Moréas, Paul Fort, Mallarmé, Verlaine, Oscar Wilde, Arsène Houssaye, whose 'secretary' she was one day to be. To earn her living, she became a rider at the Hippodrome in the Avenue de l'Alma (at that time under the direction of Charles Zidler), and then a cashier at the Universal Exhibition of 1889. Under the protection of Charles Zidler, she joined the Moulin Rouge.

Her gentleness and her breeding won the respect of the other performers. Dressed always in red, with a black hat, sometimes rather heavily made-up, she resembled, it was said, an orchid without the poison. Bending her pliant body until her back was practically touching the dusty floor, she danced with restraint, holding her petticoats until, with her leg extended, she tapped out the rhythm of *Orphée aux enfers* (Orpheus in the Underworld). She became the only dancer who was permitted to wear coloured undergarments, while her companions had to be satisfied with white – scarcely matching the reality beneath. Her improvisations earned ovations. Applause represented her main wealth, since she was not paid. That did not trouble her – rather the contrary. Later on when, of necessity, she took a fee, she lost, by her own admission, her 'customary pleasure'. It was an attitude to life which led her regularly to forsake the dance hall in the Place Blanche, only to return with renewed satisfaction. Each time she reappeared the whole audience would be on its feet, singing 'The Return of Avril'! Such popularity, naturally, could only provoke jealousies. A story was put about that she was a school teacher who had been dismissed (the ultimate disgrace!), when she did not even possess a certificate of primary education. La Goulue asserted that 'she is a humbug and she'll finish up as a frightful little bourgeoise'. That was not really how it turned out.

Between appearances at the Moulin Rouge, we also find her dancing at the Jardin de Paris, at the Eldorado, at the Tabarin and at the Théâtre Sarah Bernhardt, miming at the Folies Bergère, partnering Mistinguett at the Casino de Paris, queen of the cancan at London's Palace Theatre and in Madrid, a transatlantic comedienne in *The Belle of New York*, then with the Bouffes Parisiens in

THE WHO'S-WHO OF THE CANCAN

Grille d'Égout
(Drainage Grating)

She had been a school-mistress. It was Henri Rochefort who gave her the name, on account of the gaps between her teeth. The contrast between her and La Goulue is startling. Meticulous in her work, gayer, more voluptuous, her performance was not so much exciting as amusing; she raised the *chahut* to the level of a gavotte. She was intelligent, frank and well brought-up, tending to seek the company of those from which she could learn something new. Thus she became the teacher and close friend of Réjane, who asked her to dance in Meilhac's *Ma Cousine*. Its success did not, however, measure up to her hopes. She withdrew from the entertainment world, and finished her days in the obscurity of a caretaker's lodge.

La Môme Fromage
(The Cheese Kid)

Her nickname derives from the slang, whereby the name 'Fromage' (Cheese) is applied to the youngest in the workshop. Thus, at the start of her career, La Môme Fromage was the youngest of the apprentices in a leading dressmaker's in the Rue du Quatre Septembre. She had short legs and wide shoulders. It was said that La Goulue was rather fond of her, in a way not readily acknowledged in those days.

La Sauterelle
(The Grasshopper)

Very acrobatic, and the indefatigable member of the troupe. She ended up running a bar in Rheims.

Nini Patte en l'Air
(Nini Foot-in-the Air)

Brunette, ugly and vulgar. According to the English writer Arthur Symons, her nickname derived from her individual trick, 'a particular quiver of the foot as the leg is held rigid in the air'. Her real name was Hervé. She claimed to be a widow

and was accustomed to use the name of 'the Widow Monier'. The success of the quadrille gave her the idea of opening a French Cancan School, a dance academy which was for some time the nursery of the quadrille, numbering La Sirène, Cigarette, Étoile Filante, Follette, Eglantine and Épi d'Or among its pupils. The last two even obtained a booking in London, together with Jeanne Fees, known as Demi-Siphon, who died after suffering an injury while doing the splits.

The school's reputation was to deteriorate rapidly. According to the newspapers, these activities were only a cover. Nini, they said, boarded the girls under her roof and admitted members of the male sex to her classes! Some time after this first scandal, worse was to be alleged about her singing classes. Indignant, she gave up teaching and retired to the provinces, where she married. There she apparently settled down happily, though always hurt by what, to her dying day, she believed to have been a conspiracy.

La Môme Cri Cri, La Tonkinoise, Georgette Macarona

The last of these owed her nickname to her complete mastery of the art of the belly-dance. These three sisters, whose father was a poulterer on the Boulevard Montparnasse, tried several times to steal the show from La Goulue. They were unsuccessful.

Rayon d'Or
(Ray of Gold)

She was tall and sandy-haired. Her real name was Chrétiennot. Her nickname had nothing to do with a social status which made her an exception, being the only priestess of the cancan who managed to make her fortune. The reason for this was that, at the beginning of 1890, she went off with a customer, a rich American who had come to France to show off the latest improvements to Thomas Edison's phonograph. The happy pair

became gold prospectors in Alaska, struck it rich and became multi-millionaires. Homesick, Rayon d'Or managed to persuade her partner to go and live in Paris. However, one day, his taste for adventure got the better of him and she consented to follow. They embarked on a boat for New York and that was the last anyone ever heard of them.

La Mistral

A dancer who, away from the Moulin Rouge, encountered many disappointments. Like La Goulue, she ended up selling paper streamers and balls of confetti in the bars of Montmartre.

Other dancers, in alphabetical order:

Arc en Ciel
Camélia
La Canadienne
Cascadeuse
Cha-Hu-Ka-O
Cigale
Clair de Lune
La Comète
Diamant
Eclipse
L'Étoile filante
La Follette
Galipette
Gavrochinette
La Gazelle
Gigue
La Grenouille
La Grue
Hirondelle
La Japonaise
Miss Rigolette
La Môme Caca
Muguet la Limonnière
Myosotis
La Panthère
Pâquerette
Pigeonnette
La Pirouette
Risette
Serpentine
Serpolette
La Sylphide
La Torpille
La Tour Eiffel
Vif-Argent
Violette
Vol au Vent

The fee for their performance was six to eight francs per day. In addition an allowance was paid by the management to cover laundry expenses.

Claudine à Paris, and even as a tragedy actress, playing Anitra in *Peer Gynt* – a genre of which she confessed she understood nothing but which satisfied her natural curiosity, her taste for variety and her need for culture.

A varied professional existence matched her private life. 'There were certainly those who loved me,' she says in her autobiography. 'I loved in return, though each time in a different way. On this score, I hope that I may be pardoned.'

Her love affairs were many, indeed countless. Her lovers included Auguste Renoir, who painted her portrait; Alphonse Allais, who asked her to marry him and then, on being refused, pursued her along the Rue Trudaine, revolver in hand, half laughing, half weeping; a prince who, madly in love with her, wanted them to die together; and an American in whose company she passed several happy years in New York.

In her heart these lovers were always of lesser importance than her friends: her doctor, Théodore de Wyzema, of whom she said 'I have never met a being who could be compared to him', and Henri de Toulouse-Lautrec, whom she was one of the few in the Place Blanche not to scorn. He wrote about her: 'She is as delicate as a narcissus flower, and as pale.'

In due course the birth of a son would quell her craze for life and for dancing. 'The years of discretion have arrived at last – I should say the years of senility, when we commit follies no more.'

In 1910 she married the painter Maurice Biais and retired to Jouy-en-Josas, where the years passed happily until the death of her companion.

Finding herself penniless, she settled down discreetly, almost anonymously, in an old people's home, where she passed her days embroidering and knitting, never referring to her brilliant past except with a few close friends. She declared that she preferred her provincial peace to the frenetic life of a Paris which she no longer recognised. She returned to it only once with pleasure. In 1941, her most faithful admirers tracked her down and arranged a celebration in her honour in the capital, a final appearance which was also her grand finale. Before a mesmerised audience, she danced an improvised ballet and, in that instant, rediscovered all the grace of her youth, a miracle which she explained in her own way.

'In spite of my white hairs and all that people say, I can let myself be carried away by music. Perhaps it is one of the many ways of expressing ourselves which the world likes to describe as madness. Well, that may be so, but it has always been agreeable and comforting to me, helping me through life, and I have remained a slave to its enchantment.

'If there are dance halls in the other life, it is quite possible that I shall be invited to perform the *Danse Macabre* . . .'

La Torpille

La Goulue

La Môme Fromage

Observations on the cancan

'This quadrille possesses a number of features which render it memorable: the cool indecency of the women, the eager crowd six-deep around the stage, having come in the hope of seeing something daring, their excitement being communicated to the performers.' (a reporter of the day)

'The dancers' skirts, some twelve metres in circumference, were of panels and frothy lace, as were the drawers. The effect of the black stockings against this snowy whiteness was to emphasise the shape of the legs.'
(Jane Avril)

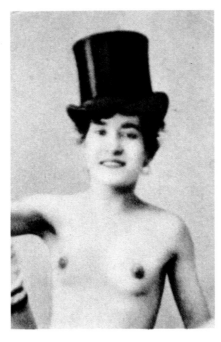

La Goulue

Nini Patte en l'Air

THE QUEENS of the CANCAN

Miss Rigolette

Hirondelle

Grille d'Égout

La Sauterelle

Rayon d'Or

The Audience at the Moulin Rouge

The cancan by J.F. Raffaelli, on whom Toulouse-Lautrec based his own technique

The main hall of the Moulin Rouge with the cancan in progress: the whole hall erupts . . .

Every evening at eight o'clock the working class public would stream along to the Moulin Rouge: menial workers, shop-assistants, dressmakers and the residents of the Place Blanche all came to enjoy themselves on the pretext of drinking a cup of coffee.

Half-past nine would herald the arrival of the tradespeople and businessmen seeking to forget their worries, students, elegant women, lords and ladies, ambassadors, royalty, visiting foreigners, and those whose social standing obliged them to adopt a subterfuge for frequenting low company. Artists wanting to share the emotions of the public, the better to understand it, politicians declaring that, in the Place Blanche, they are able to probe the reality of their opponents' souls better than anywhere else, priests in plain clothes whose duty it is, they assure us, to experience the sins of the flesh 'in the field' . . .

Several times a week the evenings would go on much later than planned. Charles Zidler gave his dancers full per-mission to enjoy themselves and even to kick over the traces after the show. Thus, for their own amusement, they would perform the most extraordinary steps. Fluttering about before the large mirrors in the hall, they had no difficulty at all in persuading the regulars of the estab-lishment to join them. For a quarter of an hour the orchestra would contribute the rhythm and then, in unison, the audience would take over. This was the signal for a cacophony which would sometimes last until dawn. Highly practised ears were needed to distinguish the laughter, the singing, and the distinctive sound made by the explosion of champagne corks. Shirt-fronts and detachable collars became limp, top hats rolled across the floor and garters were converted into arm-bands. It was the legend of *La Vie Parisienne* come to life in the most joyous fashion.

An advertisement for the Moulin Rouge

Valentin Le Désossé
The Man in the Quadrille

What of the man behind the mask of Valentin le Désossé? If statistics from the period are to be believed, he danced on more than one hundred thousand occasions. His biography, however, is as slim as was his body. His real name was Jacques Renaudin, the son of a notary of Sceaux, and during the daytime he led the exemplary life of a perfectly respectable gentleman. In the mornings he would ride through the Bois

Valentin Le Désossé: the only photograph which shows him in his ordinary clothes

de Boulogne or fish from the bank of the Seine. Malicious tongues even declared that he had no need of a line, being so long himself! In the afternoons he would carry out a few minor duties in the family practice. Then, in the evenings, he would cross Paris to Montmartre, to become the foil of La Goulue. A first glimpse of this unique individual, who must have been approaching fifty then, would have aroused curiosity. He resembled an ill-nourished acrobat and, to quote Yvette Guilbert, seemed to dress himself in ready-made suits from the cheaper suburban tailors. His permanent attire consisted of a black frock-coat and yellow trousers, supplemented by a dented and shiny top hat. Chewing without any apparent lassitude on an everlasting cigar, his outstanding features were a large nose and enormous feet. He seemed to be perpetually sleep-walking – until the orchestra struck up the first notes of the quadrille. Once he started to dance, his agility and the precision with which he moved his arms and legs, as if made of rubber, were a source of wonderment. Certainly his profile tended to incite laughter, but his extravagant and harmonious movements were acclaimed by an enthusiastic audience. Every evening he was carried off by his partners in triumph.

Quite unlike the 'gigolos who make ladies dance', he had an excellent reputation as a gentleman. Courteous and reserved, he would accept the invitation of a drink only provided that he could return the compliment without delay. This did not prevent rumours of the most outrageous kind from circulating about him. He was said to be capable of entwining himself like a snake around a standard lamp; it was whispered that he refused to accept any kind of fee; it was asserted that his father had cut him off without a penny.

All his secrets Valentin took with him when, in 1895, he left the Moulin Rouge, disappearing into the night with the same agility he had displayed on the stage. He is reported to have died in 1906, but, apart from brief reappearances, all trace of him was lost. Some said that to earn his living, he had opened a *bistrot* in the Rue Coquillière, while others insisted that he had been employed as a manual worker in a lift factory, using the false name of Père Dupont. A journalist of the day, certain of the resemblance, turned up at the alley where he worked with the objective of wringing the truth from him, but in vain. Claude-André Puget wrote a comedy based on the story of this unusual man. Its four acts and five scenes were presented on the stage of the Théâtre Michel on 21 October 1932, with Pierre Fresnay in the leading role, Hélène Perdrière, Jeanne Cheirel and Polaire. Although a hit, it did nothing further to lift even a corner of the curtain covering one of the most mysterious heroes of show business.

CURRENT EVENTS IN 1889

The year when the Moulin Rouge revolution began was one of unrest and disturbances. Earthquakes were experienced in America, Switzerland, Austria, England, Spain and even France. In politics unrest was also in full swing. General Boulanger lost the election and promptly went into exile in Belgium.

In France, interest was concentrated on the colony of Indo-China, the conquest of which was in full swing, and cultural life was passing through difficult days. At the Gymnase, Alphonse Daudet had put on *La Lutte pour la vie* (The Struggle for Life) a five-act drama which is completely forgotten today. No one paid any attention to Paul Claudel's poem *Tête d'or* or, come to that, to an 'Essay on direct data from the consciousness', by a certain Bergson.

On the other hand, the completion of the building of the Eiffel Tower and the opening of the Universal Exhibition were downright popular successes.

This was the society, searching for the basis of its economic and political future, into which the Moulin Rouge was born.

Valentin and La Goulue, by Barabandy

35

JOSEPH OLLER: The Father of the MOULIN ROUGE

For Joseph Oller, the Moulin Rouge was the summit of an exceptional Parisian life which, in his early years, could hardly have been predicted. He was born in Terrassa, a town in Spanish

Not only the cancan was danced at the Moulin Rouge; there were also the mattchiche, the waltz, the quadrille, the bolero, the seguidilla to name but a few others

Catalonia, but in 1841, when he was two years old, his parents went to settle in Paris. As an adolescent he was already deeply fond of the city, which Baron Haussmann was then in the course of improving and extending. He frequented the Reine Blanche, the Élysée-Montmartre, the Bal Mabille, the Moulin de la Galette, and the cafés patronised by writers. When he was seventeen his father sent him to Bilbao to learn Spanish. There he discovered cock-fighting and was an avid observer of the quarrels which broke out among the crowd over the placing of bets. He found the resultant disorder intolerable and thereupon devised a remedy. Going to the organ-

isers, he suggested the introduction of a gambling rule which was both simple and fair, and this was immediately adopted.

Betting continued to preoccupy him on his return to Paris, in the field of horse-racing. In those days no bets were laid on the racecourses themselves, and certain privileged people gathered in clubs which were described, rather pompously, as 'for the encouragement of horse-breeding'. The general public had to be content with *La poule*, a kind of sweep-stake even easier to understand than the *Tac-o-Tac*. Before the start of a race, numbered pieces of paper, representing the horses on the card, were put into a hat. This was then shaken, and the person who drew out the number of the winning horse pocketed all the stake money.

Joseph Oller devised a system based on the one he had tried in Bilbao. To put it into practice, he opened an office on the Boulevard Magenta. It was so successful that soon he was selling tickets, first from caravans painted yellow and black, and then from kiosks. In 1867 he introduced an improved version of his system, and created the 'tote'. With his headquarters on the Boulevard des Italiens, he also started a newspaper, *Le Bulletin des Courses*. His path seemed to have been decided, but political and legal circumstances conspired to bring about a change of direction. The tote was accused by the Republicans of being 'a plot hatched by the Second Empire to distract the people's attention from matters of public concern' and in 1874 it was banned. Joseph Oller decided to transfer his attentions to his other love, entertainment. He purchased a café, the Baden, and transformed it into a concert hall, advertising it as the *Fantaisies Oller*. He had entered a world in which he was destined to be one of the princes. In 1878, at the same spot, he opened the Théâtre des Nouveautés, where the operettas, comedies and farces he put on enjoyed great popularity.

In 1885 Oller opened the big Rochechouart public baths, 600 square metres in area, with 500 cubicles

arranged in five galleries, each 1600 metres long, and a gymnasium and Turkish baths for relaxation and hydrotherapy. It represented a revolution at that time, but was not a financial success. The number of bathers was insufficient to cover the running costs and the enterprise came to nothing.

Oller was not to be beaten: the entertainment business had become an addiction. In the Faubourg Saint-Honoré, at the foot of a large flight of steps designed by Charles Garnier, the architect of the Paris Opéra, he created the Arènes Nautiques, soon renamed the Nouveau Cirque, where he put on a circus in the winter, replacing it with a swimming pool when spring came around. He installed the first tip-up seats in the history of the theatre; at the end of the circus season they were taken out and the bathers were able to stretch out on the area around the pool. Another success to his name! The whole arrangement was described by the technicians as 'completely unique', while journalists called it 'the eighth wonder of the world'. During the summer, when his usual clients deserted the capital to patronise seasonally fashionable watering places, Joseph Oller offered international attractions. Thus the well-to-do flocked to enjoy mimes, horses, elephants, and delightful water-nymphs performing in the pool. The clowns Footitt and Chocolat, Paul and Louis Fratellini, Antonio Medrano and the Darios all received Paris's approval.

The establishment finally closed its doors in 1926, the building being sold and converted to become the future Salle Pleyel.

In 1887 the government re-legalised the tote and Joseph Oller returned to the world of racehorses, which he had never really abandoned. In 1880 he had actually converted some land into racecourses, at Maisons-Laffitte and at Saint-Germain, while in 1882 he had registered the patents covering a system for the

illumination of the course by electricity, and an automatic alarm, designed to stop the issuing of betting slips immediately the start of a race was signalled. From the profits which he made on these two activities, he was able to open an amusement park at 28 Boulevard des Capucines, featuring the Montagnes Russes, a switchback railway. The layout used a series of wooden cabins, imported from England, which the Parisians took to with enthusiasm.

Two years later the Universal Exhibition was held and Joseph Oller built the Moulin Rouge on the site of the famous Reine Blanche dance hall. Even before it was finished he knew that it was to be the culmination of his life's work. This establishment, he told his associates, was going to be the most magnificent of all the temples dedicated to music and dancing. No one actually laughed in his face, but what encouragement he received was without conviction, and no belief was expressed in the success of his venture. Yet, from the opening night,

the public was as enthusiastic as the detractors had been pessimistic. Oller then handed over the reins to Charles Zidler. The latter had excellent references, having just been running the Hippodrome, a wooden hall near the Place de l'Alma, where big equestrian shows were staged.

For three years the two men shared a complete understanding. The reason for the rift between them, on the thousandth day of their partnership, remains as mysterious now as it was then. There was talk of 'management problems', of 'conflict between the staff and the performers, dependent on the mood of the director'. Some even said that Zidler was the real creator of the Moulin Rouge, and that Oller was nothing but an impostor. It was a sad finale.

This was a passing incident which seemed not to trouble Joseph Oller. He offered the post of director to his brother Jean, just returned from the Argentine, where he had been organising horse-races. After this he expanded his empire by buying the Jardin de Paris, a celebrated pleasure garden just off the Champs-Élysées. In due course it was decided that the Grand Palais, which was to be the centre-piece of the 1900 Universal Exhibition, should be built on that site. He did not, however, leave the area, for he re-established himself 200 metres away. The Jardin de Paris was a high-class amusement park for a very smart clientele. It included variety and theatrical entertainments, a dance hall, a circus, bars, rifle ranges, exhibitions of models, slides, and even a photographic salon for those who wished to keep a souvenir of their visit. It constituted an annexe to the Moulin Rouge for, every evening, a short play, a mime or several Andalusian, Tyrolean and Hungarian scenes would be followed by the appearance of La Goulue, Nini Patte en l'Air and Valentin le Désossé with their frenetic quadrilles and their frantic waltzing. This was preceded at about eleven o'clock by five horses

pulling the omnibus which carried spectators and dancers alike from the dance hall in Montmartre to the Champs-Élysées. Like the far-sighted businessman he was, Oller had discovered the best way of doubling the takings from his most dedicated customers.

Several months after his split with Zidler, on 12 April 1893, he opened the Olympia. For its site he chose that of the now-defunct Montagnes Russes, on the Boulevard des Capucines. He proposed to make of this *hangar* (lean-to hall) a place of entertainment where 'the luxury and beauty would surpass anything yet seen in Paris'. He could not speak English, but he discovered that *hangar*, when translated into the language of Shakespeare, meant 'hall', and he therefore gave this new establishment the name of 'Music-hall'. The bill included ballets and other high quality entertainments. The brothers Isola were appointed as directors of what, six decades on, was to become the empire of Bruno Coquatrix. Two years later, in the cellars (which today house the Olympia Tavern), Oller opened a waxworks museum, presenting a panoramic history of the world, from the Passion of Christ up to events of the current day, via the French Revolution.

All this did not mean that he was neglecting his first love. On 2 June 1891 a new law was enacted which officially resurrected the tote. The horse-racing companies immediately entrusted the official organisation of the betting on the capital's racecourses to him, and he set up a printing press to provide the racing companies with bulletins and betting slips. The benefits of his system survive to this day.

In 1905 he was delegated by the Minister of the Interior to arrange the visit to Paris of the young King Alphonse III of Spain, who was coming to France for the first time. The powers-that-be used this opportunity to bestow upon him the title of 'Minister for Public Entertainment without portfolio' – official recognition. When not involved in meetings or travelling around Europe, Joseph Oller passed his time in the company of his closest friends – among them Georges Courteline, who remained one of his most faithful companions. He had a fertile imagination, was always ready for new adventures, and remained young in heart to the end of his days. At the age of seventy he preferred the bicycle and the horse to the motor car, although he had been one of its first users. He died on 19 April 1922 after three days of illness – the first he had ever suffered in his life. He had one regret, as he confided shortly before his death to someone who asked if he was satisfied with his achievements:

'Not entirely. I would have liked to have done more . . .'

CHARLES ZIDLER:
The Watcher from the Wings

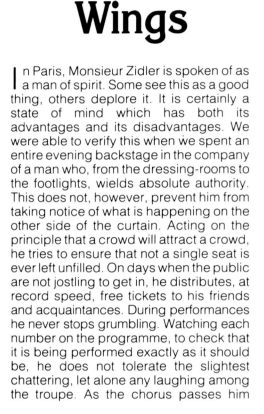

In Paris, Monsieur Zidler is spoken of as a man of spirit. Some see this as a good thing, others deplore it. It is certainly a state of mind which has both its advantages and its disadvantages. We were able to verify this when we spent an entire evening backstage in the company of a man who, from the dressing-rooms to the footlights, wields absolute authority. This does not, however, prevent him from taking notice of what is happening on the other side of the curtain. Acting on the principle that a crowd will attract a crowd, he tries to ensure that not a single seat is ever left unfilled. On days when the public are not jostling to get in, he distributes, at record speed, free tickets to his friends and acquaintances. During performances he never stops grumbling. Watching each number on the programme, to check that it is being performed exactly as it should be, he does not tolerate the slightest chattering, let alone any laughing among the troupe. As the chorus passes him before going on the stage, some comment is always on his lips: 'Paulette, don't make eyes at the gallery! Gaby, stop laughing! Louise, your drawers are showing! Camélia, don't wriggle like that!' It seems that the young ladies referred to do not take such remarks amiss. On the contrary, they value the eye of a professional whose experience cannot be denied.

'Before I joined Joseph Oller in the Place Blanche, I had all kinds of jobs,' he told us after the finale and the encores. 'At the age of ten, I was a tanner by the River Bièvre; by the time I was fourteen, I had learnt to read and write. I have also been the director of the Hippodrome, a magnificent wooden hall near the Place de l'Alma, where I organised equestrian spectaculars, gladiatorial combats, processions, chariot races and tournaments.' By abandoning rapiers in favour of peaceful feathers, he has done well and so has the Moulin Rouge.

Sunday evening suppers

At the instigation of Charles Destemps, the mayor of Rheims and editor of *Gil Blas*, it became traditional, every Sunday after the performance, for the whole troupe to meet in two adjoining apartments opposite the Moulin Rouge. There Charles Zidler would ladle out the soup to little dressmakers, street-walkers and grand courtesans alike. No one missed out on these gatherings, which were proof that the world of entertainment was, more than ever, one big family.

Yvette Guilbert

The Great National Diseuse

Yvette Guilbert was not simply the immortal performer of Xanrof's *Le Fiacre* (actually created by Félicia Mallet, an artist completely forgotten today). Dubbed 'The Great National Diseuse (Monologist)' by her faithful followers, she experienced poverty, scan-

---

The visitors' book of Moulin Rouge regulars

Alphonse Allais
Maurice Barrès
Tristan Bernard — at that time the sports director of the Buffalo cycle track, between the Porte de Champerret and the Porte des Ternes
Sarah Bernhardt
Léon Bloy
Maurice Donnay
Edmond Haraucourt
Louis Legrand, painter and disciple of Toulouse-Lautrec
Jean Lorrain
Guy de Maupassant
Montoya
Jean Moréas
Xavier Privas, poet and song-writer of the Butte
Jules Renard
Jean Richepin
Francisque Sarcey
Laurent Tailhade
Oscar Wilde
Juan Cardona, Spanish painter, who produced a poster of the show
Paul Roig, an artist mainly known for his anarchistic ideas
Jules Chéret, inventor of the lithographic multi-colour poster
Ignacio Zuloaga, Santiago Rossinyol, Ramon Casas, Miguel Utrillo, Charles-Lucien Léandre, Abel Faivre, Jean-Louis Forain, Caran d'Ache, Jean-François Raffaelli — all fashionable painters of the day

The cost of a ticket for the Moulin Rouge

2 francs – Normal days
3 francs – Gala nights
10 sous – Sunday afternoons

Performances at 8.00 p.m.
Dancing at 10.00 p.m.

---

dal and glory. Her career began at the Moulin Rouge in 1890, in the days of the *café-concert*, in the guise of *Nurse Valérie*. Her reception by the public was extremely tepid. The caricature was perfect: her hair was smoothed and drawn under the traditional pale blue cowl, her dress was hidden under a long cloak buttoned from the neck to the hem. Nevertheless, her comic song, recounting the misadventures of an English nurse required to look after rich gentlemen who were, although sick, amorously inclined towards their 'maid-of-all-work', scarcely attracted any attention from the audience.

The young Yvette Guilbert was not in the least discouraged. It was not the first time since the day of her one and only triumph, in an amateur company performing *L'Île de Tulipatan* by Jacques Offenbach. She had not yet found her way, but she knew she had a vocation. She had begun as a model and salesgirl in the shoe department of the Magasins du Printemps before, the story goes, being carried off by an Italian prince. Her real apprenticeship was to be in the hard school of the *cafés-concerts*. At the Eldorado the applause was muted. At the casino in Lyons she was booed and left the show at the end of the second performance. There were days when she could not afford to eat, and she began to feel she had had enough. The engagement at the Moulin Rouge, which she owed to Charles Zidler's confidence in her, was a question of survival. Overnight she had left the Eden Concert, owing a considerable sum for the broken contract to a director who had clearly no idea of her abilities. Needless to say, she had not a penny in the world and, to make matters worse, she was having to care for her sick mother.

*   *
*   *

The first few weeks were very difficult. Yvette was earning twenty francs a day. The miracle arrived in the form of an article in *Gil Blas*. René Maizeroy, a writer popular at the time, asserted that on no account should this 'strange creature' be missed. He added that her white

---

dress, reaching down to her feet, made her a much more distinguished woman than her contemporaries. He approved of the originality of her black gloves on a *café-concert* stage, where it was traditional to appear wearing white ones. Had he known the reason for this choice, he would no doubt have written of meanness rather than genius! For the artiste this colour was in fact a means of avoiding ruinous laundry charges. However, not only society but also painters, sculptors, song-writers and poets heeded the recommendation of the man of letters and, every evening, reserved an ever-louder ovation for the singer who was in the course of becoming a prima donna. In March 1891 Jehan Sarrazin, the director of the Divan Japonais, invited her to come and sing in his cabaret after her performance at the Moulin Rouge. Followed, as soon as her turn was finished, by faithful deserters from the Place Blanche, she tried out a new repertoire with a character whom she thought of as satirical, but whom the critics described as 'morbid', 'macabre' or even 'divinely perverse'. Edmond de Goncourt himself said that she was 'a very great tragic actress who could cause an anguishing constriction of the heart'. She rapidly became the symbol for decadent women, the embodiment of the *fin-de-siècle*. Émile Zola, Jules Renard and Maurice Donnay were numbered among her unwavering supporters.

*
*   *

It was the start of a career which was to take her as far as North America, with triumphs in Paris, at the Concert Parisien, the Scala and the Champs-Élysées, but which did not prevent her, after 1900, from enjoying a happy private life as a married woman. The man in her life brought her the affection and admiration which enabled her to forget the scorn, not to say masochism, of the directors she had worked for in her early days. Employers whom, in her biography, she lists and whom Prévert would not have disowned.

'Former innkeepers, purveyors of spirits at four sous a glass, butter sellers in the market, jewellery brokers, a barkeeper from Marseilles, a laundress, a tanner, a swimming instructor, a diver, a washer-up. And even a toothless old master mason who, when he paid me, complained: "A thousand francs for singing for thirty minutes! I could have had three metres of wall for that price."'

'Those enigmatic shoulders — like those of a man — which seem never to come to an end and which, even should they be uncovered as far as the hips, would never succeed in being immodest.'

(Jean Lorrain)

GALA NIGHTS

11 February 1890: The arrival of Le Pétomane (The Farter)

The words will undoubtedly become immortal: 'The only artist who pays no author's rights.' Physically, appearances are not in his favour: small in stature, hair cut short, a Kaiser Wilhelm moustache, an expressionless face. Yet, what brilliance when the spot-lights are directed upon him. Messieurs Oller and Zidler had promised us an attraction of an exceptional kind, and neither we nor the public were disappointed. Picture the flushed faces, tears streaming down their cheeks, picture the ladies stifling their laughter, carried off in distress by nurses in white, suddenly appearing from nowhere. It was a good quarter of an hour before we recovered our breath. The reason for it all is somewhat delicate to describe. Suffice it to say that this man, a certain Pujol, appeared before us wearing a red coat and black satin trousers. He didn't sing, he did imitations of . . . er, of . . . well, look, if his name isn't sufficient to allow you to guess what we're trying to say (which we doubt), below is the conversation between Charles Zidler and this blithe performer on the occasion of their first meeting. We were able to get hold of it, but the responsibility for their words we leave entirely to the two protagonists.

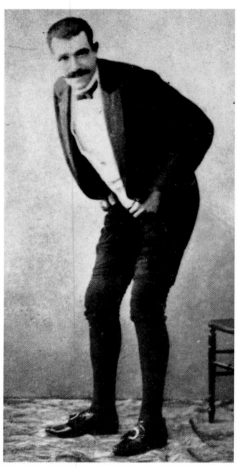

Le Pétomane in his favourite position

Charles Zidler: What exactly is your speciality?

Le Pétomane: Well, Monsieur, take it that I have an aspiratory anus or, to put it another way, my anus is of such elasticity that I can open and close it at will.

Charles Zidler: I see. Go on.

Le Pétomane: It is a fact, Monsieur, that through this providential opening I can absorb any quantity of liquid with which you wish to supply me.

(Charles Zidler hands him a large bowl of water – from the tap, not even mineral – and he does the necessary. His pants are provided with a hole in the appropriate place. He empties the bowl in no time and immediately refills it. A slight aroma of sulphur permeates the room.)

Le Pétomane: I haven't finished! After this . . . what you might call, enema, I can expel odour-free gases ad infinitum. The secret of my process lies in the acoustic fidelity of the sounds I produce.

Charles Zidler: So, in fact, you sing through your behind!

Le Pétomane: Exactly Monsieur. Tenor, one! Baritone, two! Bass, three! Contralto, four! Soprano, five! Now, a vocal exercise!

You may imagine the demonstration and the contract which, between guffaws, Charles Zidler got him to sign.

It should be added that Monsieur Oller, who was responsible for the stage setting (oh yes, there was one) for the turn, had thought of everything. The audience accompanied the phenomenon in chorus, while a confederate planted in the crowd played the part of disbeliever marvellously. He climbed up on to the stage to check that it was no trick, and that the performer was not hiding anything – anywhere . . . It was extraordinarily funny. Were we not afraid of being accused of vulgarity, we would even suggest that an explosion of laughter is guaranteed.

A cylinder recording of this 'entertainment' was made, and is a great rarity. For years it has amused those who, never having visited Paris, have been unable to appreciate this short-lived star for themselves.

9 March 1890

Monsieur Henri de Toulouse-Lautrec is gifted with a true sense of the ridiculous. He reports the following incident, of which he himself was the victim, which took place last night at the Moulin Rouge: 'I had placed my stick on the table, as I do every evening. It has been specially made to suit my height, to enable me to walk without too much difficulty. As I was standing up, a customer called to me: "Monsieur, don't forget your pencil." It was very unkind, but most funny.'

22 April 1890

The latest witticism from Monsieur de Toulouse-Lautrec: Whenever he goes anywhere, he asks, if possible, to be seated on a chair normally reserved for small children, adding:

'I shall be more comfortable on that than on the *Bottin Mondain* (Society Directory) or a dictionary, and high society and the *Académie française* will be grateful.'

12 May 1890

A Moulin Rouge regular has told us the following story, which took place last night before his own eyes. Two women were arguing at the table next to Monsieur Lautrec. They were discussing the purity of the pedigree of the dog which one of them held on a lead.

'It's frightfully ugly,' said the other.

To which the dog's owner retorted:

'Look at his black muzzle. That's the unmistakable sign of his pedigree.' Then, turning towards Henri de Toulouse-Lautrec, she added:

'Is it not so, Monsieur, that one can be frightfully ugly and yet of a very high pedigree?'

'To whom are you referring, Madame?' was the artist's only reply.

9 October 1890

Ever since this morning, Joseph Oller has been telling everyone the latest of Monsieur Lautrec's witticisms.

'Last night, I asked him which of the dancers he would like to sleep with.

"None of them," he answered immediately. "If they make love with the same energy as they dance the cancan, my poor carcass would be crushed to death."'

26 October 1890

Last night at the Moulin Rouge there was very nearly a diplomatic incident, if not the start of a new war between France and England. His Highness the Prince of

IN THE WINGS

Wales, the future Edward VII, on a private visit to Paris, had booked a table, for the purpose of discovering for himself this famous quadrille whose reputation has already reached the other side of the Channel. Recognising him, La Goulue, leg in the air and head in her petticoats, called out without any hesitation:

'Hey, Wales, the champagne's on you!'

As can be imagined, a murmur immediately ran round the hall. Happily, His Royal Highness blinked behind the smoke from his Havana, but did not flinch. He even smiled and presented the dancer with a bottle of the *meilleur cru*. It's what they call *noblesse oblige*.

20 December 1890

Every evening the main attraction at the entrance to the Moulin Rouge is Marcel Legay, the poet of Montmartre. With arm upraised, he recites a verse of his own composition, which is unlikely to achieve any success beyond the pavement of the Place Blanche. Judge for yourselves:

Moulin-Rouge, Moulin-Rouge
pour qui mouds-tu, Moulin-Rouge?
Pour la mort ou pour l'amour?
Pour qui mouds-tu jusqu'au jour?

(Moulin Rouge, Moulin Rouge,
For whom are you grinding, Moulin Rouge?
Can it be death or is love your corn?
For whom are you grinding until the dawn?)

11 February 1891

The repartee of La Goulue will never cease to amaze us. We had another demonstration of this last night, during the visit of Prince Alexis, the cousin of the Tsar. The story is worth the telling. At the end of the performance His Highness, who was accompanied by his retinue and surrounded by considerable security, ordered an aide-de-camp to go and ask the troupe to dance the *ruskaia*. The reply reached him in the form of a great burst of laughter from the star of the quadrille. In no way discouraged by this refusal, the Russian prince ordered champagne for all the ladies concerned and demanded a repeat of the cancan.

La Goulue shrugged her shoulders. To try to persuade her to provide the desired encore, Charles Zidler explained to her that it was a Grand Duke who was making the request and that he could not be refused. To this she retorted, with a frankness which bordered on naivety:

'What's so extraordinary about this Grand Duke? When I was little, I saw plenty of them – in a cage at the zoo.'

10 March 1891

La Goulue had spent the day in the Bois de Boulogne, in the company of Henri de Toulouse-Lautrec. That evening, to those who had visions of a lovers' meeting, the queen of the quadrille replied:

'I asked him to come along because I wanted to frighten off anyone who might try to accost me.'

27 April 1891

Extract from the diary of Jules Renard:

'Last night at the Moulin Rouge . . . It is sad to find oneself ignored by the woman one finds attractive. A little girl wearing socks, her legs bare, doing the splits. I would have been glad to have been her protector. I would also like to have been the conductor of the orchestra, the conductor of it all. Ah, the warts of vanity!'

10 September 1892

Monsieur Charles Zidler is leaving the Moulin Rouge 'for health reasons'. This news, which was announced officially this morning, has come as no surprise. For some months no one has been unaware of the considerable friction that has existed between the director and the dancers, and even some of the regular customers. It is a sad end to a great adventure which has lasted for three years. Joseph Oller has dealt with a situation where the characters of the two parties had become incompatible by immediately placing his brother, Monsieur Jean Oller, at the head of the establishment. Yvette Guilbert has demonstrated her support for the former director by sending him the following note:

'You possess a genius for the creation of popular pleasure in the very highest sense of the word, and for entertaining the people, with subtle differences according to the quality of the audience to be amused. No one can replace you.'

15 September 1894

Being circulated around the dressing

rooms of the Moulin Rouge this evening is the virulent article published in *La Justice* over the signature of Georges Clemenceau. It is the culmination of a quarrel which has been going on for several months between supporters and opponents of Yvette Guilbert, one of the leading performers of the *café-concert* in the Place Blanche. At the centre of the dispute is the permanent disagreement between the singer and Toulouse-Lautrec. Everybody knows that she has dubbed him 'the Quasimodo of art' and that, on the only drawing he has given her, she wrote 'You little monster, you've made me look terrible'. This time it was a preliminary sketch for a poster that unleashed the prima donna's thunderbolts.

'For the love of God, don't make me look so ugly,' she said, deeply offended. 'A number of people who have come to see me, including my mother, were shocked when they saw your colour sketch.'

Jean Lorrain, our well-known Parisian chronicler, immediately approved this outburst in an inflammatory article. Georges Clemenceau has now calmed things down by drawing attention to the accuracy of the analysis and the supernatural dimension given to the singer by the painter. Affair now closed – until the next time. The characters of the two protagonists suggest that matters will certainly not rest there.

27 April 1895

The fine weather seems to be here to stay. This forecast was the method chosen by the management of the Moulin Rouge to announce the arrangements for the staging of shows during the summer. When the skies are blue, the entertainment will take place in the gardens. If it rains, the concerts and quadrilles will move under cover in the vast hall. On the programme will be the most popular music and dance productions of the year, under the direction of Messieurs Mabille and Gouvain.

12 November 1897

Notice to clients: The Moulin Rouge will be closed for the day, owing to the funeral of Charles Zidler, former director of the establishment.

23 October 1902

Last night, for the first time, the Moulin Rouge experienced the benefit of the Métro, with the opening of a station in the Place Blanche. It should attract a whole new clientele to Montmartre's lively establishment.

II
THE FIRST REVUES

Mlle MINTE
danseuse du Moulin Rouge.

19 April 1890

Presentation of a programme of dancing, singing and mime, entitled *Circassiens et Circassiennes*.

3 May 1890

Presentation of a musical entertainment entitled *Les Belles Orientales*.

13 December 1894

The first appearance of Paul-Louis Flers, song-writer and future director of the establishment. Production of *A la pointe du pied* (On Tip-toe), scenes of Montmartre devised by Paul-Louis Flers and performed by the Oller dancers.

23 February 1895

The first combined musical show and public dance, henceforth presented every evening at ten o'clock, and featuring Germaine Ety, Kamona, Daubreuil and Bloch.

13 March 1895

A new programme which included *Mon ami Polissard* (My Friend Polissard), a sketch by Pericaud, Villemer and Delormel.

27 March 1895

Première of *La Cornette*, operetta by Bernicat. Stars of the evening were three girls from Andalusia, whose dances were encored.

5 October 1895

Première of *La Mariée du Moulin Rouge* (The Bride of the Moulin Rouge), a Montmartre sketch.

16 November 1895

Presentation of *Coco Bel Oeil*, an operetta which served as the finale to the regular evening show.

14 December 1895

Presentation of *Ah Chaleur*, a new minirevue by Paul-Louis Flers.

5 April 1896

Presentation of an operetta-mime, *On demande Arlequin* (Where's Harlequin?), by F. Bernicat.

29 September 1896

The show returned to its winter quarters with, as the finale, *Mademoiselle Loulotte*, a mini-operetta by Victor Roger.

2 October 1896

Première of *Le Cirque Pougers*, farce in one act.

13 December 1896

Première of the end-of-year revue, *Les Caucaseries de la Butte*, by Messieurs Fordyce and Davin de Champelos.

16 March 1897

In addition to the usual programme, *Au coq huppé*, an operetta by Banes. The cast included Messieurs Gaillard, Poquelin and Hotlair, and Mesdemoiselles Dufresny and Mary Hett.

11 December 1897

Première of *Viv' la Butte*, a revue by Eugène Lemercier, with Mesdemoiselles Mary Hett, Dufresny, Phillip, Lancy and Marsa, and Messieurs Roger, Latouche and Amond.

16 December 1898

Neuf à dix (Nine to Ten), a fantasy-revue by Edme Paze, with Muguet, Lancy and Daris.

THE MOULIN ROUGE PROGRAMMES

Sinoel, a music-hall comic before becoming one of the most popular supporting actors in the cinema

21 June 1895

Monsieur Joseph Oller announces the arrival of fresh attractions to take part in the show: Miss Nelly, a young and ravishing English comedienne, the Kitchens and Osbornes with their hilarious eccentricities, Pauline, a second Paulin, as well as those new singing and dancing discoveries, Jenny Cook, Daubreuil, Luciani, Gourez and Andrée Phillip.

2 May 1896

Monsieur Joseph Oller announces a new show bill, with Sevrane, Yvonne Renaix and Yvette Ica. The success of Marcel Legay, for whom this show represents well-merited recognition, should also be noted.

19 July 1896

Yet more new attractions at the Moulin Rouge! Mademoiselle Domoge, Roger M., the Haytoni Brothers, as well as Dufay, the gayest of our comediennes. And not forgetting Miss Jenny, whose performance the day before yesterday on the first level of the Eiffel Tower drew the attention of a select audience, among whom were the representative of the Chinese cultural delegation, which is visiting Paris.

1 September 1896

The new indoor programme at the Moulin Rouge: Ninon Duverneil, Jenny Cook, Raignaud, Suzanne d'An and Dickson.

10 May 1897
The Jardin de Paris at the Moulin Rouge

The famous show on the Champs-Élysées has been exiled to the Place Blanche for the summer. This is due to the preparations for the next Universal Exhibition, which has also obliged Joseph Oller to abandon the site proposed for the Grand Palais, and occupy another a few hundred metres further away. Until this is opened, which is expected to be at the end of September, four programmes have been planned in the Place Blanche for the clientele of the Jardin de Paris.

18 May 1897

Shows with Mesdames Naya, Dufresny, Wrain and Kamouna, and Messieurs Roger and Poquelin, as well the Mabille orchestra. *Fin de siècle* dances performed by Grille d'Égout, Serpolette and Clair de Lune.

1 August 1897

New attractions: Berthomier and Zents, Margareth and Jullian, Maréchal and Dufor.

19 August 1897

Return of Mademoiselle Lancey. With, in addition, Jenny Cook, Lily Destrey, Flon Flon and Giselle, Messieurs Roger, Dufor, Jiggy and the Holhens.

5 September 1897

Noteworthy début of Mesdemoiselles Célina Bobe, Nelsa, Lancy and Marsa, Messieurs Meyriac and Cambe, and the Kitchen and Osborne clowns.

30 September 1897

New show with the Dumond Minstrels, Italian street singers.

1 April 1898

New cast for the show preceding the dancing. On the bill Mesdemoiselles Nelsa, Darièle, Naedia, Manais Muller and Renée Aveline, together with the jugglers Tremay and Lena, Aderamis, burlesque acrobats, and the Stanley and Henderson quartet.

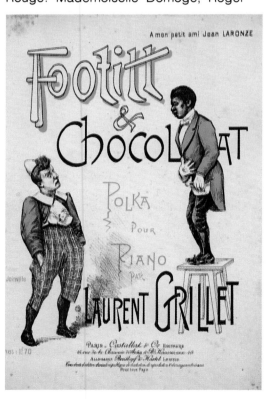

Footitt in his clowning turn

6 May 1898

New show with Denise d'Évian, a deserter from the Scala, the juggler Léa d'Asty, the acrobat sisters Caïra, and Max Dearly, emulator of the much-missed Paul Legrand.

21 July 1898

A show with the hunchbacked acrobat Léonardi, Dodok and Lena, and Miss Virginie Ferrando, the graceful tightrope-walker. Mademoiselle Valor appeared a number of times, in the different guises of Joan of Arc, Mary Queen of Scots, Madame de Sévigné, Marie-Antoinette, Madame Rolland and Madame de Staël.

8 September 1898

The graceful juggler Léa d'Asty, Madeleine Dones, Mademoiselle Ha-Naës and the duettists Nerval and Schneider.

19 October 1898

A new star in a new style: Myletta the Bohemian, a young fortune-teller, whose beauty is itself mysterious.

2 November 1898

The Snowdrops, eight English dancers, and the Animissofs, Franco-Russian duettists.

8 April 1899

The duo of Arnal Jonnis and Professor Thérèsez with their Magnetic Act.

5 May 1899

The virtuoso musical clown Bi-Bo-Bi and the elegant and lissom Léa d'Asty.

5 August 1899

The Mannons in their burlesque mime and Miss Edith Russel with her five pretty goats.

2 September 1899

The Andrels troupe and the suggestive barefoot dance performed by Miss Helen Constantine.

1 October 1899

The Rossi sisters, excellent mimers, Madame Lucette Best and Mademoiselle Andrée Chambault.

1 November 1899

Monsieur Daubreuil, Mesdemoiselles Mathilde Gomez, in her Spanish and Neapolitan repertoire, and Blanche d'Arvilly, with her Spanish-Montmartre songs, and the Hayton brothers, with their eccentric comedy.

1 December 1899

Annie Barret, singer, and the beautiful Vabrey.

2 March 1900

Paula Brebion, the well-known star. Mademoiselle Renée d'Almy, a star-to-be.

26 May 1900

In the large dance hall the Bunko Hungarian orchestra, alternating with that conducted so brilliantly by Messieurs Mabille and Gauvin.

30 June 1900

After the show finishes in the garden, everyone crowds into the dance hall where, each evening on the bandstand, a gipsy orchestra plays the intoxicating waltzes of Strauss and Fahrbach.

4 September 1900

Immediately after the show, and before the dancing begins, the Coros de Clavie, a Catalan choral society consisting of 450 singers, performs a few pieces in the main hall, accompanied by the Mabille orchestra.

24 November 1900

Mademoiselle Laetitia in Paulette Darty's repertoire, Miss Gara with her American dances, and Anita, the captivating Andalusian ballerina.

15 December 1900

The graceful Beany Smart with his fashionable cycling displays.

1 March 1901

Mademoiselle Bian-Ka.

27 March 1901

Foscolo, the graceful deserter from the Scala.

12 December 1901

An attractive Viennese dancer, who wishes to retain her anonymity, reveals herself to the audience, using the masculine name of John Land.

8 February 1902

Performers in masquerade, Zizi Papillon and the Hatcaps, acrobatic English dancers.

18 October 1902

The graceful Emma Georges and the hilarious Georges.

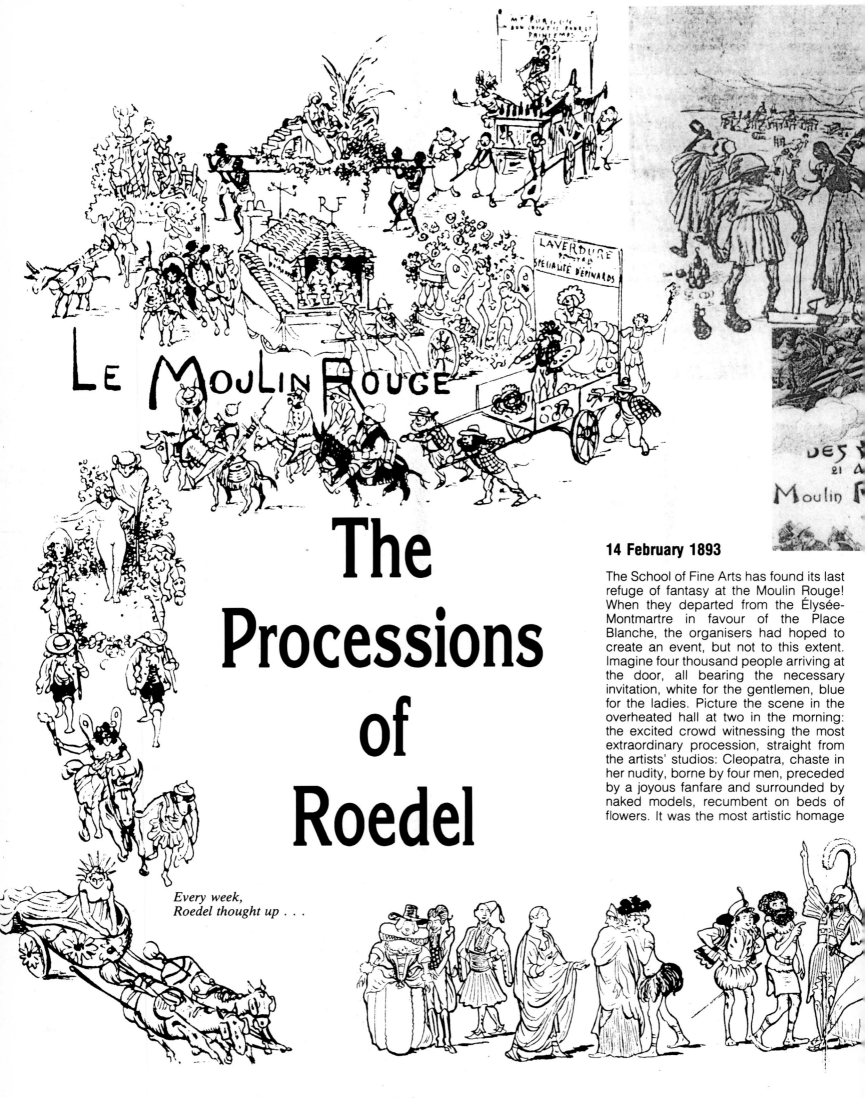

Le Moulin Rouge

The Processions of Roedel

Every week,
Roedel thought up . . .

14 February 1893

The School of Fine Arts has found its last refuge of fantasy at the Moulin Rouge! When they departed from the Élysée-Montmartre in favour of the Place Blanche, the organisers had hoped to create an event, but not to this extent. Imagine four thousand people arriving at the door, all bearing the necessary invitation, white for the gentlemen, blue for the ladies. Picture the scene in the overheated hall at two in the morning: the excited crowd witnessing the most extraordinary procession, straight from the artists' studios: Cleopatra, chaste in her nudity, borne by four men, preceded by a joyous fanfare and surrounded by naked models, recumbent on beds of flowers. It was the most artistic homage

. . . a new procession, based on a theme from mythology, fairy tales, the Classics, the countryside, history .

The invitation card which was the start of the scandal

to art, beauty and love. 'On the contrary, it was a deed of extreme gravity and unacceptable immodesty,' the officials of the General Society of Protest Against Public Licentiousness asserted, in all seriousness, this morning. An investigation was instigated into the organisers of the ball. The principal witness for the prosecution was none other than Mademoiselle Weber, otherwise known as La Goulue. A most curious attitude, considering her reputation! The hearing was fixed for June; those partial to court cases which are out of the ordinary will surely not deprive themselves of this small pleasure . . .

14 June 1893

After lengthy examination of the witnesses for the prosecution, and above all for the defence, as well as the various charges, N° 11 criminal court delivered its judgment: Henri Guillaume, organiser of the Quat'z'Arts Ball, Sarah Brown and Manon, accused of appearing on the stage in a state of extreme nudity, were sentenced − to a fine of one hundred francs, with time to pay! Since the verdict took into account the artistic and disinter-

ested nature of the offence committed, it was considered to be effectively an acquittal. Clearly extremely contented, those responsible for the Quat'z'Arts Ball immediately announced that next year's would be taking place, at the Moulin Rouge, on the usual date.

... of the Moulin Rouge. No detail was left to chance in the creation of the most magnificent costum

... which were, however ...

... worn only for a single evenin

The subsequent Quat'z' Arts balls:

2 April 1894: The wounds of the previous year had not yet healed. No nudity and very ample costumes. The reaction of one regular customer: 'What's this, the Salvation Army?'

5 April 1895: The ball returned to the magnificence and gaiety of 1893, with armies of warriors wearing helmets and bearing swords, a caravan of camels and the waving of multi-coloured banners.

17 April 1896: A strange fairyland of multi-coloured costumes with Roman legionaries in full uniform.

9 April 1897, 22 April 1898, 21 April 1899, 6 April 1900, 26 April 1901: The balls became ever more magnificent, with elephants, horses, caves, a recon-

struction of the Egyptian campaign and extremely effective ancient costumes. A student spectacle never equalled.

Every Saturday, at half-past eleven . . .

. . . the gaudy procession would enter the hall . . .

the utmost splendour in the service of decadence

Illustrations made at the time by the painter Louis Morin

The Catalogue of the Redoutes

With the quadrille at the height of its glory, Joseph Oller decided to offer Parisians who loved songs and fun even more joyous festivities and even more beautiful shows. He thus reinstated the ancient tradition of the masked ball in evening dress, which is called a *Redoute*. The designer Roedel was appointed the grand organiser of processions and chose his assistants every Saturday, at eleven o'clock. His principal themes were taken from history. Success was immediate. For five months in the year, from 1894 to 1902, the whole of Paris jostled to applaud the most brilliant *tableaux vivants* in the world. Sometimes there would be arguments about who was to be allowed to appear, however briefly, among the walkers-on. To understand why, we need only examine the complete list of those unforgettable Saturday night displays.

Roedel took great care over every detail of his redoutes; he illustrated the programmes himself

RECORD OF EVENTS

15 December 1894: 'The procession of Bacchus'. The God of Wine, symbol of tragedy and the poetic arts, he became the patron of these evenings.

27 December 1894: The Venetian Carnival.

12 January 1895: The great national epics, from the Revolution to the current day, illustrated with military uniforms.

26 January 1895: Venice in the sixteenth century.

22 February 1895: Old Paris, with a reconstruction of the Cour des Miracles (an old district frequented by beggars and vagabonds).

4 December 1895: Cavalcade and Grand Military Parade.

4 January 1896: The descent through the *Courtille* (a kind of enclosed garden). At the head of the procession the mask of Lord Seymour, better known under the name of Milord l'Arsouille (a debauched character).

18 January 1896: The Festival of Fools.

1 February 1896: The Procession of the Queen of the Bacchanalia.

15 February 1896: The Spanish Festival.

29 February 1896: The Carnival of Louis-Philippe.

12 March 1896: *Redoute* for mid-Lent: 'The angry cow'.

19 December 1896: Burlesque *redoute*: 'The sale of Diane de Bougie'.

23 January 1897: Artistic Bohemia.

30 January 1897: The Great Imperial Age. Military and allegorical parade.

6 February 1897: 'The return to Mecca'. *Redoute* of current Parisian life.

13 March 1897: 'The Festival of Love', paying tribute to Watteau.

26 March 1897: 'Cavalcade of the Students'.

17 April 1897: 'The Festival of Spring'.

1 May 1897: *Redoute* dedicated to Nicolas Charlet, coinciding with the unveiling of the monument erected to the memory of the famous painter of the Napoleonic era.

20 November 1897: Festival in ancient Athens.

27 November 1897: The Procession of the Hours. An evocation of cheerful times.

7 December 1897: 'Sambre et Meuse'. Commemoration of the victors of the battles of Jemmapes and Valmy.

24 December 1897: 'Noël, Noël'.

8 January 1898: The Parade of the Kings, including the King of Yvetot, Gambrinus, the playing card Kings and Henri IV.

12 February 1898: 'Wine and the vine', with Bacchus escorted by old Silenus and a procession of bacchanales.

5 March 1898: 'Valmy', with a military and allegorical parade to the tune of the march *Sambre et Meuse*. At the head of the procession, Renée d'Harcely representing the Republic, from the recent effigy called 'The Sower', by the sculptor Louis-Oscar Roty.

9 April 1898: 'The triumph of Phryné', coinciding with the last day of Lent.

26 November 1898: 'Mars and Venus', with an Olympian procession. The warriors of Fontenoy marching alongside the Army of the Sambre et Meuse, together with battalions of pretty girls.

24 December 1898: 'Christmas in Montmartre'.

7 January 1899: 'The Three Kings in Montmartre', with, as the procession disperses, the cutting and distribution of a giant twelfth-night cake.

21 January 1899: 'Who shall have the apple?', with a procession of all the Olympian Gods.

1 April 1899: 'The Flowerhead'.

23 December 1899: 'Christmas in Montmartre' – new version.

6 January 1900: 'Long live the King', with giant cake.

20 January 1900: 'The procession of Venus', attended by Parisian high society on its way to the Opéra.

15 February 1900: 'Who shall have the apple?'

31 March 1900: ' Off to Cythera'.

14 April 1900: 'The Festival of Spring'. Procession of the girls of Montmartre in flower.

13 October 1900: 'The procession of Venus', with a Senegalese Venus, attended by a troupe of Indochinese dancers.

13 November 1900: 'Nymphs and Sirens'.

24 December 1900: 'Christmas in Montmartre', in six scenes: Midnight in Brittany, Midnight in the street, Truffled poultry, Midnight at Nisis's, Midnight at the Inn, Midnight on duty.

19 January 1901: 'Furbelows and face-powder', with quadrilles by the Clodoches and revellers in fancy dress. Scenes based on: The boudoir, Under arms, Going to the ball, The masked ball, Flirting, Going home.

16 February 1901: 'Here come the masks', with scenes of carnival from ancient times to the present day.

3 April 1901: 'The Rascal of Spring'.

24 December 1901: 'Christmas Eve at the

à Georges Courteline

Moulin', with a giant Christmas Tree and the giving of presents to the establishment's faithful supporters.

18 January 1902: 'Muhammad's Paradise'.

15 February 1902: 'Rabelais'. Scenes from the lives of Gargantua and Pantagruel.

15 March 1902: 'In the harem'. Oriental life.

29 March 1902: 'The Festival of Spring: Love and Flowers'.

17 August 1899: The following publicity notice was published in all the Paris dailies:

Where could one spend a more agreeable time, breathing the fresh air, than at the Moulin Rouge, in its pretty garden, whether listening to the enjoyable concert or watching the entertainment offered by this establishment's famous dancers?

THE GREAT PRIVATE FUNCTIONS

Throughout the years, the Moulin Rouge has been the frequent location for Parisian events of all kinds.

On private evenings, on public ones, on evenings devoted to sport or to horseracing, Steinlen was also at the Moulin Rouge, where nothing escaped his sharp eyes

IN THE WINGS

18 January 1898: The Moulin Rouge in Danger!

There is a rumour running around Paris – the Moulin Rouge is closing down! The fall in receipts due to competition from the Casino de Paris and other entertainment spots has become so great that Joseph Oller was thought to have decided to put the key under the mat, although the story has been expressly denied by the individual involved. The building is not up for sale and the establishment which, in ten years, has become one of the most renowned in the world will continue to function.

'The Moulin Rouge has become the meeting-place of the capital,' he explained. 'No foreigner, passing through Paris, fails to visit it. I promise you, in the coming months, festivals of even greater brilliance.'

From the horse's mouth . . .

The Grand Prix horse-races

Between 1895 and 1900 all the 'Evening Festivities' forming the conclusion to the most important meetings: the Grand Prix d'Automne at Longchamp, the Derby at Chantilly, the Grand International Steeplechase at Auteuil . . .

The sporting evenings:

Introduction to the pleasures of cycling. Such evenings were unusual, exceptional occasions.

7 February 1895: a gathering of the 'Unpuncturables', a group of dramatic artists who took part in regular cycle rides, wearing jersey and leggings like the champions.

21 November 1896: *Vélo-Redoute*, with a procession of bicycles, tandems, three-man and four-man machines.

26 December 1896: special night associated with the fourth Bicycle Exhibition.

16 April 1899: demonstration by the womens' skating polo team.

3 January 1900: demonstration of wrestling by Norlah, the famous Turkish wrestler.

Poetry evenings:

On Saturday nights regular gatherings were attended by the poet-songwriters including, in particular, two of the leading lights of the day: Marcel Legay and You Ling.

Classical evenings:

Every Good Friday between 1895 and 1902 classical concerts were presented, after the regular show: fifty musicians under the direction of Messieurs Mabille and Gouvain, the conductors of the dance orchestra.

Children's matinées:

Each Shrove Monday and at mid-Lent between 1895 and 1902, masked balls in evening-dress were held for children under ten. They offered various entertainments, Punch and Judy shows, presents for each child and set dances and farandoles.

Other evening entertainments:

15 April 1896: draw for the 'angry cow' tombola.

1 June 1896: 'intellectual art' evening, with contributions from Mary Helt, Yvonne Renaix, Philippa, Norba and the songwriter Poussin.

6 October 1896: special afternoon performance, presented to coincide with the Franco-Russian celebrations.

15 December 1898: opening of the pierrettes' dance.

4 July 1902: celebration of American Independence Day.

GALA NIGHTS

7 February 1901

Last night saw an unbroken procession of luxurious carriages in front of the handsome establishment in Montmartre, where the whole of sophisticated and fashionable Paris joined the light-hearted set which forms its habitual clientele. The reason for this effusion of elegance was the return of the singer Blanche d'Arvilly, whose name blazing from the posters was enough to bring the high and low of boulevardier Paris to the Butte. She was the complete mistress of her art, full of nuances, feeling and Parisian grace. As for her costumes, these were utter marvels, wonderfully adapted to her songs, of which *La Masseuse* was typical and one which she delivered bewitchingly.

The return of the Montagnes Russes switchback railway at the Moulin Rouge
8 May 1901

As everybody will remember, the Montagnes Russes were, a quarter of a century ago, the most original of all the amusement parks in Paris. Built in England and set up on the Boulevard des Capucines, they were an attraction to Parisians and tourists alike. Joseph Oller, their creator, was so fond of them that he has just announced their reopening in the gardens of the Moulin Rouge. Pending their official inauguration, scheduled for 22 May, the management, for the benefit of artists, has introduced a competition for a new poster depicting them. Five hundred francs in prize money will be shared between the best six entries, to be judged by a jury to be formed by Messieurs Jules Choret, Grasset, Mucha, Luncis and Jeanniot. All the entries will be on display in the hall of the Moulin Rouge for the week commencing 21 May.

A few figures for the Moulin Rouge
25 June 1901

The computation is an easy one: the takings on the Métro amount to 125 francs per hour; those for the Montagnes Russes are 3 francs per hour. To put it another way, the new three-tier Montagnes Russes have become the star turn of an establishment which is attracting more and more patrons every day. Many people unhesitatingly have ten or fifteen goes at a time. At the beginning of the month the jury set up to judge the poster competition for this attraction awarded first prize to Monsieur Whidopff, the second to René Péau and the third to Vallhourat. Last week, during the evening festivities, fireworks were let off from the topmost point of the Montagnes Russes, providing the finest illuminations we have seen for a long time.

17 August 1901

A patron of the Moulin Rouge has just made a very interesting calculation. Between 6 October 1889 and the present day, the sails of the mill have made four million eight hundred thousand revolutions. This is equal to a third of the total number of visitors since the dance hall opened. These figures can be believed with absolute confidence, for the person who produced them is, in fact, one of our most brilliant statisticians.

Moulin Rouge: new rumours
16 June 1902

For the moment it is nothing more than a rumour: that the Moulin Rouge is to be converted into a big music hall – another Olympia or Folies-Bergère. It is also said that Monsieur Paul-Louis Flers, the author of revues which have been particularly popular with the public for the past two years, will take over the management of the new establishment. Such stories have been strenuously denied by Joseph Oller – yet again. The atmosphere in the area of the Place Blanche persuades us to believe him. The universal popularity of the Moulin Rouge was proved by its success during the last Exhibition. Every evening a crowd of Parisians, provincials and, above all, foreigners gather there to enjoy themselves, whether for the excellent concert performed by the group of outstanding artists, the quadrille, both eccentric and ultra-Parisian, or the many games installed in the establishment. Nevertheless, in private, Joseph Oller professes himself, it seems, 'tired' of assuming all these responsibilities, while seeing the takings regularly decreasing. It is also being said that the fees offered to the artists have been reduced and that the size of the orchestra is on the point of being reduced also. Furthermore, the public dance hall is no longer in fashion. The Rue de Clichy, ballets, mime and the entertainments offered by Messieurs Armand Després and Louis Borney at the Casino de Paris are what are now drawing the public. All these rumours are therefore not without their foundation. The wind is blowing from another direction, and it is not towards Montmartre.

The Curtain Falls on the MOULIN ROUGE

29 December 1902: The last dance

Last night the Moulin Rouge saw its last quadrille. Thus the funeral has taken place, but it was not of the highest class. Those who had known and appreciated the panache of the cancan, the back-chat of La Goulue and the exceptional agility of Valentin le Désossé found it difficult to endure the comparison. In place of the joyous orchestra of the much-loved Mabille, what did we hear?

You'll never guess – a mechanical organ! The din of its music shattered the ears and the hearts of the faithful adherents of former years. Thus this legendary dance hall has passed away unmourned by the sound of drum or trumpet. The shadow of La Goulue was everywhere present in a hall where, for the last time, thronged some of the pioneers of the cancan: Jane Avril, Grille d'Égout, La Môme Fromage and Valentin le Désossé – stars whose names cannot mean very much in the minds of a fashionable Paris which has seen great changes. This last evening will

have been a minor event in Paris; it will make a greater impact in London and Chicago, where the reputation of the Place Blanche, happily, has remained intact. Where do we go from here? The new management has announced its reopening for next month, with 'even more beautiful' decorations and an 'even more outstanding' programme. We should like to see it. It will require much imagination on the part of Monsieur P-L Flers to expunge the memory of those five quadrilles a day, which were worth one *louis* to the dancers. That was a time when pleasure was to be found in a hell, the road to which is perhaps, today, no longer paved with good intentions.

IN THE WINGS
29 November 1902

Now it's official. The Moulin Rouge dance hall will be changed to a variety theatre next January. Monsieur Paul-Louis Flers will be its director and will bear responsibility for the thousand and one details of the new decor. He has said that 'it will be in the best of taste and great pains will be taken', and has placed the plans and their execution in the hands of Monsieur Niermans, the very artistic architect who has demonstrated his talent many times. The new hall is scheduled to open at the end of January 1903.

Valentin le Désossé's statement

'Today is no ordinary day. I should like to express my thanks to all the management, all the staff, the customers and the employees, and above all to all those women who have pursued me for so many years.'

On the Place Blanche: the entrance to the Moulin Rouge in 1894

CHANGE of OWNERSHIP

The Universal Exhibition of 1900 was fatal to the Moulin Rouge of Joseph Oller, Toulouse-Lautrec and La Goulue. The quadrille was by then popular only with a few sentimentalists and foreigners who were unaware of the change in fashion. It needed only a few months before the takings were no longer covering the outgoings, and the financial situation became so disquieting that, in 1902, Joseph Oller was prepared to consider an offer from a company headed by the dramatic author Max Maurey. He retained the ownership of

The commère and compere: the traditional presenters of the revue

the building, but handed over responsibility for the artistic activities. Major work was then begun to transform the dance hall into another of the variety theatres which were then experiencing increasing popular success.

The architect Niermans fitted out a hall glowing with white and orange velvet, and Paul-Louis Flers, the revue writer of the moment, accepted the post of director. His programme was then much more ambitious than his libretti. His reign was distinguished, but lasted for only nine months — long enough to yield three

shows and to create routines which, after his departure, were to establish themselves as traditions. The *apéritif-concert* in the garden became the meeting-place for the idle rich from four until seven on summer afternoons. In summer, said the advertisements, the Moulin Rouge provided the favourite relaxation for all true Parisians. In the highest social circles it was the custom to make advance reservations for the front-row seats, the boxes and the orchestra stalls. One could leave and then return to see the best numbers in the show, between eight and eleven o'clock, at quarter-past, half-past and a quarter-to the hour. The performance not to be missed was the French cancan — now the French quadrille, but still as rhythmical.

In the basement was an enormous tavern-restaurant, featuring a Tyrolean orchestra with blaring brass instruments, and boxing matches. Unfortunately, its success was not to measure up to the promoters' dreams.

Between 1903 and 1914, directors were to come and go almost as frequently as the play-bills were changed. The list is impressive: Georges Judic, Charles Montcharmont, Valette and Monza, Victor Silvestre, Joseph Oller himself in 1906, trying to return to the tiller of the boat he

In the days of colonies, oriental dancers were very much the fashion

had first launched, Max Viterbo, Edmond Brouette, Charles Aumont, Paul Ruez, Peter Carin, Jean Fabert . . . Their problems were financial, unconcerned with the shows, and they did not prevent the public from remaining faithful to the Place Blanche. Every evening it crowded through the doors of what had been dubbed the 'joyous Moulin Rouge', to enjoy satires on current events and the audacious sets whose influence can still be discerned today. It applauded scenery, costumes and casts of productions of a sumptuousness previously un-

The Moulin Rouge all ablaze at the turn of the century

equalled. The shows were discussed late into the night, at dinner-parties attended by the most elegant and distinguished personalities. Thus men of the world, men-about-town, writers and artists rubbed shoulders with members of sober and respectable American, English and German families who, wearing false noses or dark glasses, studied every detail of this place of ruination with the same concentration they had given to the Mona Lisa or Napoleon's tomb.

Those were the days when the revue, having invaded the music-hall, was taking over the theatre. Every establishment worthy of that name was obliged to include one in its programme, and it mattered not what it was, though the leaflets always proclaimed it 'the best'.

Thus one performer succeeded another, for the most part forgotten today, though deserving their places in the show business temple of the immortals. Their names can be found in a detailed list of the revues, which continued until 27 February 1915. On that night, a huge fire destroyed the auditorium and the lobby. Fortunately the stage, the exits, the dressing rooms and the frontage all escaped. Joseph Oller took his successive tenants to court, with the object of determining their respective responsibility for the origin of the disaster. On 6 December 1915 Jean Fabert was required to restore the establishment at his own expense. The First World War prevented all attempts to settle the affair, and it was to be ten years before the Moulin Rouge rose again from its ashes.

PAUL-LOUIS FLERS:

The King of Revue

When he took over as director of the Moulin Rouge, Paul-Louis Flers was not an unknown. For nearly ten years he had captured the public taste, and his revues had been box-office draws in all the *cafés-concerts* and music-halls of Paris. His real name was Pujol, this fellow with the thin face, the hook nose, the little moustache and the mischievous eyes. He was an inveterate worker, who had at his service a valuable team of ghost-writers who enabled him to meet his obligations. Every Thursday he held a meeting of his assistants, floated an idea, proposed the reworking of an old one and pocketed the work of his collaborators, uttering the time-honoured phrase: 'I'll see if I can make something out of this.' Jacques-Charles and, in particular, the celebrated Rip were both, for a few months, members of a team which was resolutely anglophile. Paul-Louis Flers had a great partiality for the English style and liked only British music, which was

Paul-Louis Flers, by Bertys

also in vogue with the general public.

He thus held all the right cards to carry out in the Place Blanche the ambitious scheme on which he had decided: to make the Moulin Rouge the leading variety theatre in Paris.

First of all he made important innovations. Frequent visits to the Wintergarten in Berlin and to Ronacher's in Vienna had imbued him with the idea of providing Paris with an establishment even more beautiful and even more comfortable than those huge music-halls. He therefore fitted out a spacious lobby and – a sensational innovation – a restaurant from which everything could be seen and heard. Arranged behind the seats in the circle were tables which immediately became the most sought-after in Paris. He cherished high ambitions for staging, too. The revues in *his* Moulin Rouge would abandon former well-trodden paths and, in their luxury and vigour, would exceed all which purported to be the finest and youngest in Paris. Thus, he announced the opening of *Tu marches?*, a revue by Adrien Vély which had a cast of no fewer than one hundred and fifty performers. The first part contained original numbers which were changed every fortnight and were destined, it was said, to cause a sensation. Two months later, the musical comedy *The Belle of New York* was a shattering success and the box offices were besieged by ticket seekers. In November 1903 he presented *T'en as un oeil* before, to everyone's surprise, relinquishing the director's chair which had fitted him so well. He indicated that he wanted to devote himself solely to his writing, and handed over his responsibilities to the ex-director of the Châtelet, Georges Judic. Success remained with him for many years both in the Place Blanche and elsewhere. He discovered outstanding talents such as Phroso, Tom Hearn and the renowned dancer Norman French, who later taught Maurice Chevalier and had an enormous influence on his career. It would be difficult to imagine a better recommendation.

IN THE WINGS

5 March 1903

The gala night planned to coincide with the opening of the Moulin Rouge variety theatre, which had been scheduled for this evening, has been put off until tomorrow, to allow last-minute alterations of the scenery for the Kingdom of Saxony, requiring a further evening of rehearsals.

7 March 1903

Missives are arriving at the Moulin Rouge in their hundreds, begging for 'just a little corner somewhere'. Alas, to quote Polin, there is nothing left – not a thing!

18 March 1903

Such is success, Paul-Louis Flers has just had to replace three rows of seats in the lower circle with restaurant tables. An extra hundred places are now available every evening, to meet the needs of those who, despite remarkable dedication, do not manage to secure places for the Moulin Rouge variety show.

12 June 1903

Unusual spectacle in the Place Blanche. A crowd gathered in front of the entrance to the Moulin Rouge variety theatre, complaining of no longer being able to find boxes and seats to see *The Belle of New York*. The management put out a statement expressing their regrets and pointing out that it was only in this theatre that there had been no increase in the price of the seats. A warning to those who, encouraged by the success of the entertainment business, indulge in an apparently very profitable 'black market'.

4 August 1903

The Moulin Rouge is once more the rendez-vous of the caricaturists. Every evening they gather there to sketch the scenes in *The Belle of New York*. This week we sighted, solemnly installed in their seats, those well-known artists Abel Faivre, Caran d'Ache, Testéonide, Jacques-Charles and Léandre, the author of a very witty piece about this operetta.

12 August 1903

Short conversation overheard in the corridors of the Moulin Rouge:

'You, in Paris, at this time of year? You, the sportsman, the society man, the king of elegance? *And* in the middle of the week too!

'I've given it all up. I've taken to coming to the Moulin Rouge every evening, to see *The Belle of New York*. I've ditched everything else for that. For the countryside I have the Moulin Rouge's marvellous garden, which is good enough for me. I find myself unable to exist for one month without enjoying the delicious Marville, the hilarious Claudius and all the other performers in this wonderful operetta.'

And that unwavering supporter of *The Belle of New York*, the Count of F—— moved off, humming a popular air from the show.

GALA NIGHTS AT THE MOULIN

5 March 1903:
TU MARCHES?
(YOU'RE GOING?)

Revue by Adrien Vély and Charles Clairville.

With Alexandre Colas, Charles Reschal, Victor Lejal, Carlos Avril, Ellen Baxone, Loulou Mabel, Mado Minty and Marguerite Fournier.

Mea culpa! Several months ago, when our adored Moulin Rouge closed, we were hardly fair to the new owners of this legendary dance hall. It really seemed very difficult, not to say impossible, to surpass the achievements of Joseph Oller and Charles Zidler during those great days in the Place Blanche. Today we are not ashamed to admit that we were wrong. We emerged from the opening night still dazzled by the countless wonders that Monsieur Paul-Louis Flers has produced. The present has only one link with the past – a name known throughout the world: Monsieur Paul-Louis Flers, the famous revue author now stands revealed as a most brilliant director. His first advantage is to be blessed with facilities which match his ambitions. Committing the fitting-out of this latest rendezvous of elegant Paris to Monsieur Niermans was a marvellous idea. The work of this popular architect has a calm, luxurious modernity, unobtrusively setting off to advantage beautiful shoulders and attractive costumes. It is immense, gay and luminous, and the scenery and the décor combine to make it the handsomest place of entertainment in the world. By taking the tables in the restaurant by storm, the public has acknowledged this. Glory and long life to the theatre which serves dinner too! The variety turns are particularly well chosen and very much out of the ordinary. The Fassios are dizzy and youthful acrobats, the Deprients are gymnasts of incomparable daring, Miss Ada Bell and Edwards are skilful jugglers, while Cook and Miss Rothert have already taken London by storm. Discovered by P-L Flers himself, they should arouse the admiration of Parisians too.

As for *Tu marches?*, the 'crazy and witty' revue by Adrien Vély, this promises to eclipse all others of its kind, not only by the wittiness of its author and the talent of its performers, but also by its dazzling scenery and its opulent costumes. One hundred and fifty artists, ten sets! Masterpieces by Amable: the castle wall at Elsinore, the kingdom of Saxony with a hundred women, dressed in sumptuous costumes and adornments, ranged up a huge staircase which begins in the roof of the Moulin Rouge and consists of no fewer than one hundred and ninety-two steps. It is impossible to describe in all their detail the incredible settings for Hamlet, for the master of ceremonies, for Bob l'Amour's garage, for the Director of the Bouffes and his English company, which were followed by a homeric cake-walk danced by a newspaper editor, Jean Lorrain, La Belle Otéro, Little Tich and Liane de Pougy. The 'Chariot race', the admir-

able scenery by Jambon, and the 'Forest of Moulins Rouges', the apotheosis of fairyland, merit equal praise. In establishing his claim to be the leading 'star finder', the new director has taken the risk of placing at the top of the bill three young discoveries: Ellen Baxone, the comedienne, is not yet seventeen; the principal dancer, Mado Minty, is scarcely eighteen; and the third star, Miss Loulu Mabel, is a very rich American whose beauty threatens to outdo the lustre of our own 'Professional Beauties'. She wants, she says, to 'sacrifice everything' to the pleasure of acting and dancing. She is unlikely to end up the loser and should quickly profit from the publicity.

11 April 1903:
LE GATEAU D'OR
(THE GOLDEN CAKE)

At the Moulin Rouge it's one big laugh! That's what we were promised, and P-L Flers has kept his word. It's a long time since we have been so entertained anywhere in Paris.

Last night dancers, both French and British, came to compete for the title of world champion of the cake-walk. This

'The Belle of New York': the finale

IN THE WINGS

2 October 1903

There's a trial of strength taking place at the Moulin Rouge. Don't worry, there's not the least sign of conflict to be seen. After the boxing match three weeks ago, between the two lightweights Joe Parker and George Cooper, today we have the world championship of strength, the Golden Gauntlet.

There are no towering hulks, glistening with sweat, to be seen. These are good-looking young men, athletes possessing symmetry of form and finely-jointed limbs, well-proportioned and graceful giants, aware of the beauty of physical force and of the aesthetics of outline. The favourite is Elisseieff, the terrible Cossack, while among the many outsiders one notes Maspoli, from Lyons, who is one of the best-known. In England recently he won the envied title of weight-lifting champion. The first prize is a celebrated work of art, bought not long ago by the Council of Paris. It is 'Nudes in the Storm' by the sculptor Raoul Larche.

The evening has been organised jointly by the Athletic Club of Saint Petersburg and *L'Auto*, the magazine under the very competent editorship of Henri Desgrange. The event was used to carry out a genuine scientific experiment. In order to find out how far man's energy can be taken, it is essential to know the limit of his physical strength. The best way to arrive at this would seem to be to gather together athletes from all fields, in brotherly endeavours. This evening at the Moulin Rouge, as you will have gathered, unity has, more than ever, meant strength.

The representatives:

Serge Elisseieff (Russia), Pierre Bonnes (France), Charles Pourée (France), Victorius (France), Émile Deriaz (Switzerland), Jacques Roumageon (France), Gabriel Lassartesse (France), Alfredo Gonzalo (Spain), Jean Calvet (France), Louis David (France).

There will be three heats before the final contest:

Single extended arm with 20 kilo weight (in the hand or from a ring)
Lift with one hand or short halter
Snatch by hand, on the bar or short halter, according to personal preference.

We look forward to an epic contest between Elisseieff and Bonnes.

17 November 1903

The following is a portrait of Louise Balthy, in the form of a publicity enclosure circulated with the leading Parisian dailies:

'Balthy! Who's Balthy?'
'Everyone knows who Balthy is!'
'Really?'
'She's fantastic, she's exuberance personified!'
'What about it?'
'She's the singer with the vibrant and engaging voice.'
'Anything else?'
'She's the most audacious of mimics!'
'Go on.'
'She's the most moving of actresses . . . when she wants to be!'
'Tell me more!'
'For the theatre or the music-hall which has on its stage she is the surest and the most brilliant attraction, the goose that lays the golden eggs. Balthy the Star!'
'And where is she appearing at the moment?'
'At the Moulin Rouge, in the revue *T'en as un oeil!*'

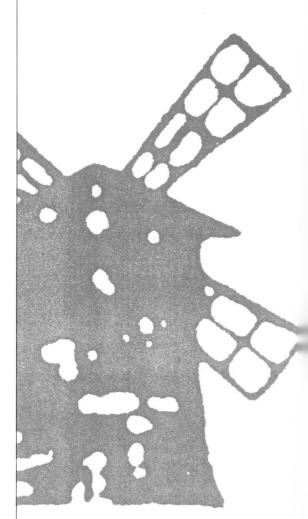

was the ostensible reason for an evening of surprises. Picture the grand staircase lined with an exclusively feminine guard of honour to welcome the audience's arrival. Add to that a gipsy supper, served by Julien, the most dedicated of *maîtres d'hôtel*, a breakfast referred to as 'a select hop' and, to cries of joy, the dances, judged by the most beautiful actresses in Paris: Lyse Berty (Capucines), Marcelle Bordo (Nouveautés), Suzanne Carlix (Gymnase), Chavita (Opéra-Comique), Paulette Darty (Scala), Diéterle (Bouffes Parisiens), Jameson and Lucy Jousset (Palais Royal), Hughetto (La Scala of Milan), Marie Laparcerie (on the staff of *Gil Blas*), Pernyn (Variétés), Léa Piron (Opéra), Yvonne de Rycke (Athénée), Jane Yvon (Variétés) and Ellen Baxone (Moulin Rouge). The jury was chaired by the impetuous and whimsical Louise Balthy, whose verve and sense of aptitude is well known. The winner received the Golden Cake and twenty thousand francs worth of *objets d'art* and gifts. The major prize amongst these, valued at eight thousand francs, was a magnificently wooded piece of land in the park of Beauséjour, in the middle of the forest of Sainte Geneviéve, one hour from Paris. It was natural that the last bouquet should be symbolised by trees.

30 April 1903:
THE BELLE OF NEW YORK

American spectacular operetta by Hugh Morton.
Adapted by: Paul Gavault.
Music: Gustave Kerker.
Costumes by Pascaud.
Scenery by Amable.

With Marie Marville (Fifi)
Maurice Claudius (Bob)
Ellen Baxone (the cashier)
Charles Reschal (Ichabod Branson)
Victor Lejal (Badaboum Pacha)
Portal (Harry)
Marien (Blinky Bill)
Carlos Avril (the pianist)
Giralduc (Cora)
Marguerite Fournier (Kissie Pom Pom)
Marcelle Fabry (the Chinese woman)
and Miss Williams (a working girl)

The most famous American operetta in the world at the Moulin Rouge! A world event that is not to be missed, not only by fashionable Paris, but also by fashionable London and fashionable New York. That was the evening which we have just spent in the Place Blanche. It was a party given in honour of the American colony in Paris, at which the ambassador himself made sure he was represented, by his private secretary. It

'The Belle of New York': the principal players

was a triumph for the performers, who were applauded the moment the curtain rose. The story is a very simple one: the conquest of Harry Bronson by the young Fifi, to whose charms he is initially oblivious. Two hundred performances are assured, with outstanding artists. Mademoiselle Ellen Baxone sings more prettily and exquisitely than ever, Madame Girlduc is herself, in other words excellent, Mademoiselle Marguerite Fournier would exhaust a critic's brains if he were to award her all the words of praise which she deserves. Reschal, Carlos Avril and Lejal surpass themselves, a very difficult feat, it must be said. As for the exquisite Cocktail sisters, who flit about amid shafts of gilded light, fairy scenery and Chinese palaces, they play the only French girls in a show where all the characters are English. It's enough to make one think that American girls will soon be more exquisite than French ones . . .

20 January 1904:
VOLUPTATA

Spectacular operetta in two acts by Paul-Louis Flers
Music by Paul Marcelles.

With Sulbac, Hamilton, Charles Reschal, Fernand Frey, Carlos Avril, Anna Tariol, Dorgère and the Cocktails.
Orchestra directed by G. Goublier.
Costumes by Landolff.

Paul-Louis Flers has decided that the form of variety show which he has made popular at the Moulin Rouge over the past year is now sufficiently established to allow him to take flight elsewhere on his own wings. He has therefore relinquished his directorial duties and returned to writing. For this return to his original profession he has chosen the field of operetta in which he has often given us proof of his talent. The two-act *Voluptata* is a marvel of Parisian entertainment, and one of the finest and most sensitive which we have had the chance to see for a long time. A festive evening, attended by Her Highness Elegance and His Majesty Good Taste, a mixture of laughter and poetry! The scenery for the third scene was worth the journey on its own: a verdant, flower-decked garden, a natural river meandering across the stage, and the Cocktails in the exquisite costume of eighteenth-century peasants, gathering daisies from the grass and plucking their petals as they sang. Also to be praised is the talent of the orchestra conductor, Gustave Goublier, the only one, to our knowledge, to wield the baton wearing white gloves. We must also report the first steps of a new American dance, ragtime, performed by eight delectable young women. Finally, what does the leading protagonist think of his piece? In the wings, at the end of

IN THE WINGS

20 November 1903

A statistics enthusiast has claimed that, at each performance of *T'en as un oeil!*, there are one million nine hundred and seventy-three thousand francs in the theatre. This is made up of eight thousand francs in takings, eighty thousand for the costumes, thirty thousand for the scenery, fifteen thousand for the show horses, two hundred and forty thousand for the jewellery on the stage, and fifteen thousand for that in the boxes and the orchestra stalls.

24 November 1903

From last night the Moulin Rouge has a new and outstanding entertainer. His name is Norman French, and he is a comic dancer who is currently the rage of London. He is an impeccable gentleman, with an astounding suppleness. We have doubtless not heard the last of him in Paris.

1 December 1903

There is a new wind of correspondence blowing through revue. Never before, it seems, has an artiste received in her mail so many emotional communications from anonymous admirers. That great performer Louise Balthy, who is applauded each evening in *T'en as un oeil!*, receives dozens of missives, some touching in their naivety, others climbing up to lyricism and treading – O Montmartre! – the heights of Mount Parnassus.

13 January 1904:
A SHORT INTERVIEW

'Louise Balthy, you're actually going to leave the Moulin Rouge at the height of your success there?'

'Yes, another ten performances and I shall have come to the end of my contract.'

'What are you proposing to do? After all, an artist of your calibre doesn't take a rest in the middle of the theatre season.'

'But my programme has been decided for a long time – I'm going abroad! I shall be in England where, as a result of an exchange of letters which I found very flattering, I shall be singing in a very attractive number of fashionable salons to which I have been invited. To tell the truth, London Society is not as strait-laced as is made out. Since my repertoire also includes serious ballads and more conformist songs than I usually sing in my revues, I can tackle all kinds of audience.'

12 July 1904

The management of the Moulin Rouge has discovered a most unusual form of publicity to make *The Toreador* – the success of the summer – known to the widest possible public. Using indelible ink, they have printed, on the completely bald head of a dedicated retainer, the title of this highly successful operetta. Several times a day this stalwart, who has the appearance of a gentleman, seats himself on the terraces of fashionable restaurants and the big cafés. He then removes his hat, thus revealing the illuminated advertisement to an amused public. The success of the stunt on the spot is immediate, and this apparently extends to the box-office of the variety theatre on the Place Blanche.

4 August 1904

The audience which attended last night's performance of *The Toreador* have not yet got over it. The amiable prince was to be seen on the stage and in the stalls at one and the same time. The explanation, however, is simple: the artist's double in the stalls was Mr Grossmith, who created the role in the English version of the show, visiting Paris in the company of Ivan Caryll, one of the composers of the music of this gayest of operettas.

31 August 1904

With *The Toreador* enjoying its great success, Monsieur Chausson, Chairman of the Board, administrator elect, and director of the Moulin Rouge, has handed over control to the new occupiers: Messieurs Montcharmont and Melchissedec. Monsieur Fabius de Champville, secretary to the former director, has followed him into retirement. He will be replaced by Monsieur Robert Dieudonné. We wish the new management good luck and every success.

5 November 1904

The recipe concocted by the new management is bringing results! The latest rage among Parisians is to appear, all dressed up, in the last act of *La Revue du Moulin*. You actually appear on the stage! Everyone whom fashionable Paris considers to be in the swim – the 'toffs' as they're called – gets a special kick out of finding himself in front of the footlights, surrounded by so many pretty girls in their glittering costumes.

Anna Tariol and her partners in 'Voluptata'

the performance, Paul-Louis Flers exclaimed:

'The last action of Paul-Louis Flers, director, was to commission a piece from Paul-Louis Flers, writer. My God, let's hope he hasn't made a blunder!'

30 January 1904:
LE BAL DES MINUINETTES

At a time when physical exercise seems to have become the principal preoccupation of our fellow-citizens, here we have the Moulin Rouge offering us this evening the first sporting ball. The event will be stylish and Parisian, but unusual in that, before the Boston and the two-step, one hundred and fifty competitors, charming artists who are all appearing at the theatres, *cafés-concerts* and music-halls of Paris, will take part in unique contests: a lovely legs competition, an egg-and-spoon race, a bicycle race with an electrical machine of a new type, a tug-of-war, and climbing the greasy pole, from which various delightful objects are suspended. Prize money worth twenty thousand francs is at stake! The jury with the task of examining the results will be the epitome of elegance. Mademoiselle Liane de Pougy has agreed to occupy the chair, and around her, in charming costumes, we may list Mesdemoiselles Louise Bignon, Anna Tariol, Alice Bonheur, Gaby Deslys, Suzanne Derval, Arlette Dorgère, Debary, Faber, Jousset, De Leka, Louly d'Auray, Yvonne de Ricke, Berthe Siredi, and not forgetting, of course, the beautiful Marville and the charming Ellen Baxone.

We should also mention the exceptional performance by the party of Scottish workmen who, in twenty minutes — between eleven forty and midnight, to be precise — succeeded in removing all the seats and installing the track and the dance floor in their place. This feat they accomplish every year in London, at Covent Garden. They seem to have lost none of their expertise through crossing the Channel.

3 March 1904:
OFFENBACH REVUE

Spectacular mime revue.

With Liane de Pougy, Xavière de Leka, Anna Tariol, the Cocktails, Sulbac, Charles Reschal, Jacquet, Carlos Avril, Victor Lejal and Fernand Frey.

Xavière de Leka: as celebrated off-stage as on

If you like marching, counter-marching, the two-step, the cake-walk and lullabies, don't miss the new spectacular mime revue at the Moulin Rouge. For an hour and a half over two hundred different tunes, each more alluring, more gracious than the other, fill the place with their joyful sound. After that, you have the entrance of the charming Liane de Pougy. Delightfully dressed, charming, the essence of grace and simplicity, the 'best comedienne of our *demi-mondaines*' as she has been described, is a sensation in the part of Mademoiselle Flonflon. To play the part she returned at very short notice from the depths of Portugal, and she has not regretted it. Since the disappearance of her famous pearl necklace, hardly a smile has been seen on her lips. This success should enable her to rediscover her customary zest. I should tell you that she has just finished a *roman à clef*, which is soon destined to create quite a furore in the theatrical world.

The presence on stage should also be noted of a real English Lord. Although he has a private income of three hundred thousand francs, Lord N, 'The man with the grip of iron', as they call him in London, works simply for the pleasure of it. He is a gentleman of dazzling style and Herculean strength. His courtesy is exemplary – except when anyone treads on his toes. He is then capable, we are assured, of justifying – at your cost – the name which the British have given him. Admire him by all means, but stand back – an essential precaution for your own comfort and safety!

15 April 1904:
LYSISTRATA

German operetta adapted by Paul-Louis Flers.
Music by Paul Lincke.

With Germain Gallois, Xavière de Leka, Jane Yannick, Angèle Gril, Gaby Boisset, Mimi James, Bianca Pierre, Déa de Corlay, Suzy, Berthe Nanon, Sulbac, Fernand Frey, Carlos Avril and Charles Reschal.

Scenery by Marion and Théo.

The little sister of *The Belle of New York* has come to Paris for the summer! That's what Paul-Louis Flers promised us, and he has kept his word by giving us *Lysistrata*, the famous German operetta, performed more than five thousand times in Austria, in Germany, and nearly ten thousand times in America and England. For Paris the book has been rewritten from start to finish, scenes have been added and the score strengthened with additional songs, as is the way in England. The result is a measure of the effort exerted. The appearance in Lysistrata's house of illuminated lines of verse creates an absolutely magical effect, and the quartet, with the illuminated words twinkling in the grass and in the sky, is perhaps the prettiest part of the score. The perfection of the performance alone renders it worthy of the Opéra-Comique. As for the *tableaux vivants*, these are, in our opinion, the last word in art. The Etruscan Cup, the Purveyor of Love, the Bones Players, Isis, Jupiter and the Jade Column, posed by models with perfect figures from the Quat'z' Arts, evoked long murmurs of admiration. Also to be mentioned are the whistling fauns, a scene in the temple of Bacchus, the marvellous kicks-in-the-back dance and, above all, Germaine Gallois in the leading role. We applauded her with immense pleasure; at last the most beautiful woman in Paris is no longer content to play comedy parts. Those who remember her success in *La Mascotte* at the Gaîté, will have no difficulty in picturing the ovation which she received from the audience last night.

The poster and the principal characters in 'The Toreador' (opposite)

18 June 1904:
THE TOREADOR

English operetta in two acts and four scenes, adapted by A. Fordyce and Jacques Bousquet.
Music by Ivan Caryll and Lionel Monckton.

With Ellen Baxone (replaced at the end of August by Lacombe), Yannick, Suzy Mabelle, Rousselière, Compton and de Villiers.

With Claudius and Prince, Charles Reschal, Carlos Avril, Sablanc and de Verneuil.

'Have you seen that little piece?' This is the question which is on everyone's lips on the boulevards this morning. For a full ten minutes this small part kept the lucky audience at the first night of *The Toreador* convulsed with laughter.

It is an English operetta which has been performed all over the world, and which only Parisians still have not seen. This extraordinary scene, played by Claudius and Prince, a deserter from the Variétés, is the star turn of a delightful show whose welcome rivals that of *The Belle of New York*, which may be remembered as a great triumph.

The allure of beauty competes with the hilarity of the plot and the luxury of the production. As it departed, the delighted crowd was humming *The Language of the Flowers*. It was the perfect ending to an evening which was a bouquet of joy.

7 December 1904:
LA FÊTE DE L'AUTOMOBILE
(THE FESTIVAL OF THE MOTOR CAR)

That elegant music-hall in the Place Blanche has been invaded by the world of the motor car. Tonight, between half-past midnight and five a.m., we were present at the extraordinary *Redoute* which the whole of Paris has been talking about for the last fortnight, and we were not disappointed. *La Presse* and *L'Auto*, the organisers of the evening, have found a worthy means of celebrating the opening of the *Salon de l'Automobile*. Among the crowd were well-dressed women, but mainly it consisted of men in black suits and driving caps, while on stage was the most entertaining of revues, appropriate to the occasion. First of all there was the return of Polaire. She tells us that she has definitely left a *café-concert* which she hates, for some very interesting parts in the theatre. Just for one evening she agreed to sing some comic songs once more, provided that the words were by Martin Galle, that brilliant journalist on *La Presse*, a wish that you may be sure was granted. After that, Thérèse Cernay confessed that she was 'the walker-on with the graceful walk'. Also to be mentioned are the excellent Frey, the Mathurins in a series of sporting monologues, Marguerite Deval, a maestro conducting *Teuf-Teuf* (Chuff-chuff), a 'motor car march' composed for the occasion by Edouard Mathé, the performance of a *Traffic accident polka*, a tombola based on 'the breakdown' and, above all, the extraordinary reconstruction of the 'Café of Mourmelon-le Petit', a dump in the provinces, in all its horror, all its gaiety and all its sadness. Highly improbable nonsense, but so well parodied as to be inspired.

One should also not forget the procession composed of highly comical scenes of motoring life and the amusing competitions − contests as bizarre as they were sporting − judged by eminent personalities, among whom were Mesdames Le Bargy and Cora Laparcerie, Marguerite Deval, Polaire, Louise Bignon, Marthe Régnier, Mégard, Bianca Duhamel, Cléo de Mérode, Angèle Héraud, Ellen Baxone and Alice Nory. Certainly a *Redoute* in the grand tradition which one had thought lost for ever, but which has returned to us with gusto, as you can imagine. When's the next one?

27 December 1904:
NEZ PARTOUT
(NOSY PARKER)

Fantasy by Jacques Ferny, Vincent Hispa and Robert Dieudonné.

With the inimitable Little Tich and other attractions: Kara, the king of the jugglers, the

Ferraris, *fin-de-siècle* dancers, Baggessen, Lowell and Lowell, and the Cocktails.

9 April 1905:
THE TOREADOR (revival)

English operetta in two acts and four, scenes adapted by A. Fordyce and Jacques Bousquet.
Music by Ivan Caryll and Lionel Monckton.

Prince, who later achieved fame in the cinema under the name of Rigodin

With Prince, Claudius, Villers, Ed Roze and Fernal.
With Duberny, Jane Delorme, Mars-Pearl, Mortann, Katty Wale, Mauriane and the Ginger Girls.

26 September 1905:
LA MARISKA

Ballet-mime in one act and three scenes by Jean Lorrain.
Music by Narici.

Orchestra under the direction of Goublier.
Produced by G. Saracco, ballet-master.
Scenery by Visconti.
Costumes by Landolff.

With Trouhanowa, André, Schmidt, Ghisio, Beaudier, Gardès, Adèle, Bertora, Hart, Martinet, Rescally, Phili, Seymour, Riquier, Canot and Collinet.

With Paglieri, G. Sarraco, Tzitrine, Rizzo, Chevalier, Cressonnier, Émile and Danielle.

The management of the Moulin Rouge has just achieved a master stroke by engaging the famous dancer Natasha Trouhanowa. *La Mariska* is a ballet-mime which scored a great success at Monte-Carlo and, since then, pretty well everywhere that it has been performed by its graceful interpreter. She is on stage continuously, miming and dancing, supple, winning, energetic, amorous, voluptuous, and dominating everything with the supreme impetus of her noble, electrifying passion. She possesses an inner choreographic sense; her supple body bends and undulates with exquisite charm and her legs form designs of an unrivalled, elegant and new artistry.

The originality of the plot is not a factor in its success. The theme, which is very well portrayed by our colleague Jean Lorrain, is of an extreme simplicity. A Bohemian girl, Mariska, who is one of a group of gipsy players, sees a rich Magyar enter the inn where she is dancing. Both are instantly infatuated with one another; she falls into the noble visitor's arms − and then falls asleep. It never happens any other way in Hungary! The girl dreams that the nobleman has married her and that he has ordered a feast in her honour. But the musicians of her tribe burst in, with the intention of carrying her off. She tries to escape. The Magyar, not understanding what has just taken place, sends her sprawling. She awakens and realizes that her dream was in the nature of a warning. She tears herself free from a fatal passion which seemed to offer more of dreams than of riches, and returns to her own people.

The music is very pleasant to the ear and the costumes cannot be faulted. Natasha is resplendent, both in her Bohemian's rags and in her white, silver-embroidered festive robe, a diadem in her hair and goodness knows how many roubles-worth of diamonds on her bosom. She truly deserves the title which fashionable Paris has bestowed upon her: 'Trouhanowa the Charmer'.

6 May 1905:
EGLÉ ou L'ENFANT À LA VACHE
(EGLÉ or THE COW'S CHILD)

Operetta is dead! The fault lies, they say, in the dearth of good productions which are worthy of the public's attention. It is the main topic of conversation behind the scenes of Parisian music-halls. To remedy this state of affairs the management of the Moulin Rouge has hit on the ingenious idea of bringing together librettists popular with the public and a composer whose career has known continual success. The first, Émile Moreau, who was one of the writers responsible for *Madame Sans-Gêne*, has had his successes, and his collaboration with Victorien Sardou was a very happy one. As for the second, Claude Terrasse, all are agreed in describing him as a worthy successor to Offenbach and Hervé. The result has lived up to our hopes. This piece of farcical mythology is an admirable way, albeit a very whimsical one, of filling the gaps in the classical education of those who have forgotten the exceedingly precious lessons of their schooldays. It is the best way of obtaining 'everything you want to know' about the fifteen years spent in Colchide by the Argonauts in the search for the Golden Fleece, about Telamon, Jason, Orpheus, Castor and Pollux, about the reasons which impelled Jupiter to change the nymph Io into a cow and about the fate of Eglé, the daughter born from this love-affair. The importance of problems such as these will not be lost on anyone. That is, so long as the house is full at the Moulin Rouge every evening.

31 October 1905:
T'EN AS UN OEIL!
(TAKE A GLANCE AT IT)

Revue in two acts and twelve scenes by Henry Fursy and Charles Mougel.
Music arranged by Gustave Goublier.
Costumes designed by Japhet and made by Pascaud.
Scenery by Amable, Ronsin and Cornil.

With Louise Balthy (Caroline, the Tyrolean doll, the negress)
Ellen Baxone (the dyer, the errand-girl)
Marie Marville (La Guérinière, La Tiare)
Sulbac (the schoolmaster, the emperor, the Tyrolean doll, Mephistopheles)
Jacquet (the counsellor, the apache, the good judge, M. Crachat)
Charles Reschal (M. Vigoureux, the prince)
Fernand Frey (Paul Mounet, the tragic actor, the Grand Duke)
Victor Lejal (the administrator, the sergeant)
Carlos Avril (a soldier, a paymaster)

Also: Alberthal, Eugénie, Ed Withney, together with Liliane, de Leka, Arlington, Berthe Manon, Charlotte Jernon, Suzy, Kelly, Mimi James, et al.

With the famous Cocktails.

It seems that the word 'impossible' does not figure in P-L Flers's vocabulary. To offer a more marvellous show than *The Belle of New York* would appear to smack of Utopia. Today's reality exceeds the affection which we have for what we already consider to be one of the most sumptuous productions we have ever seen. Amongst the wonders are an exact reproduction of the racecourse at Auteuil, a riding-school at Versailles with a snow-white horse moving through all-white scenery and, above all, a 'Magic Grotto' which, we are told, is going to be reproduced in countries across the world and which took six months to design. Plus exquisite projections in the form of flowers and diamonds, with, playing among them, huge fountains, flooding the stage with splashes of light of all colours.

The performers are the equal of these displays. Marville, the most Parisian of the Belles of New York, whose song is a caress and whose look is soft poetry; Ellen Baxone, the audience's favoured child; the charming Alberthal as the facetious comedienne; and the mirthful Frey with his most effective imitations. Louise Balthy, our own great comedienne, disguised as a Tyrolean doll and then as a negress, finds parodies to her taste. It should be mentioned that she seems to be completely recovered from her motoring accident of last summer. You will no doubt recall that her vehicle crashed into a ditch and that, as the

LOUISE **BALTHY**

IN THE WINGS

19 January 1905

Bombshell from the Moulin Rouge! The management has announced the closure of the establishment for an indefinite period. The reason is urgent repair work ordered by the police.

3 April 1905

The Moulin Rouge is at last its old self. Since its reopening, its success has exceeded all the expectations of its new management. This can be ascribed to some superb entertainments, amongst which have been Fot-Gers, with his mimicry in song and his *danses nègres*, the lovely Mademoiselle de Germont, with her monologues, Monsieur Paul Toul, with his comic songs, Carmela the incomparable Spanish dancer, the four Densmores and their hilarious cat-hunt, the indescribable Linctor, the music-mad shouter, the intrepid animal tamer Romanus and the dare-devil Londe, an admirable tight-rope walker, whose perilous display astonishes and disconcerts the professionals themselves.

latter was full of water, this cushioned the impact, thus saving her life. As for Sulbac, the king of the comedians, who has come to the Moulin Rouge after twenty-one years at the Scala, he reduced the audience to unrestrained laughter when he appeared, first as a monkey and after that as the Emperor of the Sahara. Jacquet is also on the bill. In the dress of an apache, he portrays a most extraordinary captain Mandrin. Let us also salute the Cocktails, those pretty little English devils who brought the house down with their fire and their exciting costumes. Their curious little American song, *Picololo*, was on everyone's lips as they left the theatre.

The rehearsals of the show were shrouded in the greatest secrecy, and every day the doors to the stage were guarded by two policemen. The secret game was worth the candle. Only one question now remains: will it ever be possible, in another revue, to do any better? Over to Paul-Louis Flers for the answer – or, come to that, to show us, some day soon, on whatever stage he chooses.

21 January 1906:
THE REOPENING

The Moulin Rouge, that temple of pleasure, is once more a part of the Parisian scene. Last night's special show will be counted amongst the gayest and most amusing in the history of this music-hall.

Monsieur Victor Silvestre, the new director, has achieved a sensational resurrection; the most famous sails in the world will from now on be turning amid a flood of dazzling lights, sensuous flowers and brilliant music, while all the pretty girls have returned to that delightful setting which they favour before all others. Most of all, they relish the rebirth of the famous dance hall which has brought worldwide fame to La Goulue, Rayon d'Or, Grille d'Égout and other riotous and gaudy dragonflies.

There was an unfortunate delay in the opening of the doors, due to lack of familiarity in the procedure for restoring the electricity supply, after it had been out of use for some time. This incident was soon forgotten, thanks to an extensive and very well-received programme. The turns inevitably aroused thoughts of what they do best in the huge music-halls of London. We particularly commend the Scottish orchestra, a favourite of King Edward VII – young Highlanders who played the lively and picturesque melodies of their native land. Mention should also be made of Vandyke, the hilarious mimic, the jugglers Robertus and Wilfred, with their dog, all three very skilful, and not forgetting the Leitners, six marvellous Tyrolean acrobats.

This evening the entertainment continues, and we are inclined to think will do so for a long time.

14 July 1906:
THE GEISHA

English operetta in two acts.
French adaptation by Charles Clairville and Jacques Lemaire.
Music by Sidney Jones.

With Jane Petit, Spinelly, Kamouna, Élise Pujet and Jane Doe.

With Morton, Alberthal, Poudrier and Fernal.

With, as the curtain-raiser, Foscolo and The Famous Cocktails, the popular dancers.

In the end we could scarcely believe it . . . Today we have an extra reason for celebrating the national holiday. The Moulin Rouge, that favourite establishment of Parisians, provincials and foreigners alike, has once more opened its doors. After a month drifting with the tide, the tiller has been taken again by Joseph Oller, its founder. No better news could have been wished for after so many disappointments and financial ups and downs. But we must keep it to ourselves no longer – the first night fulfilled all our hopes. When the doors were opened, the old atmosphere of the great nights in the Place Blanche was there once more – a mass of carriages and motor cars such as we had not seen for a very long time. Along the whole length of the entrance hall were diners contentedly seated at their tables, as if they had been there for months. Suddenly we felt ourselves transported several years backwards in time, to a period when the Moulin Rouge was a kind of anthropological museum, and the rendezvous for all the races of the world.

As for the show itself, this was most vigorous and enjoyable. An interesting curtain-raiser prepared us for *The Geisha*, a charming English operetta. It is a masterpiece of its kind, eminently light, pleasing the eye without unduly fatiguing the mind, a mouth-watering dish of suggestive feminine display, of dazzling costumes, of exhilarating melodies, of amusing or sentimental songs, of frenzied dances, of mime, of farce and humour. It was the ideal Parisian evening.

12 September 1906:
MADAME MEPHISTO

Spectacular play in two acts and six scenes by Monréal and Blondeau.

With Thérèse Cernay and Jane Loury.

With Dekernel, Fernel and Poudrier.

With, as the curtain-raiser, the Tip Top Girls and the Alonso sisters and Kléra, the famous Spanish dancers.

A radiant and dazzling Princess of the Shadows, clearly and magnificently revealed in front of an elegant audience. That was the strange scene at the Moulin Rouge which we witnessed with delight. Madame Mephisto has taken up her residence there, for the purpose of wreaking her vengeance on her dissolute husband, perverted god and Don Juan of eternal youth. Her unfailing verve and her many metamorphoses are the source of inexhaustable gaiety. The play is the pretext for vicissitudes which are not only picturesque but impossible to describe – daring in fact – with scenery of a sparkling richness and luxury, matched in the auditorium by the first-night fashions. Throughout the evening, groups were entering, meeting others, which then replaced them, all dressed in shimmering costumes. Flamboyant imps, bespangled with silver, jockeys with golden caps, nonchalant student dandies, town councillors of martial appearance and seductive coquettes. Altogether a show which is a credit to the Oller management and the glorious Moulin, whose slowly-revolving sails seem to be driven by the breezes of indestructible gaiety.

14 November 1906:
LA REVUE DU MOULIN-ROUGE
(THE MOULIN ROUGE REVUE)

Revue in two acts and ten scenes by Lucien Boyer, Rip and Wilned.
Music by Gustave Goublier.

With Madame Devassy, Mesdemoiselles Jeanne Saulier, Paule Mab, Spinelly, Daveney, Huart, Dolmarès, Desson, de Sony, Casanova, Jane Heit, Moralys, d'Axène, Selva, de Costa and d'Arty.

With Paul Fougère, Rigaux, Harry Mass, Régiame, Strack, Yvain, Fabert, Bertou, Caulseux, Dariès, Miller, Adolpho, Cowley and Lerner.

With guest artist, the ex-'Human arrow', the intrepid Hélène Dutrier.

With the famous Scherry Girls.

The changing face of the Moulin Rouge: (left) during the 1890s, with the elephant's backside clearly visible, and (right) after the rebuilding of 1906 (photographs by Louis Levy)

Régiame, Géo, Carlos Avril and Mallet introducing the delirious burlesque in the tableau 'The Jury of the Conservatoire'

IN THE WINGS

23 January 1906

Victor Silvestre is the new director of the Moulin Rouge. On the programme: the royal Scottish orchestra in their national dress, the famous mimic Vandyke, the jugglers Robertus and Wilfrid, Homer and Davis, eccentric American dancers, the Leonis, English dancers, the six Leitners, Tyrolean acrobats, the four Delthis, the Forest clowns and the magical Fontaines. With dancing and quadrilles in the grand tradition.

27 January 1906

There is a spectacular and unusual show this evening at the Moulin Rouge: an animal contest! With cats, chickens, goats, turkeys, cocks, birds and parakeets in very great numbers. At one o'clock in the morning Mère Michel, with her cat, and Père Lustucru will make their solemn entrance. At two o'clock there will be a free tombola to be drawn by Mesdemoiselles Liane de Lancy and Suzanne Derval. The first prize will be an African donkey for a lady, fully saddled. This entertainment will be followed by dancing to the music of a fifty-piece orchestra under the direction of maestro Domergue, with *quadrilles réalistes* the *Mattchiche* and the cake-walk.

1 February 1906

Lola Hawthorne at the Moulin Rouge! This splendid and celebrated dancer opens this evening. There is no doubt that all Paris Society will be there to see and applaud this marvellous artist.

28 February 1906

Is it all over in the Place Blanche? It's official, and very sad for Paris in general and Montmartre in particular, that the Moulin Rouge has once more closed its doors. Reason? You've guessed it – change of management.

12 July 1906

Rumours of the most extravagant kind continue to circulate about the Moulin Rouge. A little while ago the idea was to nominate, as head of the establishment, Monsieur Bannel who was the able administrator of the Folies Bergère under the Isola brothers. That proposal fell through, and today another solution was found. The Oller brothers are to resume the management of the establishment which they founded seventeen years ago. For their opening programme they will be presenting operetta, dancing and other entertainments.

14 July 1906

The Moulin Rouge has been redecorated. The dress circle has been raised up so that all parts of the stage and the auditorium can now be seen from all points. Boxes with waiter service now mean that one can dine in private, without missing any part of the entertainment. Joseph Oller has done away with all the little staircases which divided the floor up into separate parts, so that there are no more steps to climb up and down as you enter the auditorium. In addition it is now possible to enter, on the same level, a renovated and enlarged garden, through an entrance opening on to the boulevard. Finally, a new electric illuminated sign indicates, for the benefit of connoisseurs of congenial idleness or attractive shows, the entrance to this Paradise Lost, which Parisians are in the process of rediscovering.

25 July 1906

A novelty! An ingenious combination of cinematography and photography, forming an interesting and astonishing entertainment being presented by Monsieur Oller at the Moulin Rouge, reproducing gestures and speech in a striking manner. An invention to keep an eye on.

1 August 1906

In response to requests from a large number of the regular customers of the Moulin Rouge, who have rightly discovered that the gardens of this celebrated music-hall make an admirably cool corner to sip an aperitif, the Messieurs Oller have decided to put on *aperitif-concerts* there, between five and seven in the evening, with the Kapossy orchestra. They begin today, entry being free.

27 October 1906

Having restored their renowned music-hall to its former popularity and fame, the Messieurs Oller have just handed it over to a new company, of which Monsieur Henri Roy is the deputy director, while artistic activities are in the hands of the journalist Max Viterbo. It is intended to reopen in early November with a spectacular revue.

27 November 1906

La Revue du Moulin is the big theatrical success of the season. The box-office queue every day is so long that the management has had to double the administrative staff.

4 January 1907: RÊVE D'ÉGYPTE (EGYPTIAN DREAM)

There was a huge and understandable commotion tonight at the Moulin Rouge. The cause was a one-act mime which was to have been included in the revue for the next ten days. After this morning's intervention by Lépine, the Prefect of Police, we doubt if this arrangement will be sustained. He is, in fact, threatening the theatre with closure if this performance is repeated before the public tonight, and we can in no way disagree with him. The whistles, trumpet blasts and assorted shouts from the audience – which drowned the music – and the seats, opera-glass cases and garlic

cloves which were thrown on to the stage confirm our view.

At first there was nothing offensive; just the story of an old scholar, immersed in the occult sciences, who falls in love with a mummy. She rises up before him, unwinds her bandages – you can picture the striptease – and begins to dance with the object of seducing him. The only thing is, the part of the old scholar is played by a woman. The dumbfounded audience then sees 'her' exchange a long and frankly erotic kiss with a mummy in a pseudo-Egyptian costume, with golden breastplates and a bracelet in the form of a snake twined around her arm.

The two ladies are well known to Parisian Society: the scholar was the Marquise de Belboeuf, the daughter of the Duc de Morny, who also answers to the name of 'Missy'; around town, she wears a dinner jacket and smokes cigars. The mummy was played by Colette Willy, the wife – in theory – of the writer Willy. Hitherto they had performed their lesbian mimes only before private audiences.

The management of the Moulin Rouge have announced that there will be a statement at the end of the afternoon. We await it with interest and impatience.

Colette, long before she had any idea of becoming president of the Académie Goncourt

24 February 1907:
LA FEUILLE DE VIGNE
(THE VINE LEAF)

Fairy operetta in two acts and ten scenes by Paul Ferrier.
Music by Henri Hirchmann.
Orchestra under the direction of Gustave Goublier.
Costumes by Japhet, made by Pascaud.

With Anne Dancrey, Mary Théry, Simone Rivière, Suzanne Iris, Dasson, Moralis, Guérita, Aryel, Norville, Berthier, Hélies, Bérangére and Pujol.

With Fernand Frey, Régiame, Carlos Avril and Daries.

In an auditorium which has been redecorated and, since yesterday, is lit by superbly sparkling crystal chandeliers, we saw a performance of the most artful of Gallic entertainments. The subject is slight, but at no time is the permissible level of taste exceeded. The action takes place in Paris, in a realm halfway between the real and the imaginary. As the scenes proceed, with admirable scenery by Ménessier, one is presented with horsewomen, horsemen, huntsmen and whippers-in. The most admired moments were incontestably the arrival of the talismans in the palace of the Queen of the Genies, and the visit to an admirable reproduction of the Grévin museum. It was spiritual, it was marvellous, it was picturesque, it was Paris.

24 April 1907:
LA LIME
(THE FILE)

Dramatic mime in one-act by Henri Ferrare.
Music by André Fijan.
Production by Desfontaines.

With Louise Bignon and de Saize, Gouget, Candrieux and Ragelin.

7 May 1907:
EGLÉ ou L'ENFANT à LA VACHE
(revival)

Operetta in two acts and five scenes by Émile Moreau.
Music by Claude Terrasse.
Costumes designed by Minon and made by Pascaud.
Scenery by Chambouleron and Mignard.

With Éva du Perret, Mathilde Commant, Dasson, Miss Barnett, Jane de Lyane, Moralis and Darvyl.

With Pougaud, Morton, Darles, Carlos Avril, Odéo, Ragelin, Gallius, de Saize, Cowley and Guerita.
And fifty dancers, directed by Madame Cernusco.

IN THE WINGS

3 January 1907

From this evening onwards, *Rêve d'Égypte*, a one-act mime by the Marquise de Belboeuf, will be included in *La Revue du Moulin*, performed by Mesdames Yssun, Colette Willy and Dasson.

4 January 1907

Faced with the scandal which arose last night over the performance of *Rêve d'Égypte*, the management of the Moulin Rouge have announced the replacement this evening of Missy by Georges Wague. He will play the part of the scholar in the mime, whose title has also been changed. It will now be called *Soleil d'Orient* (Oriental Sun).

21 July 1907

A change of management at the Moulin Rouge. The new directors, Messieurs Armand Leclerc and Edouard Brouette, have announced the forthcoming presentation of their first show, *La Revue de la femme*.

29 July 1907:
LA REVUE DE LA FEMME
(THE REVUE OF WOMANHOOD)

Spectacular revue in two acts and eight scenes by Lucien Boyer and Henri Bataille.
Production by Henri Lejeune.
Music by Gustave Goublier.
Scenery by Duboscq.
Costumes designed by Japhet and Minon, made by Pascaud.

With Mistinguett, Mealy, Allems, Lawler, O'Reilly, Deluza, Prioglio, Debièvre, Deville, Darvyl, Noinville, Delysia, Lecomte, de Costa and Aryel.

With Morton, Berthez, Sinoël, Carlos Avril, Darles, Gosset and Caudieux.

Ladies and gentlemen of Paris take heart! That great music-hall which was the glory of Montmartre is reborn at last. With the performers chosen to play the parts, the splendour of its costumes, the magnificence of its scenery and the charming interpretation of its bawdy verses, *La Revue de la femme* is one of the most sumptuous productions to have been put on for a long time. Of this fact the ovation which the cast received from the audience is undoubted evidence.

There were two star turns of rare originality: 'The path of virtue', along which one saw a procession, representing the world of Paris, of a whole batch of young and pretty women, all well known, and for whom Paquin and Lewis, those grand masters of elegance, had created marvellous costumes and hats; and 'Art and the Woman' where, amidst Duboscq's extraordinary scenery, there were portrayed all the types of woman created by the skilful pencils of Willette, Albert Guillaume, Cappiello, Abel Faivre, Gerbault, Chéret and Gibson.

Among the performers, special mention must be made of a most charming newcomer. She was the star of the Pee-wit dance, applauded yesterday by the public. Her name is Mistinguett and to us she is the very image of revue: a Parisienne full of charm and wit.

Mistinguett's first appearance at the Moulin Rouge, in its two principal scenes

Lucien Boyer

Henri Bataille

Pierre Veber, by Sem

9 October 1907

Fragson scored an undoubted success last night at the Moulin Rouge. After several songs, this excellent performer was brought back to the stage a number of times at the audience's demand.

15 December 1907

Statement from the Moulin Rouge. With effect from today, Monsieur Charles Aumont is to assume sole control of the establishment.

24 December 1907: L'AS TU REVUE?

Revue in two acts and nine scenes, with a prologue, by Lucien Boyer and Henri Bataille. Orchestra directed by Maurice Jacobi. Scenery by Bertin, Karl and Hachspill.

With Max Dearly, Cléo de Mérode, Miss May de Souza, Lucienne Malty, Stelly, Suzy Deguez, William Burtey, Becurnel, Jacquet, Poggi, Darles, Caudieux, Boucot, Dane and Beauval.

With fifty dancers and one hundred singers.

Messieurs Lucien Boyer and Henri Bataille are recidivists. After the legendary success of their *Revue de la femme*, here we are, on the first night of *L'as tu revue?*, with their names once more acclaimed by a frenzied audience. It is fair to say that we have seldom witnessed such a firework display of joyful, deafening and lively satire. All the personalities in the political world, from Toselli to Fallières, were manhandled with such verve that they must surely have been delighted. Leading a superb cast was Max Dearly, defecting from the Variétés, in the Chinaman and the aviator sketches. Miss May de Souza, the most celebrated singing star in America, won our hearts, as did Cléo de Mérode, whom we heard singing for the first time! Until now this queen of grace and beauty has kept this talent hidden from us. Also to be congratulated is William Burtey, the prince of impressionists. When he opens his mouth one seems actually to hear Paul Mounet, Coquelin, Lucien Guitry, Brasseur or Sarah Bernhardt — the finest of playbills all in one man, a further reason for proceeding forthwith to the Place Blanche.

Max Dearly

25 March 1908: SON ALTESSE L'AMOUR (HIS ROYAL HIGHNESS LOVE)

Spectacular fantasy operetta in two acts and four scenes, by Victor de Cottens and Pierre Veber.
New music and arrangements by Maurice Jacobi.
Scenery by L. Karl and E. Bertin.
Costumes by Pascaud.
Choreography directed by Marcel Caubry.

With Gaby Deslys, Juliette Mealy, Marie-Louise Labal, Alice Guerra, Frémeaux, Miss Flo.

With Fred Wright, Sulbac, Garbagni, Raiter, Baldy, Carlos Avril, Darles and Caudieux.

Gaby Deslys

Another success to be marked up to the Moulin Rouge. This one is called *Son Altesse l'Amour* and is truly royal. The audience was not mistaken in reserving an ovation for the charming Juliette Mealy, the celebrated English comedian Fred Wright, and Lucette de Liévin who also received our applause yesterday in *The Prince of Pilsen*. Gaby Deslys, with her special talent, was a great success with a number of attractive English dances, Alice Guerra earned applause as a vivacious comedienne, while Sulbac has never provoked such hearty bursts of laughter.

15 June 1908:
LA REVUE DU MOULIN
(THE MOULIN REVUE)

Revue in two acts and twelve scenes by Victor de Cottens and Lucien Boyer.
New music and arrangements by Maurice Jacobi.
Scenery by Menessier and Bertin.
Costumes by Landolff.

With Fred Wright of the Gaiety Theatre in London, Morton, Girier, Darlès, Laroche, Caudieux, Carlos Avril, Fred Pascal, Volbert Reignard and Max Dearly.

With Mistinguett, Emma Sablan, Guerra, Vera Trevor, Darcy, Darvyl, Lancret, Myrthal and Elynett.

With the Handers and Millis, speciality

dancers, and Topsy, negro dancer and singer.

With the twelve Manchester Babies.

The grand summer revue at the Moulin Rouge has now become one of the traditions of Paris. Once again this year its presentation constitutes the artistic event of the season. What can one say without producing a stream of banalities? That irresistible scenes, irreverent lines and cutting words abound? No. That the scenes evoking the Pantheon, the multilingual agents, the financier Brochette, the driver of the Taxianto and the nude are irresistible? No. That we saw a display of princely luxuriance still unequalled? No. That the performance found all the stars at the height of their careers, from Max Dearly to Fred Wright, and including Girier, the irresistible Van Putzeboom of *Occupe-toi d'Amélie*, the delicious Morton, the amusing Carlos Avril, the joyous Darlès, the exquisite May de Souza, the beautiful Alice Guerra, the pretty Belly, the spiritual Elynett and the so sweet Lucette Meyan? No. That we saw a series of dances, as unexpected as they were exceptional? Ah, yes! In particular, we should mention the partnership of Mistinguett and Fred Wright in 'The dance of the vases', and Mistinguett again, with Max Dearly, in 'The cat's eye'. This morning the steps

we saw are being described by some as 'a great stride forward in the history of music-hall', which may not be all that exaggerated.

16 October 1908:
PAR-DESSUS LES MOULINS
(ABOVE THE WINDMILLS)

Revue in two acts and nine scenes by Paul Ardot and G. and P. Briquet.
New music and arrangements by Maurice Jacobi.
Scenery by Bertin.
Costumes by Pascaud.

With Allems, Gaby Deslys, Lebergy, Guerra, Elynett, Irène Bordoni and Jane Delyane.

With Fred Wright, Morton, Cromelynck, Dambrine, Strack, Andreyor, Darlès and Caudieux.

With the twelve Manchester Babies.

Yet another triumph at the Moulin Rouge! It is becoming a habit. What more is there to say to describe the three hours of mad gaiety which we spent, applauding the delicious, irresistible new revue. Morton, in particular, is exceptional. He makes successive appearances, as a verger, as the Infante of Spain, as a character in opera and even as a lady in

Had Gaby Deslys lived, it would have changed the face of music-hall. What then would have become of Mistinguett's career?

77

IN THE WINGS

14 July 1908

Not content with being applauded and recalled innumerable times to the stage of the Moulin Rouge every evening, Max Dearly is also harvesting laurels on the racecourses. On Saturday his mare Varsovie finished first in a race at Maisons-Lafitte. Thus, in the intervals at the revue, the likeable sportsman-comedian is receiving a few extra congratulations.

20 July 1908

They remain faithful to their Paris! Max Dearly and Mistinguett have turned down offers from the biggest music-halls in London, Berlin and Vienna. All of them had invited the pair to go and perform the 'Apache dance', as they do at the Moulin Rouge with incomparable verve. Similarly Charles Aumont has just refused to transfer his revue to the Anglo-French Exhibition. Its success will be maintained, but solely in the Place Blanche.

15 August 1908

Starting this evening, *La Revue du Moulin* will have an extra number which will be without a rival: the mysterious and alarming 'Nautch dance', performed for the first time by the beautiful Sahari-Djeli. It contains a series of poses which defy the imagination. The arms bend, writhe and describe curves of an astonishing litheness. These are not simple movements of the hand and the forearm, but involve the complete arm. One has the impression of a wave motion, beginning at the shoulder, travelling down the arm and finally dying out at the fingertips. Then the movements gather speed, seem even to move against one another, and then dissolve in a disturbing harmony. The essentially artistic character of this dance presents a sharp contrast to the acrobatic whimsies of Mistinguett, Fred Wright and the Manchester Babies.

18 August 1908

Mistinguett, Max Dearly's piquant partner in the famous 'Cat's eye waltz', first renamed the '*Valse chaloupée*' and now the '*Valse sinistre*', has been laid low for a few days. No doubt she is somewhat fatigued, after so many successful appearances at the Moulin Rouge.

15 September 1908

Change of management at the Moulin Rouge: Monsieur Amédée Kahn has replaced Monsieur René Laudi as assistant manager.

19 December 1908

A special *Redoute*, for the benefit of the Musical Artists' Retirement Home has been held, the evening being introduced by Louis Mamel, the chairman of the selection committee at the Folies Bergère. There was a scene from *Le Misanthrope*, directed by Lentiner of the Comédie Française and performed by Claudius, Vibert and Dranem. There was also a competition for theatrical mad-caps, in which the first three prizes were taken by the milliner Lewis, who has just perfected the 'Lewisette' which, in a few months' time, will be seen in all hair-dos. This godsend is the solution to a problem which had been thought to be well-nigh insoluble: that of a hat to wear at the theatre.

6 March 1909

There was an extraordinary scene last night at the Moulin Rouge, during the performance of the charming revue *En l'air messieurs!*. Whistling broke out, drowning the voices of the performers during the scene – a very witty one – depicting the members of the Confédération Générale du Travail. The noise returned in greater force when a well-known delegate was portrayed giving a lesson in anti-patriotism to the children of the school at Ivry. Several people were ejected, two of them even being led off to the local police station, before being released a few moments later. In contrast, the other scenes, from '*Notre-Dame des apaches*' to '*Gars de la Moselle*', and including '*La Gigolette*', received ovations from the audience. In other words, the incidents which took place will have no effect on the future of this show.

17 August 1909

Starting this evening, Mademoiselle Polaire, with Gaston Sylvestre, will be giving a series of performances of *Ma Gosse*, a two-act play by Yves Mirande and Henri Caen. This piece will be introduced into *La Grande Revue* at a suitable point.

30 August 1909

Mademoiselle Polaire has been injured in the arm during a performance of the wild and brutal '*Danse noire*' by A. Gregoire.
The friends and admirers of this charming artist may be reassured; the injury, although painful, is not serious and will not mean that the 'Gosseline' will have to abandon her act, in which she displays her admirable artistry.

the audience. It was indescribable! Go to see and hear Dambrine impersonating Caruso – and Cromelynck singing in Belgian and Caudieux in German are also well worth the journey!

14 January 1909: EN L'AIR MESSIEURS! (UP IN THE AIR MESSIEURS!)

Revue in three acts and twenty scenes by Henri Moreau and Charles Quinel.

With Lebergy, Alice Guerra, d'Alba, Elynett, Andrée Darcy and Anthelemi.

With Dambrine, Gouget, Cromelynck, Liesse, Nemo, Darlès, Caudieux, Rousseau, Garget and Gambert.

26 June 1909: LA GRANDE REVUE DU MOULIN (THE GRAND MOULIN REVUE)

Revue in two acts and eleven scenes by Lucien Boyer and Henri Bataille.

With Mistinguett, Allems, Morton, Sinoël, Roger Ferréol, Beauval, Jane Oryan, Sidone, Leduc, Kantony, Rivers, Prévost, Debièvre and Gombert.

With the celebrated choreographic star Yetta Riouza, accompanied by twenty delectable ballerinas, directed by Sicard.

Take the same ingredients and begin again! For the authors of its summer show the new management of the Moulin Rouge has chosen Messieurs Boyer and Bataille who, two years ago, were responsible for the famous *Rèvue de la femme*, which ran for more than three hundred successful performances. So we were impatient to discover whether *La Grande Revue du Moulin* would be

It was 1909 when
Mistinguett began to
develop the character later
to be known as Titine

With her partner, she yields to the rhythm of
the tango

79

worthy of its elder sister. We were not disappointed, and the very select audience at the première last night was, it seems to us, of the same opinion. Mistinguett, with her usual spirit, gave a triumphant performance in a scene from *The Merry Widow*, while the burlesque of the famous 'Apache dance', performed by Ferréol and Morton, was encored with enthusiastic bravoes. So, more than ever, it's the Moulin Rouge which is still the place to have a good time!

30 October 1909:
MESSALINETTE

Comic opera in two acts and seven scenes by P.-L. Flers.
Music by Rodolphe Berger.
Scenery by Chambouleron and Mignard.
Costumes by Landolff.

With Marise Fairy, Le Gallo, Max Morel, Alice and Fanny de Tender, Debièvre, Dora Parnes, Brunw, Denance, Carlos Avril and Danvers.

For the last four weeks Paris has seemed dead, as the big sails of the Moulin remained immobile. Last night Montmartre roused itself at last from its torpor. In the Place Blanche, at the temple of gaiety, the triumphant song of rebirth could be heard. Monsieur Ruez, renowned for his bold initiatives, has surpassed himself. The auditorium has

been renovated with exquisite taste and the establishment has rediscovered its old spirit. As for the revival of Paul-Louis Flers's *Messalinette*, this was not the least of the evening's attractions. At last a real *French* operetta! Its success all over Europe, its three hundred days in London and its year in Berlin have been good for it. After two years' absence, it has returned to us gayer than ever. Paris, which saw the birth of its early glory, can rejoice at this well-deserved apotheosis.

2 February 1910:
LA REVUE AMOUREUSE
(THE LOVE REVUE)

Revue in thirty-two scenes by Henry Moreau and Briollet.
New music by Paul Letombe.
Produced by Max-Him.
Costumes by Landolff.
Scenery by Chambouleron and Mignard.

With Lina Ruby, Nerval, Esmée, A. Ferreal, Reine Leblanc, Edmée Lescot, Dhomas, Saidreau, Debièvre, Dutard, Danvers, R. de Villers, Ferral, Doriez, Brunw, Maffer, Lerida, Bert-Angère, Réthoré, Théo and Isvora.

This was an orgy of luxury and staging. Our eyes could scarcely credit it! Versailles, the Gardens of Babylon, the fiftieth anniversary of Solferino – and not

forgetting the Greek dances of Isadora Duncan, performed by Esmée. All this in one evening, it's too much! Paul Ruez, the agreeable director of the Moulin Rouge, who has restored it to its former splendour and popularity, is to be complimented.

27 June 1910:
TOUT EN BLEU
(ALL IN BLUE)

Fairy revue in twenty-five scenes by Henry Moreau.
New music by Paul Letombe.
Costumes by Landolff.
Scenery by Chambouleron and Mignard.

With Fernand Frey, Albens, Danvers, Dhomas, Reine Leblanc, Lina Darlan, Debièvre, Lerida, Sylvia, Verka, Vanora, Portal, Eza Berre, Strit and Bert-Angère.

The world of fashionable Paris forgathered last night at its favourite theatre to round off their Grand Prix day in an enjoyable fashion. This event happened to coincide with the first performance of Monsieur Henry Moreau's revue. Need we say more? The brilliant and ultra-select audience was unsparing with its bravoes and its encores for scenes which were as sumptuous as they were original. Among them we may mention the procession of the foolish virgins; the delightful ballet of the dead leaves; the entertaining piece about the Horse Guards; 'Boubouroclès', a beguiling parody of *Boubouroche*; Courteline's masterpiece, with Mounet-Sully, Sylvain, Albert Lambert and Sarah Bernhardt; the welcoming of Mr Roosevelt by Monsieur Fallières, with a curious concert given by the Polin agency, consisting of Dranem, Mayol, Fragson, Sulbac and Miss Campton; and, above all, the finale of the first act. The author, invoking the floods which have threatened the old river embankments of Paris and the Palace of the Louvre, recaptured the splendours of the court of Francis I and the reception of Charles V by the King of France. Before our dazzled eyes there passed heralds, standard-bearers, grandees of Spain, Prince-Electors, royal mace-bearers, marshals, ladies of the court and great nobles. It was an unprecedented artistic effort which will undoubtedly constitute the chief attraction of the Paris theatrical season.

21 October 1910:
L'AMOUR EN ESPAGNE
(LOVE IN SPAIN)
MA GOSSE
(MY YOUNGSTER)
LA BÊTE
(THE BEAST)

Revival of the play by Yves Mirande and Henry Caen.

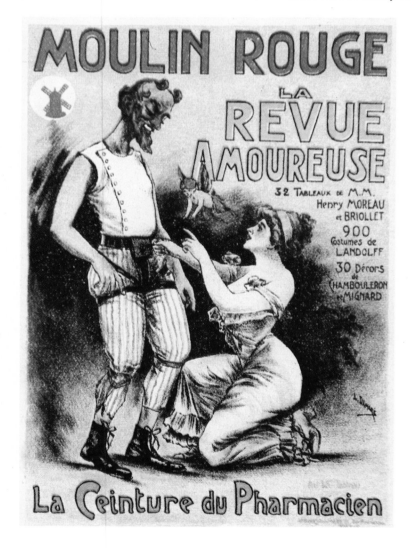

With Argentina, Polaire, Gaston Silvestre, Lucien Brulé, Bert-Angère, Portal, Lacerpète, Ida Luys, Garnier and Niomel.

On the same programme *La Bête*, a grand mime with ballets, in six scenes, after Edgar Allan Poe, with music by Emile Bonnamy, and *L'Amour en Espagne*, a spectacular operetta performed by the complete company of the Moulin Rouge together with Spanish dancers.

The wind which blows through the mountains is nothing but a light breeze compared with the wind of fear which, since last night, has been driving those glorious sails of the Moulin Rouge. In collusion with Jean Marsèle, André de Lorde, grand master of terror and intrepid explorer of horror, has just introduced a spine-chiller to the stage of the great Montmartre music-hall. Physical terror has all the greater effect when all the events, except the last, take place in an open and carefree atmosphere. The action takes place at the beginning of the last century. At the Invalides fairground, Olympia attracts the attention of a gorilla with the face of a human being which, possessed by a passion as

intense as it is bestial, breaks free from his chain and escapes through the crowd. From that moment one is gripped by the fear that the beast will find the fair one and that tragedy will strike. Both Olympia and the gorilla come to a bad end, but never mind. What we were offered was a veritable work of art.

5 November 1910: THE REOPENING OF THE DANCE HALL

Here it is at last! The genuine authentic Moulin Rouge dance hall in all its former glory. The management has had the happy idea of converting to that use the superb premises of the old tavern attached to the music-hall. A forty-piece orchestra directed by Olivier Cambon,

IN THE WINGS

20 September 1909

The management of the Moulin Rouge has just engaged Monsieur Foot Gers, who gives some very amusing impersonations of public figures in *La Grande Revue*.

8 February 1910

This evening sees the fiftieth performance of *La Revue Amoureuse* and the first presentation of 'The Chemist's Belt', a modern scene performed by Ferréal, Saidreau, Marguerite Nerval, Daguin and Grandes.

9 April 1910

A former lady-in-waiting to the Empress Eugénie was present at last night's performance of *La Revue Amoureuse*. She was so taken with the faithful re-enactment of the ceremony of the return of the troops from Italy that she was unable to hold back a cry of 'Long live the Empress'. Sometimes fiction overtakes reality.

26 April 1910

Several persons in President Roosevelt's entourage have taken advantage of their sojourn in Paris to pay a visit to the Americans' favourite music-hall, in other words the Moulin Rouge!

5 June 1910

Last night the Moulin Rouge celebrated the hundred and fiftieth performance of *La Revue Amoureuse*. In the course of the evening, the artists who have taken part in this revue, today dubbed 'the most brilliant show of the year', were frequently acclaimed by an elegant, genuine first-night 'full-house' audience.

2 July 1910

Drama last night at the Moulin Rouge. Monsieur Besnard, an artist who played in the second violins, died suddenly as he came on the stage.

13 July 1910

The Moulin Rouge has certainly brought good luck to Mademoiselle Bert-Angère. She made her debut there three years ago in very minor parts, but it was immediately noted that she was endowed with a lively mind and great imagination, and she found herself playing characters of increasing importance. Last year she learnt dancing

with Mademoiselle Sandrini, becoming one of her most brilliant pupils. Today her diction is perfect, her acting is assured and precise and one understands that one of the most applauded scenes in *Tout en bleu* is the curious dance 'Passionata' which, with her partner Monsieur Strit, she performs with extraordinary fire and choreographic science.

7 August 1910

The Moulin Rouge is running a grand poster competition. The object is to find a subject which is both new and interesting for the dance hall which is due to open in September in the magnificent hall once occupied by the old tavern. The winner, to be chosen by a special jury, will receive a cash prize in exchange for his original, which will then be lithographed.

1 September 1910

What is going on behind the scenes at the Moulin Rouge? Obviously none of the enchantment is to be found there that gains such applause on the stage. The situation, which has been confused for months, has suddenly clarified. Not before time, it might be said. On 26 August, Émile Legrand and Paul Vuillamy, the shareholders, at the instigation of the ex-director Paul Ruez, announced the dismissal of the existing directors, Messieurs Zucco, Huet, Petitjean, Maroni and Andaire. The meeting immediately nominated Paul Vuillamy, Émile Armand and Maximilien Lassez as directors. The next day, Paul Ruez, the former director, arrived at the Moulin Rouge to take possession of his office, which had been occupied for the past month by Monsieur Jean Fabert. The latter, insisting that it was he who henceforth had complete authority, attempted to prevent him by firing his pistol – 'with blanks', he affirms. 'With bullets', says Monsieur Ruez who, more alive than dead, nevertheless retreated before a summons from Monsieur Fabert's legal representative. To be continued . . .

29 October 1910

It has been announced that a settlement has been reached to the dispute which has existed between Monsieur Ruez, the ex-director of the Moulin, and the board of directors of that establishment. Paul Ruez is to reassign all his shares to the persons involved and renounce all his rights in the concern. A general meeting has just nominated Monsieur Henri Moroni as assistant director and has confirmed Monsieur Jean Fabert in his post as artistic director.

cosmopolitan dances and numerous other attractions make up a most brilliant programme. As for the old *quadrilles réalistes*, once the triumphal vehicles for La Goulue, Jane Avril, Grille d'Égout, Rayon d'Or and so many others, they have been rejuvenated and refurbished, with a charming troupe of Montmartre dancers.

13 November 1910:
CLAUDINE

Operetta based on the novels of Willy and Colette.
Music by Rodolphe Berger.
Orchestra directed by Paul Letombe.
Produced by Mévisto.

With Polaire, Marise Fairy, Yvonne Yma, Madeleine Guitty, Bert-Angère, Claudius, Colas and Regnard.

Operetta, true French operetta, gay, smart and witty, reigned triumphant last night before our dazzled eyes. After fluctuating between moving us to pity and making us laugh, the disconcerting Claudine then turned to singing. A brilliant and discerning audience, in the middle of which a large space had been reserved for the paying public, was thus presented with exquisite scenes, sometimes the stuff of dreams, and sometimes richly comical.

The first act took place at a school at Montigny, on Prizegiving Day. As the curtain rises we discovered the Gobettes, charming young girls bedecked in their finest array, and dressed in short enticing frocks. We then watched the most delightful beginning of a love story between Claudine and Renaud, before the finale, Claudine's farewells to the school. In the second act emotion reaches its peak as Claudine, in her father's house in Paris, murmurs in her distress:

Ah, why do the Fates allow
That his heart be taken by another?

This is one of the hits in a score which, by tomorrow, everyone will be singing. The last act was a veritable feast for the eyes. The scene was a smart restaurant, populated with diners and brilliant with rich costumes and sparkling lights. As for how it ends, you'll have to take yourself to the Place Blanche and find out. These few lines are simply intended to make your mouth water.

20 January 1911:
C'EST TRÈS EXCITANT
(IT'S VERY EXCITING)

Revue in twenty-seven scenes by Charles Quinel and Eugène Joulot.
New music by Paul Letombe.
Costumes by Maud Leveau.
Scenery by Chambouleron and Mignard.

With Yvonne Yma, Gaston Dupray, Fernand Frey, Jane d'Alma, Madeleine Guitty, Bertha Sylvain, Mars Pearl, Maddy Solio, Lacerpète, Jane Marney, Bert-Angère, Dupray, Gibard, Menotti, Portal and Lerida.

How much more daring are the revue writers going to become? We have grown accustomed in the music-halls to risqué situations and to ever scantier states of undress; the new scenes at the Moulin Rouge remain faithful to this tradition. Before a relaxed and joyous audience from Parisian society, *C'est très excitant* lived up to its title. It should nevertheless be said that, despite the spice with which this revue is flavoured, it shocks neither the eyes nor the ears. If its jokes are broad they are also of high quality, its frivolity is well-bred, and its taste is of the finest, never marred by the least triviality. A show, in fact, to be seen by all.

4 March 1911:
DÉVORÉES
(DEVOURED)

Accompaniment to the revue *C'est très excitant*.
Dramatic mime by George Marck.
Music by Paul Letombe.

With Valentine Petit Nerys, Yvonne Marck and the animal tamer George Marck.

There was an immensely emotional moment last night at the Moulin Rouge. It involved a dramatic mime of the most thrilling kind, the stars of which were magnificent lions, recently captured, and whose ferocity was no sham! The author, the animal tamer George Marck, himself took part, together with the delightful artist Valentine Petit and the diminutive Yvonne Marck. The plot, which was remarkably ingenious, produced as much effect by the dramatic intensity of the situations portrayed as through the participation of the wild beasts. This may be judged from the subject: an artist, painting the portrait of a female animal tamer, falls madly in love with her. The latter is coy and avoids his advances. Her unfortunate suitor bursts into tears and then, overcome, falls into a deep sleep filled with nightmares. He finds himself transported to the animal tamer's side. He goes to take her in his arms, when, suddenly, terrifying beasts arise before him. The ultimate hallucination arrives when he imagines he hears cries of pain and terror, then sees his wife and daughter devoured by the king of the beasts. Powerless to help them, he wrings his hands in despair and moans with rage, then finally awakes, to find his wife and child smiling at him. The sigh of relief was general, not only on the stage, but also in an enraptured audience, where even the most sophisticated had been entertained.

13 April 1911:
LA PETITE FRISÉE
(THE LITTLE CURLY-HAIRED GIRL)
MODERN SCHOOL

Tragi-comedy in one act by Jean Joé, followed by an Anglo-French spectacular operetta by Eugène Joullot.
Orchestra directed by Paul Letombe.

With Norman French, Bert-Angère, Morton, Rivers, Menotti, Bertha Sylvain, Lacerpète, Demony, Lerida, Myalis and Lucyane.

Last night Parisians acclaimed a new form of operetta. Beyond all question, *Modern School* represents the renovation of an exquisite style. With all due deference to our chauvinism, the success is not entirely a national one. Without the least hesitation, we warmly applauded the unpredictable or vibrating rhythms of the best work of the English and American masters. The outstanding moment was undoubtedly the 'Yankiana Rag', entertainingly danced

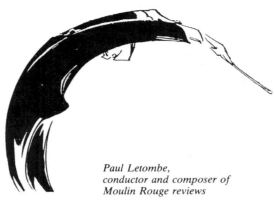

Paul Letombe,
conductor and composer of
Moulin Rouge reviews

by Norman French and Bert-Angère, which will assuredly enjoy an immense popularity.

La Petite Frisée, a dramatic comedy which precedes *Modern School*, was very amusing. In it Bert-Angère is very funny and Myalis makes a pretty urchin. One more huge success for the Moulin Rouge.

27 May 1911:
LA REVUE DU MOULIN
(THE MOULIN REVUE)

Revue in thirty-one scenes by Charles Quinel.
Orchestra directed by Paul Letombe.
Costumes by Landolff.

With Morton, Girier, Clara Faurens, Mary Max, Jane d'Alma, Leprince, Miss Lawler, Emilienne Franville, Bert-Angère, Strit, Bertha Sylvain, Villot and Menotti.

A revue for all, both Parisians and foreigners. That is the achievement of Charles Quinel.
The company includes the hundred most beautiful women in Paris, the most outstanding comics, the most polished

Apache dancers, as well as Argentinian tangos, *danses nègres* and slow waltzes, among which was 'Abouch-Abouch', for which Clara Laurens was encored by the audience. Even Offenbach was at the feast. It was being said that, from the tomb, he had given Monsieur Fabert one of the best maestros in Paris – Paul Letombe, the man it needed to lead this revue to victory.

2 August 1911:
THE BELLE OF NEW YORK
(revival)

Musical comedy by Hugh Morton, adapted by Paul Gavault.
Music by G. Kerker.
New production by Paul-Louis Flers.
Orchestra directed by Gustave Goublier.
Costumes by Landolff.

With Germaine Charley, Olga Daunal, Ida Luys, Marcelle Agly, Vilbert, Robert Casa, Strit, Fernal, Carlos Avril, the Walker Brothers and Frank Lawton.

It has been to Paris once before, and now it returns to the Moulin Rouge, to be greeted with the very same enthusiasm. Paul-Louis Flers has polished up the production, Landolff has devised two hundred costumes which are veritable jewels, and the cast has rendered brilliant artistic performances. In particular we must mention a troupe of exquisite girls, as well as Frank Lawton, the king of the whistlers. The encores came thick and fast, and will continue so for many nights to come, for as long as the illuminated sails of the Moulin Rouge fling the joyous echoes of *The Belle of New York* into the Montmartre sky.

The new finale of 'The Belle of New York'

AU MOULIN ROUGE

la Revue en Chair et... en Rosse

16 October 1911:
L'AMOUR LIBRE
(FREE LOVE)

Spectacular operetta in the style of Aristophanes in four acts by Edouard Adenis.
Music by Rodolphe Berger.
Orchestra directed by Gustave Goublier.
Costumes by Landolff.
Scenery by Amable.

With Polin, Cebron-Norbens, Pepa Bonafé, Fernand Frey, Lacerpète, Stritt, Myalis and Delyane.

20 December 1911:
LA REVUE EN CHAIR ET EN
. . . ROSSE
(THE REVUE IN THE FLESH AND IN
. . . OLD BONES)

Spectacular revue in two acts and thirty scenes by Valentin Tarault and Georges Arnould.
Produced by André Barally.
New music and arrangements by Gustave Goublier.
Costumes by Landolff.

With Sulbac, Marville, Jane Alba, Jane Merville, Lucette Clerval, Suzanne Le Priel, Netty Vignal, Resse, Géo Lole, Léon Michel, Stritt, Myalis, Lucienne Delmay, La Blanca, Saravia, Arly, de Nixo, Pepa Bonafé, Léati, Sancy, Murt, Conchita Bau, Delphin, Mafer and Lacerpète.

The event that fashionable Paris was determined not to miss – the grand winter revue at the Moulin Rouge, in a house redecorated by Jean Fabert! It was the genial director's Christmas present to his faithful public. The auditorium has been completely transformed, and scintillates with lights skilfully arranged to set off a decor which is both luxurious and agreeable, while on stage is the most unusual of music-hall entertainments. Among the more exceptional turns, we noted the presence of Anita Labartha and Séverius, two small and exquisite dancers, and most particularly that of Conchita Bau, a musical prodigy of eight summers at the most. Tomorrow's stars, without a doubt.

Sulbac and Marville, stars of 'La revue en chair et en . . . rosse'

IN THE WINGS

21 March 1911

It's the first appearance tonight, in the famous revue *C'est très excitant*, of the incomparable American artist Norman French. 'The dance of the nineteenth Kummel', the unconventional act which he performs with Bert-Angère, has been acclaimed by the public. This exceptional star combines American humour with the most original British virtuosity and the wildest of Parisian fire. It's for you to judge if he is complete.

16 June 1911

Monsieur Jean Fabert has finally just acquired a ten-year lease on the Moulin Rouge. The event will be celebrated this very day, with a festive evening, to coincide with the Grand Steeplechase. Illuminations and bonfires, with fireworks, in the gardens.

Above and below, scenes from 'La revue en chair et en . . . rosse'

*The principal performers
in 'Le Roy s'allume'*

5 April 1912:
LA BÊTE
(THE BEAST)
LE ROY S'ALLUME
(THE KING LIGHTS UP)

La Bête: Spectacular mime in six scenes by André de Lorde and Jean Marsèle.

Music by Edouard Bonnamy.

With Christine Kerf, Georges Wague and Goujet.

Le Roy s'allume: Pseudo-historical operetta in two acts and three scenes by Charles Antoine Abadie and Valentin Tarault.

Costumes by Landolff.

Scenery by Mellano de Cassina and Jean Roger.

Orchestra directed by Gustave Goublier.

With Marie Merville, Marfa d'Hervilly and Henry Lamothe.

With Jane Marville, Lacerpète, Seylis, Vissières, Sancy and Daysiris.

With the Pickart and Josefson troupes.

21 June 1912:
TAIS-TOI, TU M'AFFOLES!
(BE QUIET, YOU'RE DRIVING ME CRAZY!)

Grand summer revue in two acts and thirty scenes by Paul-Louis Flers and Eugène Héros.

Produced by André Barally.

Orchestra directed by Gustave Goublier.

Costumes by Landolff.

Scenery by Amable, Cioccari, Tirlet and Numa.

With Prince, Moricey, Nina Myral, Alice Guerra, Jane Marville, Germiane, Paula de Alba, Marcelle Arly, Sancy, Géo, Darvyl, Mafer and Barbier.

With the extraordinary Spanish dancers Iborra and Manzano and the Royal Stars troupe.

For his first show in the Place Blanche, Peter Carin, the new director, has achieved a master stroke. He made a point of choosing the two writers, Paul-Louis Flers and Eugène Héros, whose partnership has met with nothing but success wherever they have been. He received his reward last night in the shape of the most colossal success to be seen on the Butte for many a long day. The scene with Nijinski (Prince), Caruso (Moricey) and Sumurus (Nina Myral) is one of those trios of which the authors have the monopoly and which many have imitated since. 'The Dance Hall on the Road to Antin', after Gavarni, 'The Lilac Garden' and 'Liberty at the Barricades', from Delacroix, and 'The Parade of the Fatted Ox past the Café de Paris' are marvellous reconstructions. Prince, straight-faced, is very witty as the secretary of the CGT, and above all when portraying the 'The ragamuffin thief', the fake journalist who was recently in the news, having hoaxed, very plausibly it must be said, the most eminent personalities of Parisian Society. It was a succession of laughs and admiring shouts from the first cue to the final scene.

Gustave Goublier, conductor and the composer of Moulin Rouge revues

86

With Marise Fairy, Jane Marnac, Hedya, Myalis, Delyane, Jane Dyt, Lecomte, Duperré, Du Prez, De Zürka, Sinoël, Luguet, Vissières, La Blanca, Brissac, Paul Clerc and the Mirror Girls.

Can it be true? After so many imported operettas, silly enough to have disarmed the Balkans, after so many slow waltzes stretched out into three acts, here at last is an operetta worthy of the name, whose plot does not appear to have been concocted by senile old men in a sanatorium. The book is based on the Koepenick incident, which excited virtuous Germany. The good-natured Prince Otto, accom-panied by Max, a woman-chaser, finds himself in a garrison where 'there's a shortage of females'. Prevailed upon by Max, the regiment settles itself in the town of Gottenberg, where there's much fun to be had. This unscrupulous young man stirs up trouble, diverts the town hall funds to his own pocket, and seduces the burgo-master's daughter. Also involved in the story is Elsa, a princess who is engaged to Otto, although they have not yet met. She disguises herself as a young girl of Gottenberg and wins his love incognito . . . There is a whole series of improbable imbroglios from which our heroes manage to emerge — to their own good fortune, and especially to that of the public.

17 October 1912:
THE GIRLS OF GOTTENBERG

English operetta in three acts by George Grossmith and L.E. Bermann, adapted by Gabriel Timmory and Maurice de Marsan. Music by Ivan Caryll and Lionel Monckton. Produced by Peter Carin.

IN THE WINGS

3 January 1912

From tonight onwards 'Gala Fridays' will be held at the Moulin Rouge, restricted to a fashionable clientele. It will be a typically Parisian affair, including a battle of flowers and congas at the end of the second act of the successful revue *En chair et en . . . rosse*. At the same time the pretty girls in the show will hand out bouquets and gifts.

1 March 1912

The extraordinary success of *La Bête* has had repercussions in America. Messieurs André de Lorde and Marsèle have just concluded a contract with an impresario who will very shortly be taking their marvellous show overseas.

5 April 1912

The new revue at the Moulin Rouge, *Le Roy s'allume*, ought to have been called 'La Gioconda'. Its heroine is Mona Lisa herself, the girl from Florence who sat as Leonardo da Vinci's model. The plot, devised soon after the disappearance of the famous painting, tells of the passion which was aroused in Francis I when he met the celebrated young lady in the artist's house. He therefore proposed to Leonardo that they should share Mona Lisa between them, in exchange for the title of official painter to the court. The scenes in the king's bedchamber at the Louvre are ones of farce and vaudeville. Considerable liberties have been taken with the truth . . .

30 May 1912

There has been a change at the top in the Moulin Rouge. Monsieur Peter Carin, who used to be in charge at the Capucines and the Vaudeville, has been named as the director of the establishment. His motto, which he has always applied hitherto, is 'Better and better'. There should be some splendid evenings in prospect in the Place Blanche.

15 January 1913

The situation in the Place Blanche is confused, with absurd rumours in the air. Since the resignation last month of Peter Carin, the most celebrated sails in the world have not been turning well. At first the establishment was nearly taken over by Eugène Héros, Faber and Harthmann but, as a result of financial disagreements between the backers, this project failed. This did not suit Carin's purpose, the sole director remaining until a new management takes over. Having refused to pay three months' rent in advance, he has been threatened with eviction by the Oller brothers. The two parties have taken the matter to court, the verdict being expected on 21 January. The situation is one which might still be settled amicably. Monsieur Jean Fabert is believed to be about to announce the final arrangements in the establishment of a new finance company which will make him the next director of the establishment.

19 January 1913

It is for personal reasons and as a result of previous undertakings that Monsieur Louis Verneuil, with the agreement of his colleague, has asked Monsieur Jean Fabert not to put his signature to the revue which is due to open next week at the Moulin Rouge.

Officially, therefore, Monsieur Valentin Tarault will be the sole author of *Tu me fais rougir*.

28 May 1913

The Moulin Rouge had to put up closed signs last night, following sharp disagreements between the management and the artists. One of the latter, the compère of the revue *Vicieuse, va! . . .*, refused to go on stage because the management had imposed on him a fine which he considered to be undeserved. Since some fellow-artists had taken his side, it was not possible for the show to go on as normal, and the audience were reimbursed.

29 June 1913

On the occasion of the Grand Prix, a Hispano-Argentinian gala will be held tonight in honour of the delegation from the Spanish Chambers of Commerce and the Argentinian colony in Paris. The most renowned artists from the two nations will be lending their presence to an occasion which will celebrate the friendly relations uniting the kingdom of Spain and the South-American republic. On the programme will be Spanish and Argentinian songs and dances – tango, *pericón*, gipsy dance and *alegrías*, performed by Otero, Yeta Rianza, Marthe Lenclud, Christine Kerf, Maria la Bella, Gloria Star, Serjiua, Bucourt, Antonio de Bilbao, Cimarra, Pagan, Cardoco, Caïn, Loduca, Casimiro Aln, Celestino Ferrer and Edouardo Horiellos. Olé!

22 August 1913

A poster competition has been announced at the Moulin Rouge to find an original from which to produce a poster for the revue *Voui ma gosse*. Only members of the public will be entitled to vote, but the procedure will be supervised by a prestigious jury. The prizes will consist of cash and of medals.

27 January 1913: TU ME FAIS ROUGIR (YOU MAKE ME BLUSH)

Revue in two acts and twenty scenes by Valentin Tarault.
New music and arrangements by Gustave Goublier.
Production and sets by André Barally.
Orchestra directed by Raphaël Beretta.
Choreography by Pomme and La Blanca.
Costumes by Landolff.
Scenery by Cassina and Roger, Tirlet and Numa Ronsin.

With Marise Fairy, Davrigny, Maud Delorr, Pierreville, La Blanca, Miss Mabel Marlowe, Miss Eva, Debionne, Maud Dollor, Choisoeulle and Jane Merville.

With Paul Clerc, Boucot, Rivers, Du Prez, Williams, Vissières, Lucien Cotté and the Trio Gennaro.

Mademoiselle Davrigny, Boucot and Marise Fairy, by Bertys

The fortunes of the Moulin Rouge have been many and various. Under the new management of Monsieur Jean Fabert they seem to be set fair at last. His first show, *Tu me fais rougir*, lives up to the promise of its title and to the current demands of the music-hall public. In the manner of Aristophanes the revue writer has sharpened his pen on all the personalities occupying the limelight in Paris. Scenes which will delight audiences have names such as 'The Windmills of Valmy', 'Don Quixote', 'Valmy', 'Longchamp', 'The Ceremonial Dancer', 'The Festival of the Fools in 1840', 'The Farewells at Fontainebleau in 1812' and, in particular, a finale devoted to windmills of all kinds – Alphonse Daudet's, Don Quixote's, windmills in Holland, at Longchamp, at Valmy and in Montmartre. Add to this an unbelieveable profusion of pretty girls, of sensational turns such as the Trio Gennaro and, above all, of

The final scene of 'Vicieuse, va!'

dances. Just as in the good old days of La Goulue and Valentin le Désossé, at the end of each scene everyone kicked their legs up and danced with verve. There was joy in the air and sky-high dancing. It was an evening of good companionship – and very much less shocking than the title would suggest. It will enable the illuminated sails of the joyous Moulin to turn more lightly and resplendently than ever.

20 March 1913:
LA BELLE CIGARIÈRE
(THE BEAUTIFUL CIGAR GIRL)

Spectacular comic fantasy by Eugène Joullot and Benjamin Rabier.
Music by Valverde.
Orchestra directed by Raphaël Beretta.
Choreography and sets by Pomé.
Production by Brissac and Pomé.
Costumes by Landolff.
Scenery by Cassina and Roger, Tirlet and Numa.

With Pépa Bonnafé, Marguerite Dufay, Mabel Marlowe, Davrigny, Lescot, La Blanca, Cavallieri, Charletty, Garrett, Temm and Mireille Roy.

With Hasti, Ferreal, Merin, Rivers, Paul Clerc and Williany.

With the eight Flip Flap Girls.

When he took over the running of the Moulin Rouge, Monsieur Jean Fabert promised to change the programme

every two months. He has kept his word. In the part of Dolores, chosen as queen of the cigar girls at the grand carnival in Barcelona, was Pépa Bonnafé, an experienced and graceful star of operetta. As for Maria la Bella and her dancers Antonio and Pagan, in the second act they aroused justifiable enthusiasm, as did, it should be said, their colleague Isabel Migon. The scenery and the costumes were more stunning than ever, while the dances were vivid, and expressed all the gaiety of Spanish rhythm. It was Madrid translated to Montmartre, exile without the sorrow, a long journey for the price of a little ticket.

8 May 1913:
VICIEUSE, VA!
(SINNER, DEPART!)

Spectacular summer revue in two acts and thirty scenes by Fernand Rouvray and Louis Lemarchand.
New music, arrangements and direction of the orchestra by Raphaël Beretta.
Ballets and production by Léon Bucourt.

With Yetta Rianza, Davrigny, Gaby Benda, Paule Rolle, Djinn d'Iroy, Germaine Webb, Miss Eva, Miss Howe and Mina Marella.

With Serjius, Beauval, Rivers, Duprez, Marche and Mafer.

The grand summer revues at the Moulin Rouge have now achieved a worldwide reputation. They compel admiration from

IN THE WINGS
3 July 1913
This evening, the revue *Vicieuse, va!* will benefit from the addition of three new scenes – 'Do you want a jockey?', 'A dream of beauty' and 'The Russian ballet', revised and adapted by the Wanis.

Parisians and foreigners alike, by the magnificence of their productions and the wit of their authors. *Vicieuse, va!* is of this category. The finale, which is enhanced by two hundred of our prettiest Parisiennes with their radiant beauty, is a colossal artistic effort! As for the performances, these are brilliant indeed. It would be difficult to find a more delightful artist than Yetta Rianza, the brilliant dancing star of the Opéra-Comique, to add lustre, with her outstanding talent, to the most Parisian of revues. As Madame Chrysanthemum she embodies the genteel grace of Pierre Loti's heroine. Before our astonished eyes, dances from the Kasbah are intermingled with the poetic tea houses of Japan. The two scenes are not unrelated. Go and see for yourselves and, at the same time, discover that the spirit of the boulevardier has still some splendid evenings before it.

8 August 1913: MADAME CANTHARIDE

Spectacular fantasy in eight scenes by Fernand Rouvray and Louis Lemarchand.
New music, arrangements and direction of the orchestra by Raphaël Beretta.
Ballets and production by Léon Bucourt.

With Lucette de Landy, Andrée Marly, Gustave Coquet, Zidner, Rivers, Ransard and one hundred ravishing dancers.

7 October 1913: VOUI . . . MA GOSSE! (WOW . . . MY YOUNGSTER!)

Revue in forty-five scenes by Fernand Rouvray and Louis Lemarchand.
New music and arrangements by Raphaël Beretta.
Ballets, sets and production by Léon Bucourt.
Costumes by Pascaud.
Scenery by Marc-Henry, Ronsin and Laverdet, de Fleury and Saint-Aubin and de Tirlet and Numa.

With Yetta Rianza, Lucette de Landy, Andrée Marly, Rivers, Lerner, Timmy, Ransard, Alice Millet, Marche, Marignan, Sohège, Simone Kotbrune, Nina Devi, Sancy, Darclet, Williany, Duclod, Fassio and Reine Joly.

23 December 1913: FAIS VOIR . . . DIS! (LET ME SEE . . . TELL ME!)

Revue in forty-five scenes by André Dahl and Fernand Rivers.
New music and arrangements by Raphaël Beretta.
Ballets, sets and production by Léon Bucourt.
Costumes by Pascaud and Deviges-Bucourt.

With Lucette de Landy, Yvette de Brémonval, Rivers, Collen, Berthe Lecomte, Timmy, Annetta Pelucci, Fratelli, Paul Darcy, Ransard, Sohège, Hemdey, Clo Marra, Classis, Marche, Nina Walky, Reine Joly, Sancy, Bernys, Barbier, Vissières, Eadie and Ramsden, little Odette Carlia, Tom and Niel, in their kicks and bruises number.

The Moulin Rouge has been transformed into a temple of morality! Such was the unfamiliar scene we witnessed last night at the first performance of *Fair voir . . . dis!*. It was morality in a form which is impossible to resist, since it was preached by a crowd of pretty girls, gloriously undressed, in a dazzling setting. Thus, to our delighted eyes were presented in turn a restaurant doorman advising young ladies not to divert their lovers from their conjugal duties, some charming pupils from a school in Montmartre modestly removing their clothes, a new and 'proper' form of advertising, designed to modernize posters without making them deceitful, an astonishing 'Orange picking' scene and a 'Guardian angel' such as we all should possess.
So, for the sake of morality, you must hurry to the Place Blanche to applaud the new revue.

'Fais voir . . . dis!', a traditional Moulin Rouge revue, here playing at the Olympia

Jacques-Charles was the inventor of the modern variety show, with 'The Grand Revue'

La Belle d'Herlys (below, centre), was the first nude in music-hall and later Madame Jacques-Charles

26 February 1914:
L'ORGIE A BABYLONE
(THE BABYLONIAN ORGY)

Operetta in three acts and four scenes by Edouard Adenis and Rodolphe Berger.
Production and costumes by Léon Bucourt.
Orchestra and forty musicians under the direction of Raphaël Beretta.
Scenery by Roger and Damilot.
Costumes by Pascaud.

With Lucette de Landy, Girier, Gabrielle Hédia, Jan Roy, Marcel Hemdey, Timmy, Ransard, Marche, Myalis, Sancy, Dellarsenia, Bernys, Darcyle, Stella Duc, Darnoy, Valneige, Charletty, Annetta Pelucci, Sohège, La Belle d'Herlys, Jane Barbier, Romani, Darclet, Vissières, Dumas and Robert Roberty, principal dancer of the Royal Opera, Covent Garden in London.

To present an operetta on the stage of a music-hall is an enterprise both bold and arduous. The music-hall, by its very nature, demands a show whose subject is extremely simple and which can be adapted at any time. The audience may be dull-witted or foreign, and it is essential to be able to introduce at the last moment a number or a turn which has not been included by the librettist. *L'Orgie à Babylone* falls into this category. The subject, very lighthearted and delightfully bawdy, is in fact a very simple one. It is the story of a surprising adventure of which a certain queen of Babylon is for a time the dupe and a certain rogue is the hero. The latter, for whom a prophecy had foretold glory and honour, meets with the most prodigious good fortune that a very humble subject of an all-powerful ruler could aspire to. Such an adventure, you may be sure, cannot reach its end without numerous hitches and other hilarious complications along the way, forming the pre-

texts for some delightful melodies, brilliant harmonies and captivating ballets. Another gamble by Jean Fabert which has come off!

20 May 1914:
CACHE TON NU!
(HIDE YOUR NUDITY!)

Grand summer revue in forty scenes by Fernand Rouvray and Louis Lemarchand.
New music and arrangements by Raphaël Beretta.
Production and ballets by Léon Bucourt.

With Bach, Delphin, Edmond Ransard, Marcel Hamdey, Fred Marche, Vissières, Marjolie, Dumas, Hemdey, Bernys, Jeanne Perriat, Fernande Diamant, Reine Gabin, Reine Deschamps, Timmy, Clasis, Paula de Alba, Jane Barbier and La Bérat.

Bach, before he met Henri Laverne

Ever since the fashion for revue began to invade the variety theatres and music-halls of all categories, in Paris and the provinces, a certain change has been taking place in this kind of show.

Better than anyone else, Jean Fabert has understood what type of revue was needed in an establishment where people come to relax, to sit back, to smoke a cigar, and to watch rather than listen. Thus, for the gratification of the eyes, he mixes the following constituents: very short scenes played by beautiful women and skilful artists, light and shimmering costumes, a great deal of scenery, a profusion of lights, a producer of the first rank and an energetic orchestra leader.

Cache ton nu! is a model of its kind. It succeeds from start to finish, from 'The lodging room of the Touring Club de France', which portrays the misfortunes which await the unhappy tourist abandoned in Paris, to 'The Clean-out by le Wied', concerned with the current political scene, and including 'Aerial Line-shooting', a hilarious scene from military aviation, and 'Gagaphrodite', a very witty parody of the last show of the Renaissance. When one considers what is being provided elsewhere in Paris, the Moulin Rouge could have produced nothing better to show that it need fear no competition.

24 December 1914: LA LÉGENDE DES PETITS SOLDATS DE BOIS (THE LEGEND OF THE LITTLE WOODEN SOLDIERS)

Spectacular miracle play by Maurice Landay.

With Gina Barbiéri, Jeanne France, Raymonde Marly, Paulette d'Artois, Charletty, Paule Morly, Joseph Leroux, Ransard, Paul Clerc, Sinoël, René Raoult, Rivers, Vissières, ten entertainers and the whole troupe.

5 February 1915: LA REVUE TRICOLORE (THE TRICOLOUR REVUE)

Revue in ten scenes by Quinel and Moreau.

With Sinoël, Paule Morly, Maud Avril, Fred Pasca, Rivers, Marthe Sarbel, Paulette Lancret, Ransard, Miss Winnie and the Tipperary Girls, Mauville, Paulette Dartoy, Germaine Kym, Ginette Dubreuil and Alice de Tender.

At the Moulin Rouge, in *La Revue Tricolore*, one of the scenes portrays our soldiers in the trenches, and this patriotic image causes the audience to vibrate with enthusiasm. They fairly bring the house down at the appearance of the new organising genius of victory, the great victor of the Marne.

Below and opposite, four scenes from 'Cache ton nu', a revue which caught the spirit of the times

The Legend of the Apache Dance

The story of the birth of the famous *Valse chaloupée* (Apache Dance) is told by Mistinguett in her memoirs, in her own inimitable words:

'For me the history of music-hall began in the *bistrot* where I met Max Dearly. He was a great star and I was no one. When he wished me good-day, it was a wonderful moment. I met him in a *bistrot* near the Moulin Rouge. I had just got myself thrown out of the Gaîte-Rochechouart. I had cooked some herrings on the gas burners by which the dressing room — occupied by six of us — was illuminated. The smoke reached as far as the box-office. I wanted to get my own back on the director, Madame Varlet, for all her gibes. Her fingers were like sausages — cold meat with diamonds on them. When she paid us, she always found some way of being unpleasant.

"Here's your hundred sous, child, though you don't deserve them. You're so dirty. Go and use the money for a good bath."

That was precisely my role — to be dirty. I was the drain of Asnières, a main sewer. I wore green stockings, green tights, with green hair.

I had thus done what was needed to get myself thrown out, but it was a heavy blow all the same. While I was on my own in the bistrot, I had a brainwave. Dearly liked it, and I was saved.

The Apache Dance happened almost by accident, by improvisation. While we were rehearsing, he turned to me and said:

"Show me how versatile you are. See if you can follow what I do."

He danced a sort of languorous jig which I had no difficulty in imitating. Then he picked up some music from the ballet *Le Papillon* by Offenbach. Together we rehearsed the *Chaloupée*. It was a question of physiognomy. You had to express yourself, not with the feet, but with the face, with attitudes. We were very successful. Van Dongen painted a picture of our dance. Dearly wore a cloth cap and he opened my dress to expose my breasts. But that was only for the purposes of the painting.'

a Max Dearly
en grande admiration
René Bertrand

*Mistinguett and Max
Dearly: the first steps of an
Apache Dance which could
go on and on . . .*

Claudius

Dubbed 'the sage, the philosopher of the *caf'conc'*. A specialist in medleys, his hour of glory came with the perform-ances of *The Belle of New York* and *The Toreador*. Gifted with an unusual knack of improvisation, and capable of inter-rupting a scene at any moment, he specialised in the amusing, sometimes acid remark. Latecomers, ladies with large hats and persons who chattered while he was singing were his favourite targets. The dream harboured by his colleagues was to manage to make him laugh on stage – an ambition which they found impossible to realize.

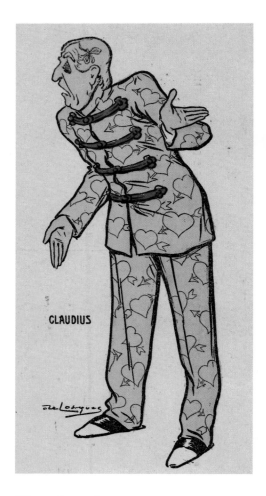

CLAUDIUS

Max Dearly

In music-hall he created the category of 'juvenile lead' and blazed the trail for a whole generation. Unlike his fellow-artists who made up their faces or dressed as clowns, he made the audi-ence laugh by sheer elegance: it was revolutionary.

Arriving in Paris from Marseilles with a recommendation from Charles Reschal, he began at the Concert Parisien. He was the youngest member of the com-

pany and opened the show, singing and dancing simultaneously: a new idea. His first success was his portrayal of *L'An-glais obstiné* (The Stubborn Englishman): after a childhood in a British circus, he found no difficulty in expressing himself in English, and even adopted a French style and accent which became his trademark.

From the start he was the darling of the fair sex and he returned the compliment. From the Concert Parisien he moved to the Scala, and then to the Variétés. His list of successes lengthened: *Le Jockey Américain* (The American Jockey), in which he mimed a complete horse-race, *Chonchette*, at the Capucines, in which he portrayed the immortal silhouette of an old actor, *A Country Girl* at the Olympia, *Miquette et sa mère* (Miquette and her mother) at the Variétés, *Le Roi* (The King), *Le Bois sacré* (The Sacred Wood), *L'Habit vert* (The Green Coat) and, above all, the *Valse chaloupée* (Apache Dance), which made Mis-tinguett's name and which he created at the Moulin Rouge during his summer break. 'This idea had been intended for the Variétés, with Eve Lavallière, using some little-known music by Jacques Offenbach. Since the director of that theatre was hostile to the proposal, I took advantage of a series of performances in the Place Blanche to put the number on there. My main problem was to find a partner of the right calibre. One evening

I left rehearsals and popped into a bar frequented by theatrical people, where I saw a young girl in tears.

'It was Mistinguett, who had just had a row with the woman in charge of the Gaîté-Rochechouart. She had exactly the sort of appearance of easy virtue that I was looking for.'

He went on to a successful career in the cinema, in operetta, with *La Vie Parisienne* and *La Belle Hélène*, and in the theatre, with *Azaïs* by Louis Verneuil and *Mon Bébé* (My Baby) by Maurice Hennequin. A supreme all-round artist.

Fragson

Harry Fragson's real name was Philippe Pot. He was born in England, in Soho, and began his career at the Cabaret de la Butte in 1891. Son of a Belgian father,

he first chose the stage name Frogson, which he later diplomatically modified to Fragson. Meeting with little success in revue, he found his true métier with songs which are still popular in France today, such as *À la Martinique, Je connais une blonde*, and *Le Long du Mis-*

souri. He was popular also with British audiences, for whom he composed *Hello, hello, who's your lady friend?* The first singer to accompany himself at the piano, he appeared at the Cigale, the Concert de l'Européen – and the Moulin Rouge. A tragedy put a premature end to his career when, in 1913, his father, from whom he was inseparable and on whom he lavished great care, shot him dead during a jealous quarrel, having discovered that, for some time, there had been a girl in his son's life and being unable to bear the thought of him harbouring feelings of tenderness, and even love, for someone else. So *caf'conc'* found itself living a Greek tragedy. Incredible, but sadly true.

titles are still remembered in France: *La Paimpolaise, Viens Poupoule, À la Martinique, À la cabane Bambou, Elle prend le boulevard Magenta, Cousine, La Polka des trottins, Les Mains de femmes, La Mattchiche.* Ignored by the upper and middle classes, and not having the necessary sex appeal to build a career as a lady-killer, this great popular star ended his life practically alone and half-paralysed, in his native town of Toulon, whose benefactor he had become by financing various projects, including a stadium and a clinic. The inspiration for a whole generation of singers, he was followed to his last resting place by only a single artist – Georgel.

Mayol, his celebrated forelock and his lucky lily, by Sem

Mayol

Félix Mayol began in 1895, in a theatre in the Rue de l'Échiquier, the Concert Parisien, which today bears his name. Every evening ordinary people from the district laughed at his often quite simple effects, and admired the charm of his voice and the preciseness of his gestures, which could often be ambiguous. In the forty-three years of his career he was noted for his blond forelock and his repertoire of comic songs, the majority of whose

Polaire

Her first poster was drawn by Toulouse-Lautrec. Her stage name she chose in Algiers, where she was born, after the Pole Star she could see in the sky. She was nicknamed 'La gommeuse épileptique' (The Epileptic Toff), because, showing off her legs and her low necklines, she was a past-mistress in the art of jigging up and down while making faces and reciting bawdy verse.

Polaire of the wasp-waist, by Losques

back to France, she tried her luck in the theatre, though without success, in *Claudine à l'école* (Claudine at school), a play which was to become famous a little later on. Changes in fashion and the disappearance of the corset dealt a fatal blow to her career. She put on weight to stay 'in the swim', but success was no longer around to greet her and she ended her life in solitude and poverty. It was said that, in rejecting her as they did, women were trying to get their revenge for the tortures they were obliged to suffer, trying – in vain – to approximate to the artiste's wasp-waist.

Polin

His real name was Pierre-Paul Marsalès. He was born in 1863 and began his career in 1886, in local concerts, before becoming one of the stars at the Eden Concert and the Alcazar d'Été. He broke the music-hall endurance record by remaining on the programme of the Scala for twenty years. On stage he armed himself with a check handkerchief into which he coughed barrack-room expressions. He introduced hundreds of songs which have remained famous in the world of French comics: *Ah Mademoiselle Rose, La Petite Tonkinoise, L'Ami Bidasse, La Caissière du Grand Café*. His influence has been considerable. Vibert, Bach and Raimu owe him a great deal. His modesty ensured that he never took any credit for it. His fame did not in fact prevent him from living a very private life. He disliked

'Max, Max, you do look a sight
Dressed as a soldier that don't have to fight'

This little ditty was dedicated to Max Lebaudy, the 'petit sucrier' (little sugar-maker) turned soldier, and was, thanks to her, taken up in chorus all over Paris. 'On stage she displayed a sort of nervous agitation, hopping from one foot to the other like a turkey on a red-hot plate,' wrote Colette about her. The two women knew one another well. At a time when the future novelist was still only the wife of Willy, they formed the first Parisian 'sisters' act. Physically she did not measure up to the standards of beauty in those days. Her skin was always tanned and she boasted a wasp-waist of a size estimated to be forty centimetres. Her nose was too large and her mouth too

wide, her chest was very high ('I've got ribs like Ravel's *Bolero*,' she was always complaining) and her hair was curly and short. The public found her muscular body and, above all, her soft eyes with the black pupils and long lids so attractive that, in 1900, a crowd assembled outside the Scala, on the Boulevard de Strasbourg, to see her getting into her cab. Her repertoire, in which she condemned vice, morphine and cocaine, gave great pleasure to the fashionable men of letters, with Jean Lorrain at their head.

One day she set off to conquer the United States. Unfortunately, her agent had announced her as 'the queen of the uglies' and 'the plainest woman in the world'. The Americans quickly discovered that it was not so – quite the contrary – and spurned her. Taking the first boat

Rip, sketched by himself, with a profile by Paul Colin

(1934), *Boissière* (1937), *Suzanne et les brigands* (1948). An honours list eloquent enough to have been included in the *Book of Records*, had it existed at that time.

Sulbac

In the world of the *cafés-concerts* he stood out from the crowd. He appeared dressed in a smock, a basket on his arm and a little hat surmounting a rubicund face with a jovial mouth. He sang songs of the countryside, and his act invariably began with four lines describing his village origins. There followed rustic monologues delivered in provincial dialect, difficult for the uninitiated to understand. His turn did not always attract sustained applause, except when he announced: 'I'm going to do the forked pear tree'. Then, standing on his head with his legs in the air, he would receive an ovation. It was a little bit of bravura on which he managed to base his whole career.

talking about himself, and he was never to be seen at public dinners. Before going on stage he shut himself up in his dressing-room; at the end of the show he would return to an ordinary life, shunning encores. 'You have to know when to get off, five minutes before the audience discover they don't want you to leave – that's the secret of success,' he was in the habit of asserting. In 1927 he died at Frette-sur-Seine as he had lived – simply, without any fuss.

Rip

His real name was Georges Thenon. He was the author of some ten comedies, a dozen operettas, countless caricatures, but above all a hundred revues, full of wit, the favourites of fashionable Paris, and which today constitute the most precious sociological records of that era. Vestiges of *Paris fin de règne, Comme le temps passe, Le Congrès s'amuse, Plus ça change* and many other successes can thus be found in the archives of the Bouffes Parisiens, the Marigny, the Daunou, the Palais Royal and the Variétés. In the place of honour are the most memorable triumphs and successes, still unequalled to this day.

Spinelly

Andrée Spinelly began at the Parisiana when she was fourteen – an infant prodigy. She matured her precocious talent in the course of many appearances on the music-hall stage. From the Fourmi she moved to the Palais du Travail, then to the Européen, the Casino de Montmartre, the Variétés, the Cigale and the Moulin Rouge, before becoming, at the Capucines, the star of *Le Cri de Paris*, Rip's first revue. Success did nothing to diminish her craving for the stage. Between 1908 and 1922 she was acclaimed by Parisian audiences in shows of which the majority are now forgotten, such as: *La Revue du Châtelet, Bigre, Vlan, Le Bonheur sous la main, Les Éclaireuses, Le Tango, Plus ça change, Une femme, six hommes et un singe, Frivolités, Kiki, Un Cochon qui sommeille, Hercule à Paris, L'École des cocottes, Le Roi, Le Fruit vert, Le Lion et la Poule, Fredaines, Le Dompteur, La Belle Amour, L'Amour à l'américaine, Déjeuner au soleil, La Bête noire.* Between two tours of Great Britain and one of the United States she found time to become one of the leading stars of the early cinema, with *Un Fil à la patte* (1925), *L'Amour à l'américaine* (1931), *Une Idylle au Caire, La Châtelaine du Liban* (1933), *Les Nuits moscovites*

Spinelly, the young star of the Moulin Rouge

The Moulin Rouge owed its post-war revival to a man who knew his music. Francis Salabert, who purchased the lease, was the most famous of French music publishers. Although deeply involved in his own business affairs, he did not treat the establishment as just a plaything, and determined to set up a good team to run it. For the management side he chose Pierre Foucret, a man who knew the entertainment world, but from the other side of the footlights. He had run the front of house for some of the greatest theatre managers. For the artistic side he was in possession of information which was worth its weight in gold: Jacques-Charles, the leading revue writer, was not on speaking terms with Léon Volterra. One had been writing and the other directing at the Casino de Paris since 1917, and they had been unanimously acclaimed. There was no time to be lost! Knowing that Jacques-Charles was due to return to Paris that very day, he decided to meet his train at the Gare Saint-Lazare. In fact, on account of a sordid business involving money, the latter was looking for a chance to leave the Rue de Clichy. Salabert immediately offered him a three-year contract.

While major renovations were undertaken in the auditorium, Jacques-Charles settled down to the writing of a revue: *New York – Montmartre*. Having been given a free hand, he felt encouraged to try out an idea on which he was keen: a show in which the stars would be American dancers! 'Expensive' is the word to describe the reaction of Pierre Foucret. With one eye on the stage and the other on the box office, he failed to see the point of that kind of expenditure. A French chorus, or even a British one, would serve the purpose! Jacques-Charles protested and in the end a compromise was found. A New York company, the Hoffmann Girls, had been the toast of London for months. Why not offer them a contract to come to Paris?

No sooner said than done. Jacques-Charles being temporarily laid up with the after-effects of a war-wound, it was Pierre Foucret who took the necessary action. However, a better manager than diplomat, he committed several *faux pas* which resulted in a deep and permanent rift with Gertrude Hoffmann.

The only possible solution lay on the other side of the Atlantic, and Jacques-Charles took the first available boat. To his surprise, on landing in the United States, he received a cable from none other than Gertrude Hoffmann. If Jacques-Charles, whom she knew by reputation, would sponsor her troupe's début in Paris, there would be no further problems. Far from it – to see her name on the Moulin Rouge bill would be an honour! The business was settled so quickly that, before returning to France, Jacques-Charles found the time to engage the Dolly Sisters as well. Named Rosie and Jenny, they were the first twins in the history of cabaret.

They would, he promised, be the stars of his second revue, which was already forming in his head. He had known them when they started out and had anticipated their success, applauding them at the Casino de Paris, following their

meteoric rise on Broadway, and seeing them exchange their false pearl necklaces for spectacular jewels. He also knew that, after their performances, they spent most of their nights attempting to break the bank in the casinos.

Finally, two days before his departure, Jacques-Charles listened to the principal melodies from a musical comedy which had been written a month earlier. The composer's name was Vincent Youmans and the show was called *No, No, Nanette*. Charmed by the lyrics, he suggested to Francis Salabert that he buy the rights for France. The latter did some quick sums. The renovation of the Moulin Rouge was greatly exceeding the original budget, and he turned the idea down. Many times in the future he was to regret this decision . . .

A few weeks later, one month behind schedule, the theatre in the Place Blanche once more opened its doors. On the first night the public jostled to applaud the new sets. In the front row sat Mistinguett. From the first few minutes, she knew that she was present on an evening of a very special significance. Without any doubt, *New York – Montmartre* relegated all the other Parisian revues to the status of antiquities. The pace set by Jacques-Charles would, in a very short time, overturn all the established rules. There was not a moment to lose; if she was to retain her title of 'queen of music-hall', she had to appear at the Moulin Rouge – and as quickly as possible.

There was one major stumbling block to this plan: some months before, she had quarrelled with Jacques-Charles. To achieve her end, therefore, she had to win round Pierre Foucret. Charming and persuasive as only she could be when she had to, she solved the problem in several meetings . . . Foucret made her, by contract, the guiding spirit of the next revue, the leading lady of the show and a co-director of the establishment! The top of the bill was still reserved, as before, for the Dolly Sisters – making them the stars on paper but not on stage, which was a very different affair. Considering themselves to be the victims of a phoney contract, they refused to take part in the show and took out proceedings against Pierre Foucret. This was far from causing Mistinguett any loss of sleep. She now had to exert all her strength in order to win the day. Sensibly, she began by making it up with Jacques-Charles. From their partnership three revues were to be born in four years. To performances in Paris were added others abroad. The last tour, to the Argentine and Brazil, which promised to be a triumph, ended in disaster. A clause in the contract had, in fact, allotted a guaranteed profit to the Moulin Rouge. Jacques-Charles, associated with the deal, swore he knew nothing of this arrangement, but in the final count found himself having to pay 800,000 francs out of his own pocket.

Feeling the injured party, he decided on revenge. Knowing that his contract was to end on 30 March 1929, and discovering that Pierre Foucret was unaware of this fact, he kept his own counsel, started the rehearsals for a new revue, and then abandoned them at dawn on the sixth day. That morning, concerned about the absence of his producer, Pierre Foucret telephoned Jacques-Charles to be told that, with effect from midnight, he was no longer a member of his crew! Picture his fury when Jacques-Charles added that he had not the slightest intention of returning – no matter how high the reward offered. Imagine Foucret's state of mind when his ex-revue writer delivered the final blow: he had just signed a long and exclusive contract with Paramount . . .

Foucret's wrath was indescribable. He found himself having to pay considerable sums in the way of indemnities to artists who had been engaged a few days earlier. He put on some variety turns and an American revue, brought the accounts up to date and then put up the shutters.

The Moulin Rouge was turned into a cinema where, for years, live artists appeared only before the showing of the film. After so many highly-coloured scenes, suddenly another, of a much darker hue, was on the stage. It was the end of a 'Belle Époque', which doubtless will never return.

The new foyer of the Moulin Rouge, and the new auditorium which was to witness Mistinguett's triumphs

JACQUES CHARLES:

The Man Who Was Revue

Jacques-Charles, the father of modern revue! Line Renaud and her fellow singers all over the world owe him a great debt. He was one of the first to devise the scene in a musical spectacular where showgirls make their way down a long staircase. Born on 14 February 1882, he was the son of the owner

of the Magasins du Pont Neuf, later to become the Samaritaine. The early death of his father prevented him from following in the family business, and he contented himself with employing his 'rag trade' upbringing in the selection of stage costumes. At 17 he was seized by the lure of journalism. He started by managing to sell news items and cartoons to any magazine which would accept them. Then by chance he made the acquaintance of Dranem. With the confidence of youth, he submitted a sketch to him, which the great artist found acceptable and which he performed for a week at the Eldorado. Not at all a bad beginning in those days! A few weeks later, he was engaged as a gossip columnist by *Gil Blas*, the paper which reported the everyday life of the *demi-mondaines*. Given the job of running a column entitled 'Tales of a Dresser', he began to be a daily backstage visitor at the Folies Bergère, the Palais de Glace, La Scala and the Moulin Rouge. In brief, all the places where, in those days, entertainment was to be found. Places in which, a few months earlier, he would never have dreamed of setting foot! Very soon his ambition was to make his living by the stage rather than by journalism. He became one of the assistants of Paul-Louis Flers, the fashionable revue writer. The latter's method was very simple: he chose the subjects and then left the job of writing the dialogue to a few carefully selected assistants. All he had to do was assemble the complete work and sign it. This 'ghost-writing', as it is called today, enabled Jacques-Charles to learn the essentials of what was to become his true vocation. In the same team a young man, seemingly very gifted, was also starting out, who was christened Rip. He also would very soon realise his true talent.

After his military service he was taken on as general secretary at the Little Palace, the temple of *caf'conc'*. A few months later the Isola brothers, owners of the Folies Bergère, the Olympia and the Parisiana, made him the general secretary of their establishments.

He began to devise parts of the revues until, in the end, he was responsible for the whole show. Three years later, with the blessing of the Isolas, he was in charge of the Olympia. On the bill were all his friends – Rip, Max Dearly, Fragson, as well as two young people for whom he predicted a glittering future – a certain Yvonne Printemps and Max Linder, who at that stage had not yet thought of trying his luck in the cinema.

On that same stage Mistinguett was hailed by the critics as the 'queen of music-hall', and in the hall he created the 'Palais de la Danse'. This was a revolutionary concept and it was to remain the leader of the Parisian dance halls.

It was at this time that there appeared in London the Futuristic Exhibition of Marinetti. It was to have an immense influence on music-hall in general, and on the career of Jacques-Charles in particular. The latter would, in fact, be the first to demonstrate it on the stage.

In 1912, while not deserting the Olympia, he took over control of the Marigny. There he put on revues in two acts and five scenes. His last show, *On s'embrase*, with Raimu, had a very short life, being on the programme for one night only, 1 August 1914. The next day the performance was cancelled a few moments before the curtain was due to rise, on account of the declaration of war. Half the cast had just been called to the colours. As for the dancers, they were all in tears because the men in their lives were about to leave for the front . . .

Jacques-Charles also took the road to the trenches. After being wounded, he spent six months in a hospital bed before setting out to return to the stage. This he was able to do through Léon Volterra, the new owner of the Casino de Paris. This extraordinary man of show business was truly self-educated. He started at the bottom of the ladder and never forgot that he owed his first little store of earnings to Jacques-Charles. Several years before, the latter had enabled him to meet his monthly bills by selling the programmes at Olympia with a phrase which was to become classic: 'I pay him fifty centimes,' he would simply call out to the audience, a fiction which delighted Jacques-Charles. Impossible to refuse a good tip in the face of such an argument! For Volterra it was to be the start of the foundation on which one day he was to build an immense fortune.

Jacques-Charles thus found himself with the job of creating the first revue for the theatre in the Rue de Clichy. It was a winner which the two partners were to repeat more than once, triumphantly topping the bill with Gaby Deslys and Harry Pilcer, and then Mistinguett and Maurice Chevalier. Between two tours, to South America and New York, he wrote with Maurice Yvain verses which were to become immortal – *Mon homme* (My man), *J'en ai marre* (I'm sick of it), and many others.

It was a financial disagreement which led to Jacques-Charles leaving the Casino de Paris for the Moulin Rouge, where he stayed for four years. His name then appeared in lights over the Paramount cinema in Paris, where he was responsible for creating super productions in the first part of the programme, which New Yorkers will never forget. Up to the war success carried him on regular journeys to London and New York. In 1945, after fifty-five years devoted to the variety stage, he decided to quit the scene.

Lucien Rimels, the last producer of the great Concert Mayol, Jacques-Charles and Jacques Crépineau: three generations, three friends united in the same love of the music-hall (1958)

He emerged to make some radio broadcasts entitled 'That's Paris' and 'The Revue of my life', consisting of interviews in which he recalled his memories, later on incorporating them in several books, work which gave him contentment until the evening of his days.

IN THE WINGS

JACQUES-CHARLES
—
MISTINGUETT
ESTRANGEMENTS AND ENTANGLEMENTS

Jacques-Charles once said of Mistinguett that she was his dearest friend and his worst enemy. Over the years, in revues and in theatres, they were always quarrelling, only to make it up later. It was a sort of love-hate relationship, a mutual jealousy typical of that between the lovers which they never were, a permanent confrontation between two persons who admired one another deeply, but who on account of their characters could only clash.

Their first encounter was when they were both newcomers. It was one evening in 1898 at the Ambassadeurs, one of the most popular *cafés-concerts* of the period. Jacques-Charles, the young gossip-writer and the lover of the comedienne of the current revue there, entered his inamorata's dressing-room, to find a dancer, both young and slim, in the act of undressing. He would have been about fifteen, and she twenty-three. She had taken the name 'Mistinguette' (with an 'e' at the end), and it was her début. She had spent the day in learning the various dodges for making herself up before going on stage. Legend has it that she was not very

pretty, with a turned-up nose and, as her companions put it, teeth 'like piano keys'. The real truth is quite different, as the photographs demonstrate – she was ravishing! No one, however, could suspect the glittering future that fate had reserved for her. Two years later they were both to be found backstage at the Eldorado. Thanks to Dranem, Jacques-Charles was in the early stages of becoming a dramatic author. In the same programme Mistinguette, to illustrate a song describing the ardour of her passion for the orchestra leader, appeared perched astride the prompt-box. It was so unexpected that the audience found itself baffled by this comedienne whose performance was 'of the epileptic variety'.

*

* *

Twelve more years were to pass before the paths of 'Miss' and Jacques-Charles would pass once more. The latter, then the director of the Olympia, engaged her as the star of *La Revue Légère*, which was to be a turning point in her career. Two years earlier she had been a revelation at the Moulin Rouge, on account of the Apache Dance, partnering Max Dearly, who was top of the bill. This time the critics and the public hailed her as the 'queen of music-hall'. Her little bit of virtuosity, completely forgotten today, was an imitation of Jacqueline Forzane, a young woman as ravishing as she was eccentric, who represented a mode of belly-dancing with an umbrella under the arm, pointed hats like Austrian shakoes, hobble-skirts and boots laced nearly to the knees, otherwise known as the *Mattchiche*.

It was a short-lived triumph, ending after only twenty performances with a bad attack of appendicitis. It was nevertheless an event which was to strengthen the links between them. Several weeks later, Miss's fiancé, a young artist named Maurice Chevalier, set off from eastern France, where he was completing his military service. Thanks to the intervention of Jacques-Charles, he had just been posted to Fontainebleau. Mistinguett found herself unable to bear his absence any longer, and the director of the Olympia simply did what was necessary to apply balm to the artiste's heart.

From now on, their paths to success were to cross time and again. Off stage, Jacques-Charles was a privileged observer of the relationship – often a stormy one – between 'Miss' and Maurice Chevalier. On stage, for a revue at the Casino de Paris entitled *Paris qui jazz*, he wrote, in collaboration with Albert Willemetz and Maurice Yvain, a song called *Mon homme* (My man). When he accompanied her to New York, he risked a prison sentence on her behalf. To do her a good turn he was carrying in one of his suitcases a dress

Mistinguett: the photographs taken during her time at the Moulin Rouge ensured her immortality

of hers which aroused the suspicions of the customs officer. How was it that a man who had sworn on his honour that he was unmarried came to be carrying such articles? Since lying constitutes one of the gravest of offences, poor Jacques-Charles imagined himself already thrown into a dungeon, like the most desperate of criminals. Luckily for him, Irving Berlin, who had come to meet him, was able to vouch for his integrity and rescue him from incarceration.

A few days later, caught in a storm on the road to Atlantic City, Jacques-Charles saved Mistinguett's life. Judging the thunder and lightning to be both close and alarming, he led her away from the tree beneath which she was sheltering from the rain. A few moments later the lightning struck the place which they had just left.

This unblemished friendship was to become stained for melancholy and wholly material reasons. Being of the opinion that the fee which had been offered her by Léon Volterra for a visit to Brazil was insufficient, she chose instead to do a tour in Buenos Aires for Madame Rasimi, the director of Bata-clan, who was very well established in South America. Since the itineraries of the performances happened to differ by only a few days, conflict was inevitable. The presence of Mistinguett did not prevent the Casino company from gaining a rapid advantage. The quarrel was pursued in the papers where Mistinguett, in her vexation, declared about her former author and friend 'and if Monsieur Jacques-Charles is despicable enough to attack a woman, he will find himself confronting me'. The polemic nearly ended in a duel between the injured party and the author of the article. In the end the reconciliation took place in Pierre Foucret's office at the Moulin Rouge. Mistinguett was so keen to be in the revue that she declared she would even accept the contract simply for the pleasure of working with her ex-enemy!

*
* *

The idyll did not endure. By the second revue, Ça, c'est Paris, fresh clouds were appearing on the horizon. Is it necessary to add these to the list of all the other gossip, the woundings, the intrigues, the schemes, the spiteful tales, the calumnies? Never mind . . . For weeks the star and her writer exchanged not a word. In the end Jacques-Charles stopped going backstage, in order not to aggravate the situation. One evening, however, he ventured a brief visit to the auditorium. 'Miss' caught sight of him and, at the end of the scene fainted away. The curtain was lowered and she was carried to her dressing room; when she opened her eyes, the anguished face before her was none other than that of Jacques-Charles. Like the heroine in the last reel of a melodrama, she fell into his arms and dissolved in tears. Regaining her composure, she recounted to him the details of a conversation which she had overheard some hours earlier. Being stretched out for a nap in the office, she had heard Pierre Foucret explaining how he had created out of nothing the entanglements which had ended in the current estrangement. His purpose had been based on the principle of divide and rule.

His machinations were to cost him dear a few months later, for it was Mistinguett herself who suggested to Jacques-Charles that he omit to remind the businessman of the date of expiry of his contract. In the end the quarrel resulted in the closure of the theatre. For once it was a dispute from which 'Miss' found herself completely disassociated.

Mistinguett dressed in glory by Gesmar

GESMAR THE METEOR

Gesmar. The name is so closely associated with the posters and the scenery of the Moulin Rouge that one has the impression that he must have lived to be a hundred. In fact he died in February 1928, when he was twenty-four years old.

Born at Nancy, he owed his start to Spinelly, one of the most popular comediennes of the day. His drawings caught her eye, and so she took him in and made him her protégé, immediately giving him the job of creating her stage costumes. At an age when he might have been expected to be studying his school-books, rather than circulating in fashionable Paris, he was famous. He became mentally disturbed. Exhausted, he attempted to put an end to his success by suicide. Happily for him, the bullet with which he had meant to achieve this end finished up in the water tank. An ability to draw well does not necessarily signify manual dexterity, as this shows. With the Spinelly residence where he was living now flooded, he was conducted to the door by the housekeeper with no further ceremony. Mistinguett, scenting something to her advantage, took over and installed him next door to her own house. He began to create all kinds of costumes and scenery for his good fairy. His ubiquity was such that, in the end, he began to be taken for Miss's son and, backstage, was referred to affectionately as 'Mama Gesmar'. He resembled an impish child, was always on the go and lived only for his work. He was an innovator in the world of costumes and was always thinking up new ideas which were instantly copied by others, although this scarcely troubled him. 'I don't care,' he always said. 'I've got plenty of other ideas!'

He worked non-stop, and all his earnings were immediately spent. He had no idea of the value of the banknotes which were handed to him, and the word 'money' he completely deleted from his vocabulary. One evening he felt feverish and, excusing himself from Mistinguett's table before the dessert was served, took to his bed. A doctor was called immediately and did not hide his concern, prescribing a treatment which demanded continuous attention. For forty-eight hours Mistinguett and Jacques-Charles took it in turns at his bedside, but all in vain. The young man was unable to recover from this unknown malady, which had started as bronchitis and finished as pneumonia.

On the day after his death Mistinguett came on stage and asked for a minute's silence in memory of this unique artist. The dancers unhesitatingly obeyed, wiping away genuine tears. It would be long before they could forget this great little man. For fifty years his drawings and his models have influenced every generation of costume designer for the music hall and the theatre. Truly a meteor which will never disappear.

110

GALA NIGHTS AT THE MOULIN

10 September 1924

Jacques-Charles, the leading creator, author and producer of Parisian Revue, has signed a three-year contract with the Moulin Rouge.

20 December 1924 – 26 August 1925
NEW YORK – MONTMARTRE

The Grand Moulin Rouge Revue in two acts and fifty scenes by Jacques-Charles.
Production by the author.
Assisted by Gertrude Hoffmann for the dances and Marcel Varnel for the sets.
Sketches by Georges Arnould, C.A. Carpentier and Palau.
American sketches adapted by Jacques-Charles (by special arrangement with E. Ray Goetz).
Lyrics by Jacques-Charles, Lucien Boyer and C.A. Carpentier.
Music by Chantrier, Charles Laurent, Moretti, Padilla, Scotto, Maurice Yvain and the most celebrated American composers.
Costumes designed by W.K. Benda, Robert Piguet, Alec Rzewusky, Montedoro, Eric Wallick and José de Zamora.
Costumes made by the Maison Pascaud and the workshops of the Moulin Rouge, under the control of Madame Langlais.

With the eighteen Gertrude Hoffmann Girls.

With Marcelle Yrven, Loulou Hegoburu, Jeanne Pirac, René Devilder, Baldini, Germaine Rieux, Sforza, Evelyn de Latour, Bizoulette, Lloyd, M.L. Shelton, Ruth Fallows, MacDonald, Wilson, Tamora, Gérard, Hughes, Nina Byron, Colette Damy, Zamora, Line Damy, Rouhier, Sylver, Delly, Emma Maitland, Laura Wamble, Wheelden, M. Gilchrist, Marie Frame, Sybil Turk, M. Smith, Boyking, Darvellys, Ducreux, Merville, Meyan, Haxonne, Nady, Lyons, Meunier, Dilan, Polette, Raiser, Carlotti, Ketty, Danny, Claire Mors, Heichert, Ney and Myriam.

With Milton, Cariel, Oy-Ra, André Berley, Darthez, Tom Thyl, Gayto, Varèze, Ludet and André Arbeau.

Forty-piece orchestra under the direction of CH. H. Laurent, conducted by Max Hoffmann for the American numbers, and accompanied by Billy Spedick, the Greatest American Drummer.

The terrible fire which once laid waste to the Moulin Rouge must now finally be laid to rest in the storage chest of bad memories. Last night, at the first performance of the *Grande Revue du Moulin-Rouge*, or *New York-Montmartre*, the flames were those of pleasure sparkling in the eyes of the guests, while it was only the applause which crackled.

Marcelle Yrven, the first star of the new Moulin Rouge

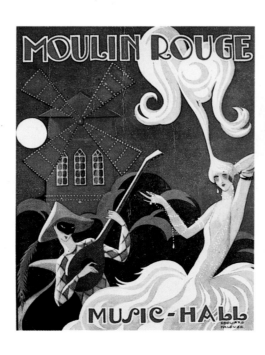

Amidst a brilliant audience we noted the late arrival of Monsieur Paul Painlevé, the Président du Conseil. The distinguished sage was somewhat distracted, having in fact arrived in time for the start of the show, but having then gone to the wrong place. He found himself in the Moulin Rouge Dance Hall, below street level. He was taken aback to find no one in the official box, but in the end realised his mistake.

We can also report the presence in the front row of our beloved Mistinguett. Although a revered star in the Americas, she nevertheless does not forget *her* Paris. Last July, you will remember, she made a brilliant return at the Casino de Paris, in a revue entitled *Bonjour Paris*. For the time being she is being very tight-lipped about her future plans. Last night one heard backstage rumours that a try-out on the stage of the Moulin Rouge was not impossible.

As for the show, that was simply delightful! A real Christmas present, delivered five days early! It was of a vitality, colour and richness which were staggering and unbelievable. We should mention a very amusing song by Milton, *La Trompette en bois* (The Wooden

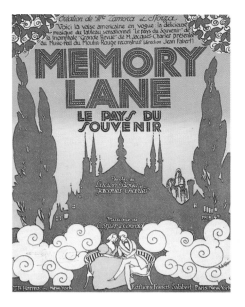

Trumpet), and in particular the first scene in the second act, 'The Stage Door', featuring, against a black background, eight dancers in evening-dresses and eight girls wrapped in magnificent cloaks. As for the first act, which takes place in different areas of New York, it seemed to have been written for the Hoffmann Girls. The rhythm was maintained right up to the final scene, thanks to the sensible treatment of the libretto by Monsieur Jacques-Charles. He has clearly taken all the lessons taught in New York, and adapted them to our own country. Thanks to him, Broadway in Paris is no longer a dream, but a reality – in the Place Blanche. We shall no doubt hear more.

From the first revue, the programme was laid down: glamour and pretty girls

The Hoffmann Girls from Broadway, in an acrobatic ballet created and directed by Gertrude Hoffmann

Milton and Baldini in 'Virginia'

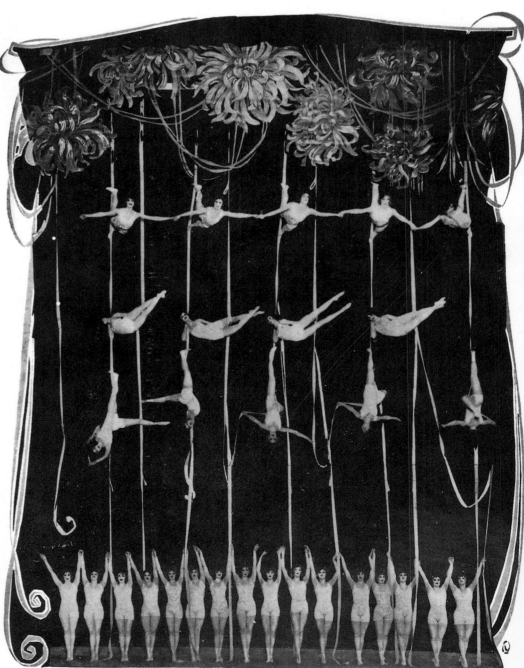

The Moulin Rouge aviary: the models transformed into birds of paradise

27 August 1925: MIEUX QUE NUE (BETTER THAN NUDE)

Revue in two acts and forty-eight scenes by Jacques-Charles.
Produced by the author.
Costumes designed by W.K. Benda, Robert Piguet, Alec Rzewusky, Montedoro, Éric Wallick and José de Zamora.

With the Gertrude Hoffmann Girls.

With Florence, Dolly, Marie, Austine, Baldini, Jeannette and Lily.
With Edmonde Guy and Biscot, the Hermanos Williams and guest star Argentina.

With Cariel, Oy-Ra, André Berley, Darthez, Tom Thyl, Gayto, Varèze, Ludet and André Arbeau.

Forty-piece orchestra under the direction of CH. H. Laurent, conducted by Max Hoffmann for the American numbers, and accompanied by Billy Spedick, the Greatest American Drummer.

Without a doubt the Moulin Rouge is really established on the road to success. In its many pleasures the new show is the equal of the previous one and will register the same triumph. It has, besides, many of the same constituents. The Hoffmann Girls, whom we shall have the pleasure of seeing in Paris for a further month, continue to provide – so to

speak – its perpetually renewed framework of joy. Once more these pretty girls, blooming with health and youth, have performed for us their different exercises, part acrobatics and part dancing. What one finds so charming is that they seem to take such pleasure in their frolics; they have in them a youthful and fluent lightheartedness. The troupe nevertheless has its élite. In particular, one of the most successful numbers was 'The thirsty dream, or the New York millionaire's cellar'. To be commended are the very personal

talents of Mademoiselles Florence, Dolly, Marie, Austine and Jeannette who evoked so wittily various liquors, from gin to Schiedam. The chief honour must, however, go to Lily, who was exquisite in the part of absinthe. Her charms would have moved the grimmest of prohibitionists.

Together with these delightful and gymnastic ballerinas, two well-loved actors constitute the stars of the revue: Edmonde Guy and Biscot. The former is no longer content simply with being the most beautiful woman in Paris; one senses that she wants to take her place among our best dancers. She is in a fair way to achieving this aim. In company with her partner, Van Duren – that superbly lithe fellow – she mimes the Adam and Eve scene with such art that grace is combined with a most elegant lightness.

In passing we should also mention an interlude which was called 'The Repopulator', whose script exceeds the bounds of decency and good taste. You may imagine what can be offered by such a theme when clumsily treated! We must not forget – what a blunder that would be – the return of the famous Spanish dancer Argentina. It would be impossible to imbue the *seguidillas*, *jotas* and those other steps of the sunny south with more quivering life, more undulating litheness, or more precision. In her hands the castanets produce sounds, now powerful, now delicate, which echo her own sensitivity and transmit the fire

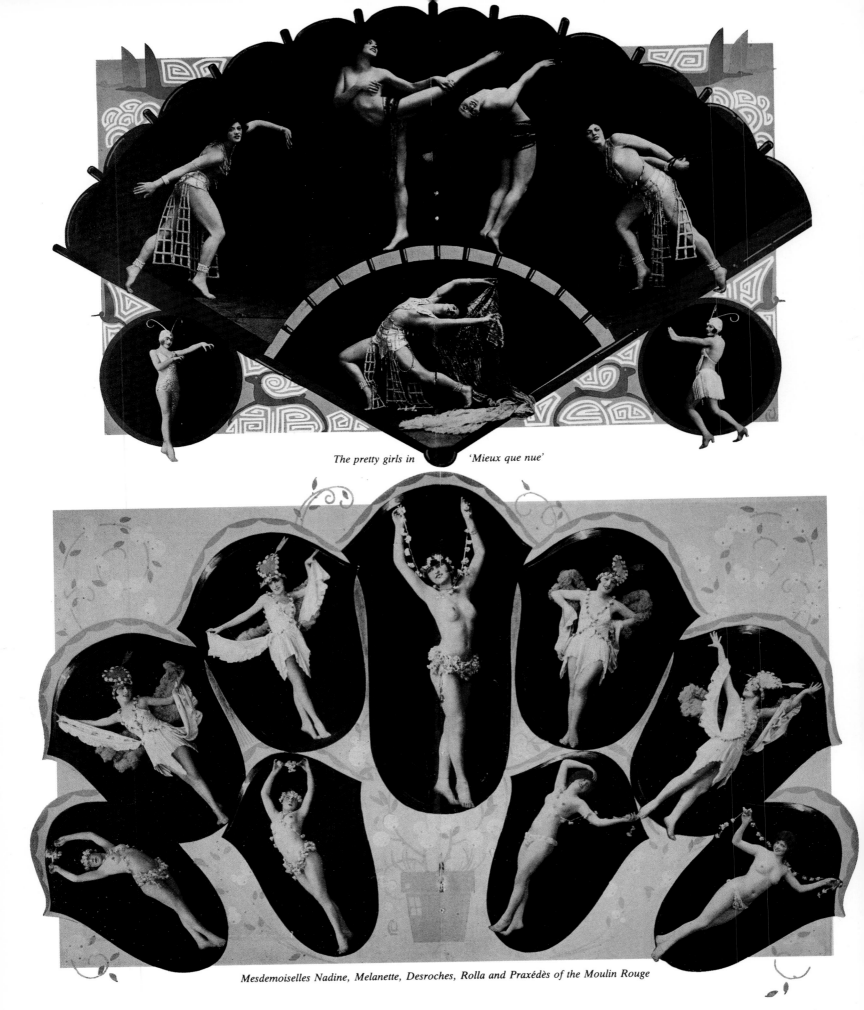

The pretty girls in 'Mieux que nue'

Mesdemoiselles Nadine, Melanette, Desroches, Rolla and Praxédès of the Moulin Rouge

which moves her. It was a moment of art and beauty which well deserved the double ovation awarded her by the audience.

Finally let us reveal that the title of the revue is derived from a number which shows a lady attired in a dress made of a material which, when subjected to various lighting effects, becomes opaque or transparent in turn. Thus we were able to watch several pretty girls undressing before our eyes, but without taking off their clothes. It is certainly ingenious, but the effect is dreadfully monotonous. The beauty of a woman who is 'better than nude' is not particularly pretty as a spectacle.

'Tout au fado' in 'La revue Mistinguett'

11 November 1925:
LA REVUE MISTINGUETT
(THE MISTINGUETT REVUE)

Grand winter revue in two acts and fifty scenes by Jacques-Charles.
Produced by Earl Leslie.
Music by José Padilla, Pierre Chagnon, Jean Lenoir, Clifford Gray, Fred Mélé and the most celebrated English and American composers.
Costumes designed by Gesmar and José de Zamora, and made under the direction of Mistinguett.

With Mistinguett and Lucienne Delahaye, Ethel and Marion Forde, Yvonne Legeay, Devilder, Colette Damy, Marcelle and Geneviève Irvin, Janeys, Liane, Suzy Bremeuse, Praxedes, Rouhier, Paulo, Marcelle Courty, Mira Delhi.

With Randall, Earl Leslie, Dréan, Henri Garat, Gayto, Tom Thyl, Blentzy, Dandy and Varèze.

With The Jackson Girls.

Forty-piece orchestra under the direction of Fred Mélé

It appears that nothing was ready and that the sewing of the dresses was completed only during the preceding night! Such improvisation, for a revue which seems to be so well controlled, augurs well for future productions! What an astonishing person Miss is – the Sarah Bernhardt of the music-hall. On her own she managed to take the place of eighteen Hoffmann Girls, who had been, moreover, thirty-six. She exhibits such zest, such courage and such vigour that she makes her audience forget all other stars, whether from the Old or the New Worlds. She is in half a dozen places at once, she changes with an ease which baffles us. As soon as she appears on the stage, all else is effaced, all else disappears. She acts with fire, she radi-

ates in the footlights. Her authority asserts itself and imposes itself from the first moment, and soon all eyes are on her alone. She slowly descends from the top of a great staircase, the immense train of a luxurious feather robe spread out behind her, as she begins to sing *Valencia*. Dressed in magnificent furs, she excites admiration. She draws applause as a horsewoman, as a music-hall star and as a pupil of a school for kissing, in a sketch which, regrettably, is in rather doubtful taste. Finally she fascinates us in a realistic scene set in the middle of a

'Miss' as a gigolette, without her feathers

been written for Marigny by Jacques-Charles and should have been presented for the first time on 2 August 1914, but the outbreak of war decided otherwise. The decision to resurrect it seems to us an excellent one.

Let us not forget other scenes, every bit as remarkable, such as the prologue, evoking the Moulin Rouge of Toulouse-Lautrec, Bruant, Jean Lorrain, Alphonse Allais, La Goulue and Valentin le Désossé. What a contrast with that of today! Next the artists took us to an enchanted garden, full of flowers, arranged in bouquets, sheaves and garlands. The dazzlement continued in the heart of an aviary of parakeets, where plumages of a thousand colours fluttered about. Finally we found ourselves regarding an astonishing curtain where sixty bird-women, lazily balanced on their perches, formed a living tapestry. A few sketches remain with us out of all this dazzlement. Dréan offered us an amusing parody of a Russian singer and an entertaining impression of the exploits of a fakir. Dorival told a few Provençal stories which had the house in fits.

There are also some new songs to report, some of which will undoubtedly do the rounds of Paris and the provinces. The varied dances enhance the attractiveness of this show. Warm applause was awarded to the Forde sisters, the charming Marion, who combines acrobatic sureness with a rare seductiveness, Miss Ruth Zackey, the delightful star of

the leading troupe of the Hoffmann Girls, the Irven sisters, with their nervous and muscular grace, and the athletic couple, the Kervas, lithe and daring. Full of natural good humour, Randal richly deserved the enthusiastic bravoes which he shared with the amusing Earl Leslie, an elegant and droll comic, who doubles as a virtuoso of the dance. Finally the orchestra itself, directed by Monsieur Fred Mélé in a wild rhythm, deserves every praise.

IN THE WINGS

6 November 1925

That morning the following advertisement was published in all the papers:

At the Moulin Rouge the work of extending and fitting it out is now complete, and the new glass proscenium will allow particularly attractive lighting effects to be produced. A complete courtyard, adjacent to the stage, has had to be roofed over to receive the new scenery and plant. The rehearsals of the revue are being actively pursued and the artists are all working hard every night. The select few who were allowed to view the presentation of the costumes and the scenery were amazed. Without doubt *La Revue Mistinguett* will be the most sumptuous and richest revue ever seen. The results of the efforts of Messieurs Foucret, Jacques-Charles, Earl Leslie and Mademoiselle Mistinguett, whose taste was responsible for the costumes, will be a truly enchanting show.

The next day a follow-up advertisement, again in all the papers:

The Moulin Rouge is pleased to announce the grand premiere of *La Revue Mistinguett*, by Jacques-Charles, with the box-office open on Monday, 9 November. Because of the armistice celebrations, the general performance will not take place until a few days later. This show, which will mark an epoch in the annals of the theatre, contains no fewer than 53 scenes, each one richer and more enchanting than the next. 'The Burning Forest' has already been ignited last night. Various devices and machinery have been used in this scene to produce a tremendous and truly impressive effect. The director of the Moulin Rouge has had to recruit a squad of security officers in order to deny access to the curious. Everywhere there are piles of lace, flowers, furs, feathers, satins, pearls and more furs. Backstage at the Moulin Rouge resembles a fable from the Thousand and One Nights.

Already, by that time, the idea of arousing expectancy and of the publicity 'teaser' announcement had arrived.

burning forest. It is night, the fire burning in the brushwood creeps ever closer. The horizon bursts into flame and great trees, burning like torches, collapse into the fiery mass. As a poor girl attacked by bandits, Mistinguett finds the pathetic tones to express the horror of this fast-moving drama, so skilfully staged. Incidentally, it seems that the scene had

'The feather robes' in 'La revue Mistinguett'

'Modern Music' in 'La revue Mistinguett'

A publicity design by Gesmar for 'Ça c'est Paris', based on his famous costume for Mistinguett

IN THE WINGS

3 February 1926

Last night saw a brawl backstage between Mistinguett and one of her girls. It took place because the latter complained of having been unfairly punished by the revue's leading lady. She, however, considering that the young girl was being too forward with Earl Leslie, refused to listen to a single word of defence. There followed from the young novice, now furious with anger, some particularly choice and unflattering words about Miss: 'You frightened old cat', 'old hag', 'grandmother'. The monologue was rounded off with 'when you kick the bucket, I'll come and dance on your grave'.

This was exactly what was needed to unlease the resultant fisticuffs, which ended with a technical knockout of the girl in the first round. Mistinguett emerged with a black eye and some hair torn out. Subsequently she made peace with her rival of the evening. And rightly so – her name is Viviane Romance.

'Les heures de la
Parisienne' in 'La revue
Mistinguett'

'Le jardin de Paris' in 'La revue Mistinguett'

IN THE WINGS

2 March 1926

It was the hundredth performance last night of *La Revue Mistinguett* at the Moulin Rouge. There were congratulations, flowers and presents backstage, but there was also gnashing of teeth. Miss had used the occasion to carry out what she called 'a boot review'.

'We all know that it is the shoe which makes the foot and the foot which makes the leg. Since, in a variety show, the leg is one of the most important features, I inspect the boots for the sake of the public. I had all the troupe's shoes laid out on the stage,' she told us. 'And, like a good junior officer, I passed them all in review.'

It was an opportunity for Miss to explain how she alone chose the girls who worked with her.

'I assure you that it is not easy to find ones who are "just right" – not too big, not too little, not too well-built, not too ugly, not too pretty. The examination is always conducted in the same fashion. The girl undresses, I examine her and, more often than not, I tell her, "Well, you won't do, you're certainly no nude. Give your address to Monsieur Earl Leslie; he may call on you to be a model." I have to undress a hundred in order to find twenty who are suitable. On the day of the premiere I dress them all myself. It's the best way I've found of keeping an eye on them. I send off to the washroom those who seem to be obstinate about their toilet, who clearly don't possess any soap at home. For me, cleanliness is of prime importance. I don't think that I could breathe during the day if I didn't take a bath every morning.'

Mistinguett in 'La forêt bleue'

'The enchanted aviary' and
'The Moulin Rouge past
and present' in 'La revue
Mistinguett'

Publicity design by Gesmar for 'Montmartre aux nues'

27 August 1926
MONTMARTRE AUX NUES
(NUDES OF MONTMARTRE)

Revue in two acts and fifty scenes by Jacques-Charles.
Produced by Earl Leslie.
Sketches by Georges Arnould.
Music by José Padilla, Fred Pearly, Pierre Chagnon, Jean Lenoir, Clifford Gray and Fred Mélé. Plus the most celebrated tunes of English and American composers.

Costumes designed by Gesmar and José de Zamora.
Costumes made under the direction of Mistinguett in the Moulin Rouge workrooms.

With Gina Palerme, Yvonne George, Marthe Berthy, Baldini, Devilder, Colette Damy, Sonia, Lapeyre, Praxédès, Milly, Marga and Fir.

With Randall, Dréan, Drosdoff, Garrick and Dandy.

With the Sparks Ballet and the Jackson Girls. Twenty-eight-piece orchestra under the direction of Fred Mélé.

Gina Palerme

With Mistinguett absent, any increase in the magnificence of the effects at the Moulin Rouge was out of the question. Clearly Monsieur Jacques-Charles's new revue is offered as an interlude, pending the return of Miss, which we trust will be soon.

Nevertheless, this show seems to us to be of sufficient quality to attract a good audience. Certain scenes, such as 'Hawaii', are not lacking in imagination. Others, such as 'The Fabulous Trains', 'The Baths' or 'The Revealing Trunks', are very ingenious and highly-coloured. As for the adaptation of 'The Flowers of Evil', it would not have failed to astonish Baudelaire, and it will undoubtedly result in the poet's discovery by not a few of the audience.

We should also mention the presence of the Spanish composer José Padilla, who was there in person to accompany his pieces. His contribution rendered a new colour to *Valencia* and *La Violetera*.

Finally we note the rhythm of the Jackson Girls. We saw them from the front, the back, the side, with their heads down, and with their legs in the air. They danced in unison, their bold movements were performed with precision, and they smiled as they did so. It may shock, but it is very attractive to see.

124

Costumes by José de Zamora for the Moulin Rouge

'Basque Pelota' in 'Montmartre aux nues'

IN THE WINGS

MISTINGUETT VERSUS THE DOLLY SISTERS

Scandal reigns at the Moulin Rouge, only a few days away from the first performance of *La Revue Mistinguett*. The Dolly Sisters, advertised as top of the bill, have announced that they have withdrawn from the show and are bringing an action against Pierre Foucret, the director of the establishment. The reason: the contract which bound them to the night-club in the Place Blanche has not been honoured. Several months ago Jacques-Charles, in whom they have complete confidence, contacted them in New York and proposed that they should appear in Paris as the stars of the show at the Moulin Rouge, and were promised their place at the top of the bill. Today they feel themselves both injured and deceived. It is true that their names still figure at the top of the bill, but in a revue where they occupy the stage for only a quarter of an hour and whose title embodies the name of Mistinguett — the star of the evening. They are therefore demanding an indemnity of five hundred and fifty thousand francs for breach of contract.

This lawsuit Jacques-Charles several days earlier tried to avoid, without success. Comprehending the seriousness of the situation, he used his influence to suggest to Rosie and Jenny that they settle their differences with Miss, on stage and in a humorous fashion. He even had an idea for the sketch in his mind. It would be called the 'Missdolly-tinguettsisters'. In the beginning they agreed, but the next day, having had the script translated, they changed their minds and, as a result, fell out with Jacques-Charles. Yet there was nothing particularly disagreeable in these verbal exchanges. Judge for yourselves:

The Dolly Sisters: 'We have a piece of business which will be very successful. Each of us comes on leading a little dog.' (They demonstrate, with two pretty little pekinese.)

Miss: 'Me too – I come on with a little dog.' (She leads an enormous bald and mangy dog out of the wings.)

The Dolly Sisters: 'Why don't we perform a scene together?'

Miss: 'That's it! We could sing a nice ballad for three voices!' (She sings a few notes, extremely out of tune.)

The Dolly Sisters (to themselves): 'That's it! She wants to make us whistle!' (aloud) 'We have another idea. We've seen it in New York, and it was a great success. We pick you up, and we keep throwing you up in the air, higher and higher.'

Miss (to herself): 'That's it! They want to smash my face in!'

In short, the case ended up going to court. Pierre Foucret was ordered to pay 550,000 francs, which the Dolly Sisters lost no time in paying to the Artists' Union. At the same time they turned the knife in the wound of their ex-employer by sharing the starring role with Maurice Chevalier at the Casino de Paris, although their participation was limited to a single reply: 'No, No, Ernest.' That didn't matter; their revenge was purely symbolic, but immensely satisfying.

21 December 1926
ÇA. . . C'EST PARIS!
(THAT'S PARIS!)
First version, with Mistinguett

Grand winter revue in two acts and sixty scenes by Jacques-Charles.
Produced by Earl Leslie.
Costumes and curtains designed by Gesmar.
Everything has been made under the direction of Mistinguett in the Moulin Rouge workrooms.
Music by José Padilla, Fred Pearly, Pierre Chagnon, Jean Lenoir, Mario Caze, Clifford Gray, Jean Boyer, Monfred Penso, Mercier, Bétove, Fred Mélé and the most celebrated English and American composers. Twenty-eight-piece orchestra under the direction of Fred Mélé.

It appears that the preparation and rehearsal of this new revue required a month's work. To judge by the results, it's highly probable! It is a very spectacular show, which presents to us a Mistinguett who is both astonishing and stupefying. Never has she demonstrated such allure, such pluck or such vigour. Received on stage in triumph, completely dominating the chorus which surrounds her, saluted by the victorious chanting of the orchestra, acclaimed by the audience, she acts with fire, she is everywhere at once, sparing no effort. First she is before us talking in a common accent, portraying the early days of Lolotte, the future music-hall star; then, flirtatious and cajoling, she is

transformed into a prostitute of 1850. Finally she is Jeannette, the little mussel fisher, being knocked about by ruffians. Half-strangled, emprisoned in a barrel, she is about to be thrown off a boat, when a fearful storm comes to her aid. She then sings Ça. . . c'est Paris!, a song by José Padilla which, in our opinion, has a very great future. It is a feast for eyes and ears, in a mixture of sumptuous costumes, diamonds, precious stones, feathers and flowers, right up to the last scene, the apotheosis of the evening, and which consists of the opening of a

coffer, covering the entire width of the stage, out of which pour gold coins. Some are effigies of the evening's star, others are alive, the most beautiful of them all, you will have guessed, being Mistinguett herself.

In the success of this golden spectacle we must include Messieurs Jacques-Charles and Earl Leslie. What ingenuity

is displayed in their scenes! The imaginary walk through the all-night restaurants of Montmartre is worth any grand ducal tour of grand dukes. The Pigall's, where the golds and the blacks are blended, and the Florida, where all shades of pink are harmonised, are a joy to the eyes. All this with, above all, pretty girls in numbers impossible to count.

'Miss and the Girls' in 'Ça c'est Paris'

Jacques-Charles (on the right) inspects his cast for 'Ça c'est Paris'

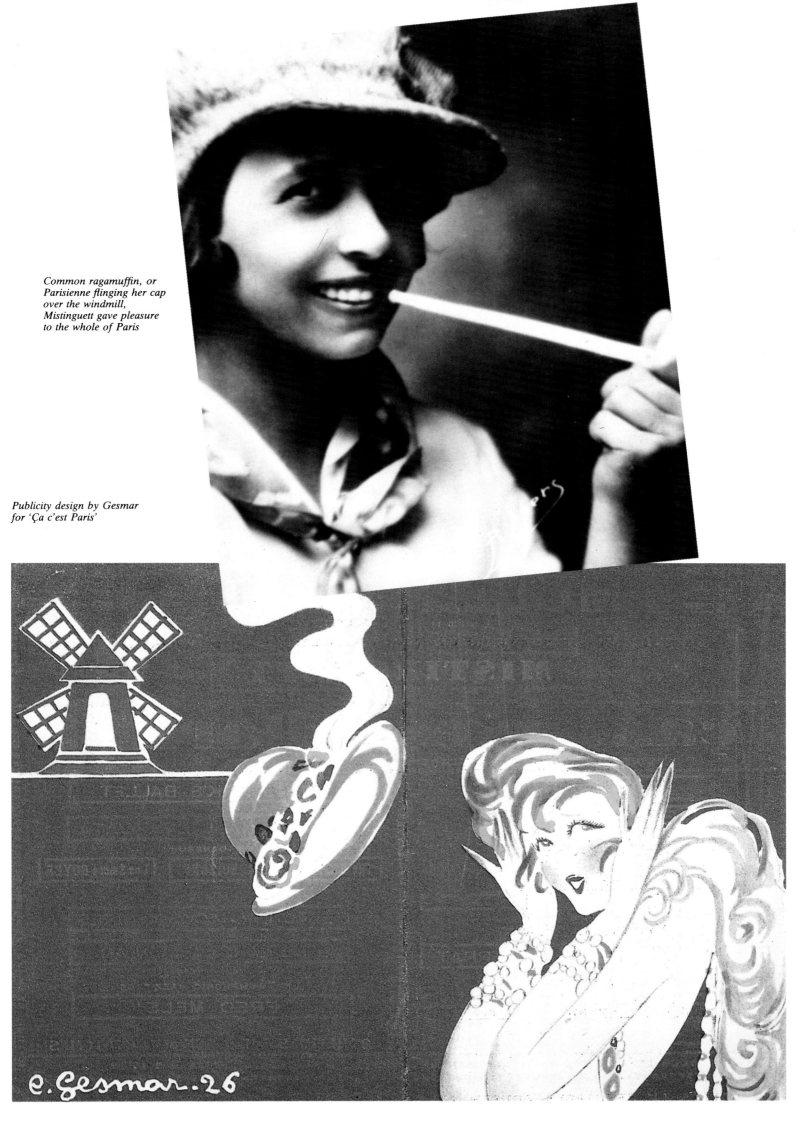

Common ragamuffin, or
Parisienne flinging her cap
over the windmill,
Mistinguett gave pleasure
to the whole of Paris

Publicity design by Gesmar
for 'Ça c'est Paris'

e. Gesmar. 26

'Ça c'est Paris': above, the finale with the entire cast.
Left, top to bottom:
'The kingdom of the dolls',
'Florida' and
'Holland!'

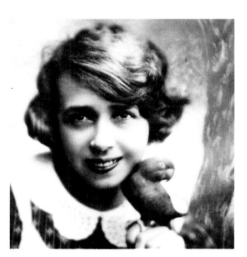

Henri Garat sings – and proves – that 'I love tall women'

2 September 1927
ÇA. . . C'EST PARIS!
Second version

Two acts and fifty scenes, by Jacques-Charles.
Produced by Earl Leslie and J.W. Jackson.
All the costumes were designed by Gesmar and made under the direction of Mistinguett in the Moulin Rouge workrooms.
Music by José Padilla, Jean Lenoir, Clifford Gray, Jean Boyer, Vincent Scotto, Fred Mélé and the most celebrated English and American composers.

With Florelle and M. Tramel.

With Marion Forde, Betty Rowland, Marthe Berthy, Janeys, Simone Mirat, Nadia Keen and Andrée Reynis.

With Henri Garat, Dandy, Varèze and Gayto.

With Spark's Ballet and the Jackson Girls. The Symphonic Jazz is under the direction of Fred Mélé.

Replace Mistinguett in a revue written exclusively for her. That's the challenge to which Mademoiselle Florelle has successfully responded with both skill and vigour. Like the famous Miss, she can adopt an infinite variety of roles, and while wearing, like her, sumptuous flowery costumes or the rags of poverty with equal elegance, she can act and sing with taste. This charming artist is but a newly-risen star, and yet we cannot doubt that she, in her turn, will soon illuminate the great sails of the Moulin.

Monsieur Jacques-Charles's brilliant revue is enriched with many scenes and

Le gros succès de LONDRES et NEW-YORK
Lancé dans la nouvelle revue
du MOULIN ROUGE

RHYTHM IS THE THING

JOHN RAITZ
ARTHUR YOUN
EVERETT LYNTON

PRIX NET
6 frs.

Marion Forde

EDITIONS FOUCRET fils (SA) 17 Rue du F? Montmartre
ancienne édition LUCIEN BRULÉ   Paris

other attractions which enhance its effect still more. It includes 'The Greatest Jazz in the World', a gigantic army of saxophones and trumpets, an impressive orchestra which plays several pieces in strict tempo. In this the conductor, Monsieur Fred Mélé, has achieved a feat, fraught with danger, which deserves high praise. As for Miss Loie Fuller's dancers, they gave us two marvellous interludes: 'The Giant Shades of Repatriation' from Peer Gynt and the 'Cake Walk' by Debussy, in which is mingled every effect of light and shade in a coruscation of colour.

Among the new artists were a pair of acrobatic dancers, Divina and Charles. As well as uncommon litheness and precision, they exhibited an astonishing daring. Finally let us report the presence of the comic Tramel, whose buffoonery is not without humour. The two sketches he played were a trifle weak, but never mind. It takes all sorts to make a world — of entertainment.

Spark's Ballet

Johnny Hudgins, Mauricet, Harry Pilcer, Dollie and Billie in 'Paris aux étoiles'

26 November 1927
PARIS AUX ÉTOILES
(STARLIT PARIS)

Grand winter revue in two acts and seventy scenes by Jacques-Charles.
Produced by the author.
Musical numbers produced by Harry Pilcer.
Music by José Padilla, Vincent Scotto, Maurice Roget, Jean Boyer, Dimitri Tiomkin, Jean Huré, Fred Mélé and the most celebrated American composers.
Costumes from models by Gesmar, George Barbier, José de Zamora, Pol Rab.
Costumes made by Max Weldy.

With Jane Aubert, Marthe Berthy, Simone Mirat, Dollie and Billie.

With Mauricet, Dandy, Harry Pilcer, Johnny Hudgins, the Jackson Girls and the Albertina Rasch Girls.
Symphonic Jazz under the direction of Fred Mélé.

For some days thousands of Parisians and foreigners have been asking the same question. What is going on behind the sealed and uncommunicative façade of the Moulin Rouge? What are Messieurs Jacques-Charles and Pierre Foucret preparing, and why are there so many secrets behind this new revue, already described as revolutionary? The instructions seem to be absolute. No one may speak. We have, however, been able to gather a few straws in the wind.

'There is no formula so good that it cannot be improved,' Pierre Foucret asserted.

'It's a secret,' Mademoiselle Jane Aubert murmured.

'No, mademoiselle, it's a conspiracy,' was the stage manager's reply. In short we were promised a formula which would be entirely new. A revue which, without sacrificing its legendary reputation of decorative richness, would be more dazzling than ever. And this would be because, for the first time, importance was to be attached to the libretto. A revue which would not be dumb, which would not be built solely on the scenery and the choreography, a revue, in short, which would not appear commonplace.

Clearly we found some astonishing things last night. Like the humourous Mauricet, who was borne into the firmament on the back of a winged dragon, we took a leap towards the stars on the sails of the Moulin. The journey seemed a very short one, since it was rather they who came to us, sliding down a Milky Way of spotlights, amid fabled landscapes and the scenery of fairyland. All in a total of seventy scenes, an astronomical figure in itself, an absolute record. There was an evocation of feminine prowess down the centuries, a little tour of Brooklyn, followed by Mexico, via Montmartre and Olympus — and we found ourselves at the foot of a temple perched on the horizon amid clouds of gold. After this we plunged into the depths below the sea, where lay the wreck of a frigate. The hull broke open, releasing the precious stones which had lain hidden within — diamonds, emeralds and sapphires, their multicoloured reflections mingling with those of coral and pearls. After the water – the fire, as the Deadly Sins performed their dance around Pluto. Under the sign of Jupiter, the show reached its grand finale – of vegetables.

As for the stars, their names are Dollie and Billie, together with Jane Aubert. The former have been the draw of Paris; it was inevitable that they would end up at the Moulin. They performed wonders with their warm voices.

The talent of Mademoiselle Aubert is not, alas, exploited to the full, which is a pity. The other artists, Johnny Hudgins, Harry Pilcer and the Albertina Rasch Girls, all come from America. While the men are known to us (Johnny Hudgins' triumph at the Ambassadeurs is not forgotten), the sixteen dancers are the rage of New York.

They dance on their points as if they had just emerged fresh from Serge Diaghilev's Ballet Russe. What joyous rockets shooting among the stars – a very successful debut!

Jane Aubert,
leading lady of
'Paris aux étoiles'

LA GLOIRE

LE PARADIS FERMÉ

POL RAB

POL RAB

Pol Rab (1899–1933), caricaturist, designer and painter, was the creator of the immortal philosopher-dogs, Ric and Rac. For the stage, he designed the costumes and scenery for several of the most famous Parisian revues. When the chanteuses réalistes were at the peak of their popularity, he was their official publicist. Among his closest friends were Marcel Achard, Pierre Lazareff and Henri Jeanson

COMEDIENNE

POL RAB

18 April 1928
PARIS QUI TOURNE
(PARIS REVOLVES)

Revue in two acts and fifty-eight scenes by Jacques-Charles and Earl Leslie.
Production, sets and dances by the authors.
Music by José Padilla, Fred Pearly, Pierre Chagnon, Renet Mercier, Vincent Scotto, Craven, Fred Mélé, Chantrier, Jean Boyer.
Costumes copied from the last models of the great designer Gesmar.
Costumes made in the Moulin Rouge workrooms.

With Mistinguett and Yvonne Legeay, Patricia Storm, Ditrix, Domenica and Duval.

With the Mazza Sisters, the Poggi Sisters and the Boyer Sisters.

With Spadaro, Carjol, Gabin, Dandy, René Blum, Jems, Pierrel, Carenzio and Thibert.

With the Jackson Roses and the Jackson Girls.
Symphonic Jazz under the direction of Fred Mélé.

To be honest, Messieurs Jacques-Charles and Earl Leslie have done a good job. The new Moulin Rouge revue needs fear no comparison with any of its predecessors. Mistinguett, sumptuously dressed and full of good humour, gave some marvellous renderings of exotic and enchanting airs, amid puppets, bells and giant butterflies fluttering their silver and black wings. She even succeeded, in a monologue, in giving a lively burlesque of herself, as quaint as it was droll. Appearing with her, let us report the debut of Gabin, a young man whose presence needs to be strengthened, but who certainly has a fine future in music-hall. Also to be remarked is the degree of influence the Dolly Sisters have had on our variety theatre. In this show there are three lots of sisters: the Mazzas, the Poggis and the Boyers. It was a show which had everything to

make it a success, but which, for some of last night's audience, took on a nightmarish quality. One sketch entitled 'The Salon of Madame Dubarry' created a feeling of dismay which we shall not easily forget. The author, Monsieur Didier Gold, tried to play for us a note which has not hitherto been heard in music-hall. What an unfortunate idea, what lack of taste! He had, in fact chosen one of the most terrible and most frightful episodes of the Terror: the arrest in her hunting lodge at Louveciennes of a woman of humble origins, who had been ennobled by royal whim to become the too-famous mistress of Louis XV. Her trial and her tragic and pitiful end on the guillotine could only revolt spectators, to whatever party they belonged. As for Mistinguett, the *grandes coquettes* are scarcely her line, and Dubarry accords neither with her physique nor the sincerity of her talent. If we may be permitted to

Mistinguett: costume and sketch by Gesmar

give a little advice to the producers of this revue, they should drop this scene as soon as possible. No one will take it amiss, most especially the public.

(This wish was to be granted a few days later. The local police authorities ordered that this scene be withdrawn. It was a decision to which Mistinguett submitted but did not approve, adding: 'In response to our "Let's go", the powers that be have said "Do it our way".')

IN THE WINGS

14 May 1928

That evening a young girl being dragged along by a wire-haired terrier entered Mistinguett's dressing room. The dog immediately made itself at home and settled in a corner where it clearly felt it belonged. The young girl, small in stature, blonde with big bright eyes and no more than fifteen years old, was called Marcelle Desboutin and she had arrived on the off-chance. She had been mad on the music-hall, ever since the day when her parents, photographers in the Rue Lepic, had sent her to the Moulin Rouge to deliver a package of reproductions of posters.

For the next few weeks Marcelle returned nearly every evening and made her way backstage. Some months later, in tribute to her ever-fresh, pinkish face, she had been dubbed 'Fraisette' ('The Little Strawberry'), and she bore this nickname while, for many years, she filled the post of Mistinguett's private secretary. She had a try-out on the stage with the chorus and succeeded in dancing perfectly out of step. It was the ideal quality to constitute the last in the troupe, the comic in a way. Very quickly she chose to remain backstage and took charge of the purse-strings — a heavy responsibility, but a decision which Miss never regretted.

'La java de Doudoune' in 'Paris qui tourne', with Jean Gabin

'Fans': Mistinguett and Tyraux with Spark's Ballet and the Jackson Girls

'The Guillotine' and
'The Execution' in
'The Dubarry', a scene
which caused a scandal

PARIS QUI TOURNE

'The Rose-garden' in 'Paris qui tourne' (below), and publicity design by Gesmar (above)

Mademoiselle Marin, Moulin Rouge dancer of flawless aestheticism

19 January 1929
ALLO, ICI PARIS
(HALLO, PARIS CALLING)

Revue in two acts and forty-five scenes by Jacques-Charles and Earl Leslie.
Production, sets and dances arranged by the authors.
Music by Fred Pearly, Pierre Chagnon, Istres, Fred Mélé, Craven, Bétove, Irving Berlin, René Sylviano, Jane Bos, Spitany, White, Mabel Wayne.

Models and costumes designed by Zig and Dolle.

With Georgius, Jean Gabin, Dandy, André Pierrel, Elsie Janis, Yvonne Legeay, Mademoiselles Margaret Jade, Suzanne Duval, Harriet Louise, the Jackson Boys and the Jackson Girls.

Symphonic Jazz under the direction of Fred Mélé.

General secretaries for the theatre: Marcel Foucret and Pierre Lazareff.

Once again Monsieur Pierre Foucret has struck hard! As the star of his new revue he has chosen the only star whose light is as brilliant as that of Mistinguett and Maurice Chevalier – Elsie Janis herself. Until now her appearances in Paris had been but few, although well-received. Elsewhere she is widely known. Two years ago she scored a triumph with *Mon homme* on all the stages in America. In London, a few months ago, she had an unprecedented success. Now, in Montmartre, she has just been given an ovation even by an audience accustomed to four years of Monsieur Jacques-Charles's hits.

At the end, she thanked everyone in fluent French, in an accent which owes more to Belleville than to Oxford. Her acting is exemplary; loud and flashy effects, regal gestures and a solemn gait are not her strong points. Rather than these she prefers simplicity and naturalness. On stage it is as if she is at home.

Yvonne Legeay, friend and understudy of Mistinguett, with her partner, Blum

She addresses the audience as she would a circle of her friends. She is kind and witty and disdains any guile or bluff. As a comedienne she is perfect; as a dancer she becomes admirable. She is the personification of lightness and litheness themselves. In addition she reveals abilities as an impersonator. The silhouettes which she formed of several popular artists were very successful. Alongside her was Georgius, the king of song and worthy heir of Paulus. He resurrected, in their former style, songs such as *L'amour boiteux*, *En revenant de la Revue* and *Frou Frou* which, half a century ago, were the rage of Paris. The joyful Dandy, as usual, filled the house with mirth; the joke about Hanch and his mule is unbelievably funny. As for Earl Leslie, always so charming to the audience, he was, of course, in his element. He danced the waltz, conducted a restless and loud jazz tune with ease, performed a sketch and acted as compère between the scenes. He has been a regular participant for four years and is thus the perfect link man, and this role does not seem the least bit disagreeable to him.

IN THE WINGS

24 January 1929

The triumph of Elsie Janis in *Allô, ici Paris*, the new revue at the Moulin Rouge, was short-lived. A few days after the first performances she was laid low with pneumonia. On doctor's orders the great American comedienne was unable to resume her place for several days.

31 January 1929

The events which take place during the hours while the theatre is closed are sometimes highly significant at the Moulin Rouge. Such is the case with the dancing competitions between the girls which are regularly organised by Monsieur Jean Fabert, who now controls the fortunes of the establishment. The one which took place yesterday demonstrated how competition between the dancers remains the best treatment for youth. There is no question of continually rehearsing the same step or of executing an unorthodox variation of the cancan. And while, in Paris, the waltz in three-time has been replaced by negro dances, those in the Place Blanche remain resolutely traditional. Thus some thirty dancers, all totally charming and none more than twenty years old, performed under the direction of Monsieur Denizart, the ballet master at the Opéra. For an hour, each in turn executed her chosen variation. Then they underwent a test of acrobatics. It made them ideally equipped for going on to tackle the mad adventure of the revue. At the end of this charming day the most beautiful costumes were rewarded in a *concours d'élégance*. Finally, sipping glasses of port, these maids of the ballet wound up their little festivity by electing their most outstanding colleague. Competition, yes, but rivalry, no.

30 March 1929

Departure of Jacques-Charles.

(The revue reopened on 6 February 1929, but closed finally at the end of the same month – due to lack of audiences, and not by any wish of Mistinguett!)

Publicity design by Delle for 'Allô, ici Paris'

La femme à la rose

Repertoire Damia

Paroles de Ch. A. Abadie
Musique de Gaston Gabaroche

Existe
Pour Piano seul
(Valse-Boston)
Pour Piano et Chant
3.50

Éditions Francis Salabert
35 Boulevard des Capucines Paris

Photo Apers

to be reported are the presence of Jean Gabin, who is becoming increasingly noteworthy in the repertoire of Maurice Chevalier, and of André Renaud with his two pianos, an astonishing virtuoso who gave brilliant renderings in the style of Liszt or Debussy. The audience listened in rapt attention to these hitherto little-known musicians and erupted in applause.

Finally the Bonjohn Girls danced and hummed the leading jazz tunes. They are reminiscent of the Ingénues, recently well-received at the Empire. They are not disagreeable to look at and very agreeable to listen to. What more could you ask for a pleasant evening?

7 June 1929
THE LEW LESLIE REVUE: BLACKBIRDS OF 1928

Production entirely conceived and staged by Lew Leslie.
Music by Jimmy McHugh.
Words by Dorothy Fields.

With a cast of stars and 100 artists, all coloured.

With the Berry Brothers.

With Aïda Ward, Adelaide Hall, Ruth Johnson and Marjorie Hubbard.

With Tim Moore, Blue Mac Allister, Mantan Moreland, Earl Tucker, Crawford Jackson, Eddie Rector and Clayton Pegbates.
The entire revue is accompanied by the famous Jazz Plantation Orchestra.

The Blackbirds are, in fact, amusing and highly-coloured birds which Messieurs Marcel Foucret and Edmond Sayag have just engaged in Paris. They are a company of coloured artists, singers, comedians, dancers and musicians

19 April 1929
VARIETY SHOW

Programme of great music-hall attractions with the Symphonic Jazz under the direction of Fred Mélé.

With Pocker and his dogs;
Gaudot, the famous musical impersonator;
The 24 Mangan Tillerettes from the Paramount Theatre;
Jean Gabin, singer-comedian;
Judex and Partner, the King of the Marksmen;
André Renaud of the National Caricature Theatre;
Léon Vanderstuyft, the world motorcycling record holder in his contest against an express;
The Bonjohn Girls, all-girl band;
Théa Alba, the woman with the multiple brains;
Amy Revere, in her fantasy choreography and Damia, the great natural singer.

With Mistinguett and Jacques-Charles departed, the show at the Moulin Rouge goes on. Monsieur Pierre Foucret is

presenting to us what he calls 'great music-hall attractions'. It is a good bill, whose leading recommendation is the name of Damia. This great artist sings *La Rue de la joie*, the lament which she first sang at the Palace, *J'ai compris* by Jean Lenoir, which she performs with much skill, *La Complainte du prisonnier*, a dramatic piece of magnificent breadth, and *Le Fou*, ending a programme of songs whose only fault lay in being too short. On the same programme was Théa Alba, dubbed the woman with five brains. Amazing! She can write five sentences in five different languages, all at the same time! She can speak more than twenty, and thus performs her number in a way to suit the audience of the evening. She insists that there is no trick; it is a gift, a training of the will. Several leading doctors have examined her, Monsieur Freud has entertained her at his home, Monsieur Pirandello has told her that she is the most curious example of a complex personality that he has seen, and Monsieur Maurice Maeterlinck has also questioned her at length. Also

MOULIN-ROUGE

LEW LESLIE'S
BLACKBIRDS

who, in America, put on a new revue every year. It is a show which does not pretend to dazzle us with the luxury of its scenery and its costumes, but rather by the quality of its effects of light and shade. A changing atmosphere where daylight and shadow contest the field, passing through all the half-tints of chiaroscuro, and of a beauty which surpasses all the most sparkling of stage settings. The opening is a surprise! It is as if one were at a comic opera! All the main themes of the revue were assembled in the space of a few minutes. Then the curtain rose to reveal the pastoral landscape of a plantation. The assembled blackbirds blended their voices, and their soft and melancholy refrain rose towards the sultry heavens. Next we found ourselves in the jungle, where the blackbirds, carried away in a frenetic dance, were transformed into firebirds. A lightly-tanned Venus, Mademoiselle Adelaide Hall, rolled the jet-black pupils of her wide eyes and sang the verses of a popular song, repeated by the company in chorus.

It was very pleasant and inspiring. After this, scenes alternated between the comic (a hilarious poker game), the dramatic (a funeral service in an atmosphere of black magic) and the frankly burlesque (the wedding of Magnolia, a comedy on the edge of a cemetery which is haunted by ghosts and living skeletons). The performance ended with a tribute to Florence Mills, the star of the company, who died last year. In brief, this show is evidence of the possible rebirth of our music hall revues. Certainly it reminded one of *La Revue Nègre* (The Negro Revue), which was a success four years ago at the Théâtre des Champs Élysées. But we noted scenes which are now excluded by Jacques-Charles because he found them too sad. On the success of this show undoubtedly depends the future of the Moulin Rouge. Has a replacement for Jacques-Charles and Mistinguett been found? It is for the audiences to give the answer.

Adelaide Hall, as seen by Paul Colin

145

IN THE WINGS

The stage door

It's on the Place Blanche, just next door to an ant-hill displaying the sign of the Taverne Cyrano. You make your way down a passageway by a working-class house, across a dismal little courtyard, past a little glass hut, along an extremely dirty board covered with pieces of paper, scribbled on, some of them torn – that's the stage door to the Moulin Rouge. Happily, once you are across the threshold, the atmosphere changes. Once the attendance sheet has been completed – Mistinguett is always the first to sign it – administrative concerns are swept from the stage. The dressing rooms, which are reached along a corridor with rich red walls, are divided into two. Those facing the courtyard are reserved for Mistinguett, the 'attractions' and the dancers. On the garden side the chorus girls and boys share a common home. All the dressing rooms, including that of the star, are similar, with mirrors mounted in blue panels and extremely harsh lighting. One would imagine oneself in a laboratory rather than a theatre. Just at one side of the stage is a large mirror – an essential fitting for the artist who, before going on stage, wishes to check her low neckline, her spangles or her jacket. A few moments before the curtain rises the atmosphere is relaxed: joking, laughter, seductions . . . But, when Mistinguett appears, silence is immediate. All take their places and will not abandon them until the end of the curtain-calls. Nothing can be more serious than the endeavour to amuse. Those who insist on the contrary are, paradoxically, not serious persons.

The audition, by Pol Rab

Garat: when 'The Road to Paradise' runs past the Moulin Rouge

In the programme of *La Revue Mistinguett*, his name appears seven times. Before becoming one of our most brilliant juvenile leads in the cinema, Henri Garat made many stage appearances.

He owed his start in variety to his sister, 'Mademoiselle Garat', one of Jacques-Charles's favourite comediennes at the Casino de Paris. He had just been released from his military service and was out of work. She managed to get him taken on as a chorus boy in the Rue de Clichy. When Jacques-Charles departed for the Moulin Rouge, Garat followed him, hoping for small parts. Imitating Maurice Chevalier, as did quite a few of his contemporaries, wearing check trousers and maroon jacket, he appeared before the audience surrounded by a host of pretty girls. Unfortunately his voice was not of a quality to match his appearance and, despite encouragement from Mistinguett, Garat rapidly recognised that a career as a singer was not for him. He crossed the Atlantic, married Harriet, a young dancer in the Hoffmann Girls, divorced her, and then made his way back to France and the Casino de Paris. He was given a small part alongside Simon-Girard, one of the big names in the theatre, but his dreams were centred on the cinema. At last one evening he thought his chance had come, in the person of an American impresario who was in the audience.

'I met him in New York, where I let him gain the impression that I was the star of the show,' he confessed to Simon-Girard before the curtain rose. 'He wants to book me for a film but, if he discovers that I am only a bit-player, he'll drop me. Please give me a break – let me take your part – just for tonight.'

Heedless of his colleague's pleas, Simon-Girard did not see why he should make such a sacrifice and refused point-blank. Desperate – nearly suicidal – Garat went on stage like an automaton. Whether by chance or fate, the first sketch which they had to play together was to change things drastically. Every evening in this scene Garat was required to shatter a chair over the head of his partner. The chair was, needless to say, a fake, designed to break apart at the first impact. Except on that particular evening. Due to the absentmindedness of a scene-shifter, it was a real and very solid chair that Simon-Girard received on the cranium. While the latter was being rushed to hospital, his understudy, who was none other than Garat, took over the part. At the end of the performance the famous American impresario, highly impressed, offered him his first film contract. *Le Congrès s'amuse* (Congress Dances), *Le Chemin du Paradis* (The Road to Paradise) and several other films made his face famous and women swoon. His tones, which had been considered too quiet for the stage, were ideal for the screen. That is what is called finding your voice.

A newcomer called Gabin junior . . .

It was a sketch in *Paris qui tourne* (Paris Revolves), entitled 'You have to know how to ask for it nicely', which saw the début of a certain Gabin, first name Jean. His father was well known for his contributions as compère of the New Year revues. It was a key role, which demanded his continual presence, as well as a large number of comedy lines. In those days the extraordinary contribution which sketches could make to a programme had not been realized. And so it was that, monologues being the centre-piece of the show, it was the compère who was the star.

Physically, undoubtedly, the two Gabins had their similarities. However, the son was as thin as his father was rotund, and set himself up in the role of the mulish 'bad boy' which bore no relationship with the rather good-natured personality of his senior.

Henri Garat's irresistible smile

The first meeting between Jean Gabin and Jacques-Charles had taken place in the latter's office a few weeks earlier. No one then imagined that he would one day be the star of Jean Renoir's *French Cancan*. The son, furnished with a recommendation from his father, was auditioned by Mistinguett in person. Finding in him a vague resemblance to Maurice Chevalier, she immediately engaged him in her company for thirty francs a day. She insisted, however, that he should sing wearing a black suit and top hat, like Maurice. He found himself on stage performing *La Java de Doudoune*.

A few rehearsals were sufficient to demonstrate that he had no gift for that kind of work. Reluctant to put him out on the street, Jacques-Charles and Mistinguett restricted him to a rôle in the revue's dramatic sketch. While still imitating Chevalier, he showed himself to be the perfect villain. Thus he discovered the road which, thanks to the cinema, was to lead him first to triumph and then to immortality.

Strange goings-on

While the renovation work in the auditorium was being completed – a month behind schedule – Jacques-Charles was putting the finishing touches to the cast by welcoming some ten 'showgirls', who had been warmly recommended by the great Ziegfeld. The girls, having been used to an America where prohibition reigned supreme, now suddenly discovered the joys of Gay Paree! Understandably, there were those who were led to raise their glasses rather more frequently than their legs. The consequences were dramatic. At rehearsals they became aggressive. Backstage, arguments broke out, which affected the rest of the troupe. The alcoholic spiral was such that, on the first night, they arrived at the Moulin Rouge still clutching their glasses! Obviously, they had toasted the revue several hours too soon. They were in a state neither to make up nor to dress. The Hoffmann Girls saved the revue from disaster by replacing them at a moment's notice. In the morning, the showgirls, having recovered their wits, arrived, made their apologies and took off for America by the first available boat. Honour was satisfied.

It was not the only incident to affect that opening night. On the previous day, during the last dress rehearsal, the stage-hands came out on strike. The reason seemed to be trifling: some of the staff were protesting against the demands of a stage manager whom they considered to be too tyrannical. According to Jacques-Charles, who related the facts in his memoirs, this man was simply asking that the stage be swept with particular care – a very minor dispute which it ought to have been possible to settle with a few carefully-chosen words, but which rapidly degenerated. In support of his stage

manager, Jacques-Charles declared frigidly that those who did not wish to obey this order could depart forthwith. Perhaps it might have been better to have guarded his tongue before uttering such sentiments. In less time than it took to shift the scenery, the stage-hands resigned *en bloc*. The incident was really simply the straw which broke the camel's back. There had clearly been no communication for days between Pierre Foucret and the staff backstage. Having

sensed the seriousness of the situation, Jacques-Charles fortunately had made contingency plans. A few minutes after the departure of the stage-hands, he introduced his secret weapon – an emergency team with whom he had worked at the Olympia, in the days before the war. They struggled through that night but, on the next day, the scenes hung together without the least incident. The tradition that the show must go on had been maintained.

Earl Leslie: the fiancé of Miss

Is there anyone who can still believe that Mistinguett was not a faithful woman? During those three revues, when she had all men at her feet, only one of them shared her life. His name was Earl Leslie and he blended naturally into the company. Tall and blond, he was born in London and had been a dancer in the Dolly Sisters' troupe at the London Pavilion. His Parisian début was at the Casino, in one of Miss's revues. It was noticeable that he preferred frequenting bars and good restaurants to the company of pretty women. Whisky and wine were, it seemed, his preferred partners. However, with Mistinguett, Cupid's dart plunged deeply into him. It took him months to convince her of the sincerity of his feelings. She was not indifferent to his charm, but several times she rejected his advances. Beside himself with despair, he drowned his sorrow in alcohol. His work, over which he took extreme care, began to suffer and he was close to losing his place. Léon Volterra then took the situation in hand and, convinced of the comedian's talent, decided to play the matchmaker. He invited the two potential turtle-doves for the weekend to a mansion which he had just bought. That very night, Oh divine surprise, Mistinguett finally yielded to her suitor's advances. Was she truly in love? Or did she wish to teach a lesson to Maurice Chevalier (who she still hoped would return to her), by showing him that she could be loved by someone younger than herself? The mystery remains unsolved. The idyll continued, with ups and downs, until the last performances of *Paris qui tourne*. From time to time, Earl Leslie succumbed to drink's temptations and this, in the end, proved fatal. On the evening of the traditional charity Hospital Ball, being a little the worse for drink, he started, backstage, to insult Miss. Between exchanges he realized that the entire company and the foremost journalists in Paris were the privileged observers of this grievous scene. Both scoop and scandal had been ensured! Blushing with shame, he fled

without even waiting to change out of his stage costume and sought refuge with Jacques-Charles. He stayed in hiding for forty-eight hours, working off the wine and his remorse. The next day, crestfallen, he made his way to the theatre. But, dancer though he remained, he was never able to recapture Miss's heart after this *faux pas*.

THE FRENCH CANCAN IN THE CRAZY YEARS

While Mistinguett was triumphant on the stage of the Moulin Rouge, the dance hall, situated in the basement, continued the tradition of the quadrille. However, Messieurs Groussot and Fabert had brought the rhythm up to date. To tell the truth, the cancan of 1925 bore very little relationship to that of earlier days. The modern Goulues and Grilles d'Égouts simply had names such as Germaine Rieux, Mercedes, Daphnée, Chloé or Mimi Anoul. The mass of lace and the multiple petticoats remained, but the cotton stockings were replaced by silk. In a hall overlooked by a gallery, sixteen young and pretty dancers, identically attired in elegant evening dresses, performed a precisely controlled ballet, which the specialists described as acrobatic. The *chahut* was no longer an essential part but, later on at night, the girls might amuse themselves. Apart from this piece of bravura, what Messieurs Sandrini and Marionno provided every week was a new mime show, the favourite rendezvous for lovers of elegant festivities and Montmartre gaiety. That's Paris!

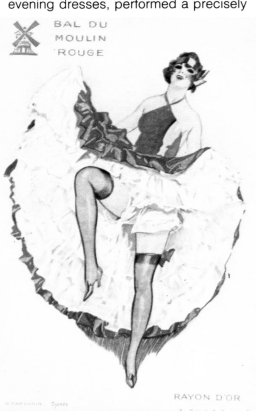

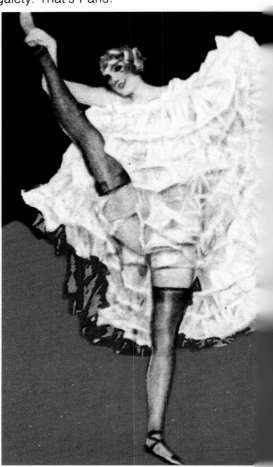

148

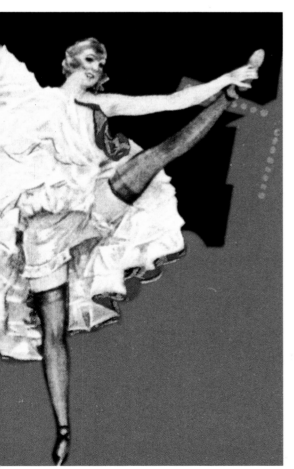

LA PANTHÈRE

FLEUR DE LOTUS

*All the steps in the cancan
retained their vigour
despite the invasion of the
Charleston and other
American rhythms*

149

THE PASSING OF THE GOLDEN AGE

Lilli Palmer, on the road to fame in Paris, before going on to London and Hollywood

Between Mistinguett's departure and the Second World War the Moulin Rouge was practically completely given over to the cinema. *La Route est belle* and *Le Roi des resquilleurs* each remained on the programme for a year. There were, however, five exceptions during this 'post-golden age'. In 1934 Maurice Catriens tried his hand at operetta: *The Land of Smiles* (with Willy Thunis) had been a success at the Gaîté-Lyrique, but this was not repeated at the Moulin Rouge. The same rebuff was suffered by *Victoria and her Hussar*. In 1937 Pierre Sandrini and Pierre Dubout, the directors of the famous Tabarin, took over the running of the Moulin Rouge dance hall, with the object of restoring to it the glamour which its universal reputation deserved. In a few days the decorator Robert Hartmann transformed the hall into an ultra-modern (for those days) night club, an essential investment for the staging of large-production ballets and dance spectaculars, which had to be models of their genre. At the time of the Universal Exhibition the New York Cotton Club was on the bill. The show which followed was only a flash in the pan and then, in 1939, before the showing of an exclusive film, Mistinguett made a return in the form of a farewell to the Moulin Rouge. It was a mini-revue with cult dancers and composers, which achieved some success only because of the names involved. The times had changed, and with them the atmosphere. The public were attracted by other forms of entertainment. It was the end of the golden age of French music-hall; no doubt it will never return.

16 December 1933:
VICTORIA ET SON HUSSARD
(VICTORIA AND HER HUSSAR)

French libretto by A. Mauprey and R. Coens. Music by Paul Abraham.
Models, scenery and costumes by Paul Larthe.

With Grazia Del Rio, Lilli Palmer (having got out of Germany, she was on her way to Hollywood, via Paris and London), Colette Fleuriot (future star of the Folies Bergère), Mercier, Peraldi and Marcel Lamy.

5 April 1936:
ENCHANTEMENT
(ENCHANTMENT)

Modern fantasy by Cheffours and Berthier.
Orchestra directed by A.J. Pasenti.

With the White Star Girls, Volbert, Susy Darys,
Nena-Sainz, Grania Venus, d'Artois, Paulette,
Mony and Ketty.

4 June 1937:
THE NEW YORK COTTON
CLUB

Lyrics and music by Benny Davis and J. Fred
Coots.
Production and dances by Clarence Rob-
inson.

With the Berry Brothers, Bill Bailey, Norton
and Margo, the Tramp Band, Whyte's Hopping Maniacs, Freddy and Ginger, Rollin
Smith, Jessye Scott and Vivian Eley.

With Teddy Hill and his Cotton Club
Orchestra.

'Elegance'
'The Cotton Plantation'
'The Jungle'
'The Suzy Q' (a new dance)
'The Wedding of Mr and Mrs Jazz'

'They've got the devil in them!' That was
the exclamation on the lips of everyone
who witnessed the Parisian debut of the
singers and dancers of the New York
Cotton Club last night. It was a triumph of
gaiety, verve, and exuberance, a mar-
riage of talent and taste, of sartorial and
musical harmony. The musicians, wearing magnificent white or beige felt hats
and splendid lilac, grey or green suits,

IN THE WINGS

THE MOST FAMOUS CABARET IN THE WORLD

In New York it's the most famous cabaret
of the thirties. It was 1923 when the
Cotton Club began its reign in Harlem.
For the past thirteen years celebrities
from all over the world, visiting New York,
have always made a detour to the little
place on Lennox Avenue. On 24 September 1936 the performers emigrated
to Broadway, an event which caused an
uproar. Ultra-conservatives predicted
failure, but it was an unprecedented
success. Three hours of applause on the
opening night, fifteen thousand in the
audiences in the first week, one hundred
thousand in the first two months.

Among them were Franklin D. Roosevelt,
the Countess of Warwick, Sir Cedric
Hardwicke, Billy Rose, Noël Coward,
Mary Pickford, Dick Powell, Johnny
Weissmuller, Cecil B. de Mille and Ernst
Lubitsch – staunch patrons for whose
pleasure nothing was left to chance:
scenery by Julian Harrison, ex-designer
of the sets for Cecil B. de Mille's
productions, costumes by Veronica,
creator of all the costumes for the Ziegfeld Follies. The shows produced their
discoveries, such as Cab Calloway and
Ethel Waters with her *Stormy Weather*,
as well as several dances, from the
Black Bottom to the Lindy Hop, and
including Truckin' and the Suzy Q. On
the Stock Exchange they call these safe
securities.

Les White's Hopping Maniacs in their original number, 'The lindy hop'

The Berry Brothers, stars of the Cotton Club

played their trumpets and tapped their feet to the plaudits of the audience. The dancers, attired in evening dresses, scaled the heights of frenzy and stepped out to an ever-faster rhythm. It was all done before unforgettable representations of the cotton plantation and the jungle, created in New York. It was Harlem finally arrived in Paris – what we have been years waiting for!

15 September 1937: PREMIER SPECTACLE MOULIN-ROUGE (THE PREMIER SHOW OF THE MOULIN ROUGE)

With Ray Ventura and his College Boys.

With the Percy-Athos Follies, the Manginis, Nanina and Joscho, and Myrio and Desha.

With the Twelve Moulin Belles.
The show presented and accompanied by Drena.

With Verdu and his ensemble.

Ray Ventura's greatest successes were always those by André Hornez and Paul Misraki

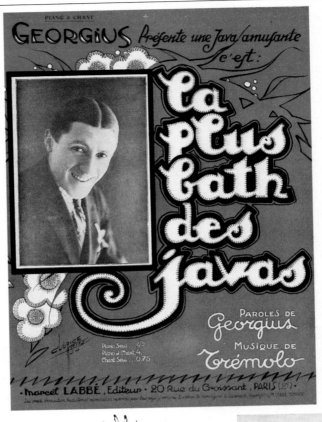

Grock also starred at the Moulin Rouge in a series of galas

The popular Georgius, whose immense talent as a writer is still to be appreciated

Georgius

His real name was Georges Guibourg and he was one of the most prolific actor-writers of the century. From 1913 until the end of the Second World War he wrote more than fifteen hundred songs. Some are still popular today: *Le lycée Papillon*, *Le Plus Bath des Javas* and others. On stage, his unfailingly distinctive style of dress – a white suit with a chrysanthemum in the button-hole – made him instantly identifiable.

Barbette,
the enigmatic discovery of
Jean Cocteau, as he was
seen both at the Moulin
Rouge and about town

Georges Milton and
André Baugé had two
of the greatest screen
successes of the period

Mistinguett, on her last appearance at the Moulin Rouge. Sketches of her dresses by Jean Dessès

10 February 1939: REFRAINS DE PARIS (SONGS OF PARIS)

With Mistinguett in her most popular numbers.
Show presented by the Gigolos Parisiens.

With Lino Carenzio, Carlos Machado, Toma, Léo Kok, Charles Richard, Léo Cady, Chevreau, Charlier and the Vivolis.

With the Fleurs d'Amour: Line, Ginette, Totoche, Martha, Maria and Paulette.

On the programme: *Ça c'est Paris, Valencia, C'est vrai, Je suis née Faubourg Saint-Denis, Mon homme, Je cherche un millionaire.*

The DARK YEARS

The he Second World War was not good for business in the night club on the Place Blanche. The dance hall below street level, run by Madame Guyol, was renamed the Robinson Moulin Rouge. There short revues such as *Folies de Montmartre* (Montmartre Follies) were staged, their only audiences consisting of German soldiers. In the main auditorium, feature films continued to be shown, preceded from time to time by music-hall turns. In July 1944, a few weeks before the liberation of Paris, Edith Piaf appeared with, early in the programme, a newcomer called Yves Montand. She had originally chosen Roger Dann, but he was unavailable. She was faced with no alternative, but saw little future for this novice who, playing the 'hepcat' in an improbable checked jacket, tried without success to perform a cowboy repertoire. 'A singer from Marseilles!' she exclaimed. 'To find him here – it's the height of vulgarity.' Worse, she described him as an amateur. He returned the compliment in full by calling her a 'gossip-monger'. The atmosphere of their first meeting may be imagined. Montand started to sing. At the end of the third verse Piaf saw the light. She knew what use could be made of this artist in music-hall, provided that he changed his style. She immediately made him wear dark trousers and shirt, which he kept to thereafter. After that, she helped him to devise his repertoire. Years later Montand said of that meeting: 'Piaf saved me time, and that was invaluable. In the end I would have changed on my own, but with her advice I passed through that stage very quickly.'

The French cancan . . . for ever!

A NEW ERA OF SUCCESS

For a while the end of the Second World War seemed to sound the death knell of the Moulin Rouge. The Robinson Moulin Rouge closed its doors, while the running of the cinema, like so many other matters at that time, came under the control of the State. It was to be another six years before the sails of the most famous windmill in the world could be seen turning once more in the sky above the Place Blanche.

In 1951 Georges France, known as Jo France and founder of the Balajo, acquired the Moulin Rouge dance hall and undertook considerable renovation work. On 1 March 1951 the basement was empty, the walls bare and the floor broken up. On 22 June the new hall opened its doors. On the programme were dances and various entertainments including, naturally, the celebrated French cancan, while from time to time special evenings were organised. The most prestigious of these took place on 19 May 1953: the twenty-fifth anniversary of the hospital charity ball, the Bal des Petits Lits Blancs, organised by Guy des Cars.

In 1955 the establishment was repurchased by Joseph and Louis Clérico, with Jean Bauchet. At first they continued the tradition of the popular dance hall established by their predecessor. Then, four years later, they tried out a new scheme, revolutionary for the Place Blanche. They installed kitchens and offered an increasingly international clientele a 'dinner-show', with revues which were very slowly to achieve a worldwide reputation – although the first one, La Revue japonaise (The Japanese Revue), was only moderately successful.

In 1962 Jean Bauchet handed over control to Jacki Clérico, the son of Joseph. It was the beginning of a new era, and of a success which still continues to this day. With ever more brilliant shows and evenings attended by royalty

Paul Heuzé, of the Institut, retains memories of his Bohemian youth in Montmartre

and the greatest international stars, the Moulin Rouge has now regained its legendary place as the leading cabaret in the world, which it should never have lost.

*
* *

In 1951 Jo France entrusted the fitting-out of the new Moulin Rouge dance hall to Henri Mahé, a leading architect of those days. Immense work was immediately undertaken. The area occupied by the old hall was dug out and enlarged. The décor chosen was a skilful compromise between the past and the present. At the entrance, on the façade, two dancers in white stucco welcomed the visitor. Descending several steps, one found oneself in a sort of vast half-

Decorative design by Paul Mahé for the new Moulin Rouge (1951)

amphitheatre, with the dance floor dominated by three tiers of seats. At the end of the hall a recessed area was reserved for the two orchestras, one for the dancing, the other for the entertainment.

As for past glories, these could be found on a wall, where there was not the slightest difficulty in recognizing La Goulue, Jane Avril, Valentin le Désossé, the Prince of Wales (later Edward VII) and Toulouse-Lautrec. A few metres away, on a pillar, posters remembered other glories of the *caf'conc'* of the *Belle Epoque*: Polaire, Yvette Guilbert, Esther Lekain, Camille Stéfani . . . Such frescoes may still be admired if you spend an evening in the

Place Blanche; this local Pantheon still remains just as Henri Mahé conceived it.

Of the garden of 1889 not the slightest trace remains today. A building has, in fact, been erected where it stood.

Although, for lack of a precise plan, it is not possible to be completely certain, it seems that today's Moulin Rouge stands pretty well in the place occupied by the original hall. As for the fifteen hundred-seat cinema, one of the largest in Paris, this was closed to the public some ten years ago and converted into a rehearsal hall, exclusively for the use of the artists in the shows and the Doriss Girls.

JEAN BAUCHET: THE MAN ON THE FLYING SAILS

Having had a brilliant career as an acrobat, Jean Bauchet started a new career in another high-risk activity – he became the owner of several casinos, at Beirut, Forges-les-Eaux and Marrakesh.

It was in the last-named that, in 1952, he encountered Joseph and Louis Clérico, there to put on their Lido show. Two years later they decided to join forces to purchase the famous Bal Tabarin. The enterprise proved complex to operate. Access to the location was not easy and

parking (even then!) was problematical.

They then turned to the Moulin Rouge, which Jo France was hoping to relinquish. Jean Bauchet, and in particular Henriette, his wife, agreed to take over the wheel of this immense boat. They engaged Doris Haug, carried out the initial modernisation and opened the way to both dinner-shows and revues. Bauchet had returned, but he was now on the other side of the pathway to the stars.

The immortal Edith Piaf

The genius of Fernand Raynaud sparkles in his different creations, from Charlie Chaplin to Grock

The Moulin Rouge Music-Hall

Between 1951 and 1960 the most prestigious top-of-the-bill artists, as well as beginners with promising futures, appeared in the fortnightly shows. Their recruitment was mainly in the hands of André Pousse, a young impresario who later became a famous comedy actor. As for the orchestra, that for the most part was under the baton of René Leroux, later to become the director of the Folies Bergère.

Among the artists who were seen were:

– Charles Trenet (between two triumphant tours of the United States)

– Charles Aznavour (his first appearance in Paris)

– Line Renaud

– Bourvil

– Philippe Clay

– Roger Pierre and Jean-Marc Thibault

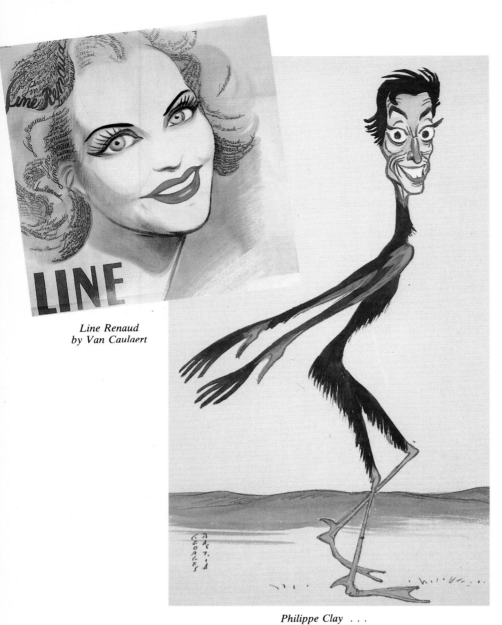

Line Renaud
by Van Caulaert

Philippe Clay . . .

Jean-Marc Thibault and Roger Pierre

– Fernand Raynaud

– Jacqueline François

– Lena Horne

– Johnnie Ray

– The Delta Rhythm Boys

– The Peter Sisters

– The Georges Rech ballet

– Florence and Frédéric (a ballet in which one of the scenes, a fishing scene, was performed by a very promising newcomer named Dany Saval).

In addition the programme included a traditional French cancan, initially directed by Pierre Bergé, and later on by Doris Haug. Among the dancers were Ginette and Annette Tanguy, the two sisters-in-law of Jean Richard.

As well as, from time to time, the surprise and unpaid services of a passing star – a practice observed by Elvis Presley each time he was in Paris, not for love of the stage but for that of a delectable dancer in the troupe, one of his favourite girl-friends.

The Peter Sisters

Bourvil sketched by Jean Bastia

Charles Trenet,
a gift from Heaven

The French cancan of the Fifties, with Jean-Louis Bert as the unforgettable Valentin le Désossé

GALA NIGHTS AT THE MOULIN

4 April 1952:
QUATRIÈME BAL DES BARBUS
(FOURTH BEARDED BALL)

Organised by the National Federation of Artists, Designers and Creative Workers and held for the benefit of the Federation's welfare fund. The evening was presided over by Robert Roquin and Alain Saint-Ogan, and the show was presented by Jacques Angelvin of *Télé-Paris*.

Competitions were held of beards, false whiskers and hairstyles.

With the Retrospective New Boppers, The Alcides, Chiquita Herrada, The Gravels, Marqueez and Dulac, Mick Micheyl and the celebrated French cancan. With Robert Rocca, introducing *La Tomate* (The Tomato).

5 April 1953:
CINQUIÈME BAL DES BARBUS
(FIFTH BEARDED BALL)

Organised by the National Federation of Artists, Designers and Creative Workers and held for the benefit of the Federation's welfare fund. The evening was presided over by Robert Roquin and Alain Saint-Ogan, and the show was presented by Jacques Angelvin of *Télé-Paris*.

Competitions were held of beards, false whiskers and hairstyles.

With Frou-Frou de Paris, Paul Arland, the Trio Pigalls, the four Bogdadis, Jean Bretonnière and the French cancan. With Robert Rocca, of *La Tomate*, and Pierre Dac.

19 May 1953:
VINGT-CINQUIÈME BAL DES PETITS LITS BLANCS
(TWENTY-FIFTH BALL OF THE LITTLE WHITE BEDS)

Presented by Léon Bailby. Artistic direction by Guy des Cars. The evening was introduced by Edmond Heuzé of the Institut de France, assisted by Annie Cordy, with:

HERVÉ MORVAN

– 'Fifty years of dance in five minutes', with the Moulin Rouge Belles and the four New Boppers.

– 'The ultra-modern customer', with Jean Davy, member of the Comédie Française, the clown Rhum, from the Médrano circus, and Christine Le Dard.

– The Likahos, the only turn in the world of authentic bullies.

– Jacques-Yves Le Toumelin, the greatest of the single-handed sailors.

– Lily Pons.

– Herta Frankel, the most amazing puppeteer of the period.

– Bing Crosby, for the first time on a European stage.

– Madeleine Robinson, 'Victoire' of the French screen.

– George and Bert Bernard, mimics who are unique in the world.

So the Silver Wedding of one of the finest charity institutions in the world has taken place in one of the most famous dance halls on the planet! An unlikely collaboration, whose success exceeded the most optimistic expectations. Judge for yourselves: an exceptional dinner served by the staff of the greatest Parisian restaurants, with, amongst others, Claude Terrail of La Tour d'Argent and Albert of Maxim's officiating in a hall overflowing with the most illustrious, from Gary Cooper, the great star of the most famous westerns, to Sonja Henie, the little fairy of the ice-rink, and not forgetting Charlie Chaplin, in an expensive suit bearing no resemblance to that worn by the Little Man. It was an act of friendship towards Léon Bailby, who was the first in France to spring to his defence on the release of *The Kid*.

On stage there were moments of emotion which we shall not forget: the traditional cancan, performed by the *corps de ballet* of the Opéra, and Jean Davy, illustrious member of the very solemn Comédie Française, accompanied by Rhum, one of the greatest of French clowns, performing the most unusual double act: a customer, both tipsy and irascible (Rhum), arrives late, bumps into everybody, insists on a table being laid for himself alone, before being served dinner by a phlegmatic *maître d'hôtel* (Davy). It was so well done that all the other diners were taken in.

Peter Ustinov himself delivered an irresistible lecture on the Bach cantatas, played by a Bavarian choir-master. Lily Pons, the great singer with the New York Metropolitan Opera, accepted an invitation, which she had always turned down, to give her famous interpretation of the Bell Song from *Lakmé*, while Josephine Baker, before beginning to sing *J'ai deux amours* (I have two loves), pre-

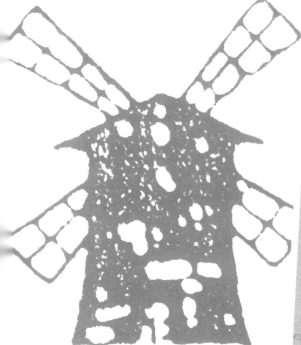

sented a tricolour bouquet composed of forget-me-nots, daisies and poppies to Chaplin who, she told us, 'loves children as much as she'. Finally, for the first time on a European stage, we applauded Bing Crosby — in English, but also in French — in the famous verses of *La Seine*.

Even the most traditional moment of the evening, the tombola, was extremely original. One of the major prizes, a Moulin Rouge dress with a belt embodying the famous sails, was made in a few minutes by Madame Bruyère in front of the audience! Congratulations are due to Guy des Cars, who had been appointed the artistic director of the show by Léon Bailby. Thanks to him, a grant of several millions will go to laboratories and research workers who, for many years, have been trying to find a cure for infantile leukaemia. The famous novelist has, not for the first time, transformed a dream into reality.

8 December 1960:
LA REVUE JAPONAISE
(THE JAPANESE REVUE)

Those who had not been warned in advance must have found the French cancan much changed. For a while the Moulin Rouge has gone Japanese. Starting last night, Henriette and Jean Bauchet are presenting the revue by Don Yada. While Japanese audiences are greeting American shows with enthusiasm, here we have the night club in the Place Blanche offering us a show which resembles the most traditional of *kabuki*.

Charmingly artistic scenes follow one another at a rapid pace — ballets and songs inspired by ancient popular legends which nevertheless seem to have nothing anachronistic about them in a Western-style spectacular. We even thought we heard, during one scene, a few notes from *Feuilles mortes* (Autumn Leaves).

The ear soon accustoms itself to the somewhat strange sounds of the music, as a succession of numbers which constitute a feast for the eyes are presented. The samurai, which we knew only from engravings, came to life before us, brandishing huge swords, while the geishas sang and danced with adorable grace. Several high-class acts were very intelligently introduced between the scenes: a gripping fight with daggers, water ballets, tight-rope walkers, jugglers, not forgetting several young girls who were practically nude, giving one the impression that Japan is perhaps in the process of discovering the art of the striptease!

赤い風車

Bal du
MOULIN ROUGE
PARIS

*Original design by O'Kley
for 'La revue japonaise'*

BAL
DU
MOULIN
ROUGE
PARIS

JACKI CLERICO: THE CONTROLLER OF THE DANCE HALL

Jacki Clérico's schoolroom was the Champs-Élysées. For today's Chairman of the Moulin Rouge learnt his trade at the Lido. Up to 1962 he held the post of its commercial director. On that date, when he was thirty-three years old, his father, Joseph Clérico, the owner of the night club, sent him on a suicide mission: to save the dance hall in the Place Blanche where, on some nights, the crowd in the auditorium actually numbered as many as forty. With him on this adventure he took Robert Rouzaud, who was responsible for publicity at the Lido, and who was immediately promoted to managing director of the Moulin Rouge.

After observing the scene for a few months, during which the existing staff were confirmed in their duties, the new Chairman announced his first show. It bore little relationship to today's spectaculars, for the budget did not exceed 350,000 francs, but it was a revue which met with general approval. Two years later the great enterprise was launched. Everything was torn down, and they started again from scratch. The stage was enlarged and, on an elevator capable of supporting a weight of two tons, a giant aquarium containing thirty-two thousand litres of filtered water was installed: it was to become celebrated throughout the world. For the first time in the history of the night club, four young girls aged from eighteen to twenty and a pair of nude dancers, called 'The Seagulls of Paris', performed a nautical ballet for the audience.

One revue followed another, with increasing success. Each one was based on a similar principle: four scenes, in which fantasy vied with the exotic, and where dolphins or even crocodiles appeared, and three variety turns of international status. Because the first two shows, *Frou Frou* and *Frisson*, were popular successes, Jacki Clérico, out of superstition, from that moment on chose only titles which began with the letter 'F'.

For *Fascination*, he installed rails with panels which allowed the stage to be extended, as well as a footbridge and the staircase on which all finales were subsequently held. In 1977 Robert Rouzaud was succeeded by Roland Léonar.

Today the Deputy Chairman's place is occupied by Jean-Jacques, Jacki's 34-year old son. Thus the succession is already ensured. The sails of the Moulin Rouge have once more been set to revolve for at least another hundred years.

HRH the Princess of Wales being welcomed by Jacki Clérico for a gala evening

THE GRAND MOULIN REVUES

20 March 1962:
CANCAN

Choreography by Doris Haug and Ruggero Angeletti.
New music by René Leroux, Hubert Degex, Jacques Solet, P. Vetheuil.
Musical director: René Leroux.
With the Doriss Girls, the Doriss Dancers, the Doriss Mannequins with Barbara Babs, Jean-Jacques Rolland, Guy Severyns, the Strong Brothers, Pier Cartier, Elsa and Waldo, Paul Berny, Cri-Cri, the Jit Bops and the Cincis.

The principal scenes:

– The Moulin Rouge in 1900
– Fever
– The Bird of Paradise
– Our Windmill of Love
– Paris Moulin Rouge: the banks of the Seine, the big stores, the Rue de la Paix, Saint-Germain-des-Prés, the Rue de Lappe, at the Moulin Rouge
– Finale with the entire company

1 April 1963:
FROU FROU

Spectacular revue.
New music by René Leroux, Jean Clauderic and P. Vetheuil.
Songs by Henri Betti.
Words by André Hornez.
Choreographer and dance mistress: Doris Haug.

Choreographer and stage director: Ruggero Angeletti.
Musical director: Michel Gamay.
Costumes and scenery: Georgio Veccia, Erté and Levasseur.

With the Doriss Dancers, the Moulin Rouge mannequins and the Renellis (Germany), Arnaut, Joan and Arnaut (United States), the Kims (Sweden), the Dalrays (Australia), Michael Allport and Jennifer (Great Britain) and the French cancan performed by Marie-Jeanne Meignier.

The principal scenes:

– Turn the pages
– The Moulin in the snow
– Peruvian Memories
– Cleopatra
– The Fair
– On the Embankment
– The Bird of Paradise
– The Moulin Rouge in 1900

15 April 1965:
FRISSON

Spectacular revue.
New music by René Leroux, Henri Betti and P. Vetheuil.
Musical arrangements: Jean Gruyer and René Leroux.
Orchestra Leader: André Dabonneville.
Words by André Hornez.
Choreographer and dance mistress: Doris Haug.
Choreographer and stage director: Ruggero Angeletti.
Costumes and scenery: Georgio Veccia, Erté and Levasseur.
With the Doriss Girls and the Belles du Moulin, the Rennos (acrobats), Luxor Gali Gali (conjuror), the Magic Aquarium (Anna Vaughan and Ralph Zaiser dancing amid fountains), the Pompoff Thedy family, Ulfi (tight-rope walker), Raspini (sleight of hand) and the French cancan performed by Marie-Jeanne Meignier.

The principal scenes:

– Rendezvous at the Moulin Rouge
– Fiesta
– The Magic Aquarium
– The Wine Harvest in Montmartre
– The Dance of the Snow
– Cleopatra
– The Moulin Rouge in 1900
– Tribute to Maurice

170

15 April 1967:
FASCINATION

A new fairy play.
New music by Henri Betti and Jean-Pierre Landreau.
Words by André Hornez.
Choreographer and dance mistress: Doris Haug.
Choreographer and stage director: Ruggero Angeletti.
Musical director: André Dabonneville.
Costumes and scenery: Georgio Veccia.

With the Doriss Girls and the Belles du Moulin, Betty Mars, Monroe (the fool with the roller), Luxor Gali Gali (fantastic illusions) and the Rennos. With the French cancan performed by Marie-Jeanne Meignier.

The principal scenes:

– Symphony of colours
– Artistic betrothal
– Intrigue in the Caribbean (with fantasies and underwater combat)
– Cascade
– Montmartre down the years: 1600 to 1967
– Grand Finale: Les Parisiennes, the enchanted gondolas and the entire company

20 March 1970:
FANTASTIC

A new fairy play.
New music by Henri Betti and Jean-Pierre Landreau.
Words by André Hornez.
Choreographer and dance mistress: Doris Haug.
Choreographer and stage director: Ruggero Angeletti.
Musical director: André Dabonneville.
Costumes and scenery: Georgio Veccia.

With the Doriss Girls and the Garçons de la Rue, Bob Bramson (skill in a ring), the Rios (how they jump!), Gene Destroy and the Marquis Family.
With the French cancan performed by Gery Atkins.

The principal scenes:

– Moulin Rouge TV magazine (various news items) with Léon Zitrone and Igor Barrère (maker of the film sequence)
– Join the dance
– Japanese daydream, with Kiki the dolphin and his friend Gillian
– The Crazy Thirties
– Love around the world
– Fantastic Grand Finale with the entire company.

29 March 1973:
FESTIVAL

A dream fantasy.
New music by Henri Betti and Jean-Pierre Landreau.
Arrangements by Pierre Delvincourt.
Words by André Hornez.
Choreographer and dance mistress: Doris Haug.
Choreographer and stage director: Ruggero Angeletti.
Musical director: André Dabonneville.
Costumes and scenery: Georgio Veccia.

With the Doriss Girls, the Belles du Moulin and the Garçons de la Rue, Bert Garden, juggler-comic, Fatima Zohra, an unusual yogi, Luxor Gali Gali, the fantastic illusionist, and the French cancan performed by René and Jackie Para. With a tribute to Maurice Chevalier: 'Oh Maurice', with Andrex.

The principal scenes:

– The animated Legend of the Moulin Rouge (in Cinemascope)
– Women are flowers
– Piracy in the Tropics (Wendy and the dolphins of Bruno Lienhardt)
– Wedding Day in eternal Russia
– Paris in 1900

1 April 1976:
FOLLEMENT

New music by Henri Betti and Jean-Pierre Landreau.
Words by André Hornez.
Choreographer and dance mistress: Doris Haug.
Choreographer and stage director: Ruggero Angeletti.
Musical director: André Dabonneville.
Costumes and scenery: Georgio Veccia.

With the Doriss Girls, Lisette Malidor, the Garçons de la Rue and the Belles du Moulin.
With Monroe (the fool with the roller), Kazbek and Zari (the prince and the slave), the Sally Brothers (attempting the impossible, youth and daring), the Pompoff Thedy Family and the French cancan performed by José Meson.

The principal scenes:

– The Chairman presents (in Cinemascope)
– Girls and guitars
– The Thousand and One Nights
– Brazil of my dreams
– The Universal Exhibition of 1900 (with the Moulin Rouge in 1900 and Lisette Malidor in the part of the woman with the jewels)
– The Moulin Rouge in 1978
– Grand *Follement* finale, with the grand telescopic and panoramic staircase, the enchanted gondolas and the flowery domes

22 December 1978:
FRÉNÉSIE

New music by Henri Betti, Don James and Pierre Delvincourt.
Additional songs by François Betti.
Words by André Hornez.
Choreographer and dance mistress: Doris Haug.
Choreographer and stage director: Ruggero Angeletti.
Musical director: André Dabonneville.
Costumes and scenery: Georgio Veccia.
With Watusi, the Doriss Girls and the Doriss Dancers.
With Monroe (the fool with the roller), the Sally Brothers (youth and daring), Luxor Gali Gali (fantastic illusions) and the French cancan.

The principal scenes:

– Invitation to the dance
– Gipsy dream
– Under Mexican skies
– 1925 in 25 minutes
– Grand finale with the entire company

Bal du Moulin Rouge

WATUSI dans frénésie 80

26 February 1983:
FEMMES, FEMMES, FEMMES

New music by Henri Betti and Jean-Pierre Landreau.
Words by André Hornez and Roland Léonar.
Choreograph by Doris Haug, Ruggero Angeletti and Larry Vickers.
Musical director: Roland Audefroy.
Costumes and scenery: Georgio Veccia.

With the Doriss Girls and Debbie de Coudreaux, with Joséphine Arnold, Steve Flanagan, Michael Ellis, Michelle Crawley, Kim Cantegreil, Tracy Morrell, Panos Metaxopoulos, Thierry Outrilla and Karl Vanderstaan.

With Hermanos Segura (talented to the tips of his toes), Elisabeth or Fabienne in the giant aquarium, the Nicolodis (youth and virtuosity), André Cagnard's horses and clowns, Marc Metral (the voice is free).

The principal scenes:

– Prologue
– In the Caribbean
– In the Wild West
– From everywhere (with the cancan of the Fifties)
– Grand Finale in Pink

12 February 1988:
FORMIDABLE

The Centenary Revue,
devised by Doris Haug and Ruggero Angeletti.
Costumes by Corrado Colabucci.
Scenery by Gaetano Castelli.
Music by Pierre Porte.
Words by Roland Léonar.
Musical director: Roland Audefroy.
Choreography by Bill Goodson.

With the Doriss Girls, The Doriss Dancers and Debbie Coudreaux, the Nicolodis (youth and virtuosity), André Cagnard's tumblers and horses, Karah-Khavak's crocodiles, Terry Parhade (a funny juggler), Marc Metral (the voice is free) and the French cancan performed by Ruggero Angeletti.

With Diane MacDonald, Grant Newsome, Herb MacCoy, Tracy Morrell, Michelle Dugan, Joséphine Arnold, Andrew Hargraves, Joachim Staaf, Gavin Mills and the company.

The principal scenes:

– Prologue: Formidable
– Under the desert sun
– Dream of Vienna
– A Centenary
– Thoughts of Maurice
– A Wink at Joséphine
– Grand Finale in red and white

DORIS HAUG:
THE LADY BEHIND THE SCENES

Sometimes the stars over Stuttgart and the sun of Casablanca can lead to the Place Blanche. As a ballet dancer in Germany, but too tall to become a prima ballerina, Doris Haug decided one day to try her luck in France.

She was engaged by the Bal Tabarin, but four months later was out of work when that establishment was shut down for good. After a short stay at La Nouvelle Eve, she started her own troupe, under the name of the Doriss Girls. Chance took her to Casablanca, in a casino being run by Jean Bauchet. In November 1957 the latter, now the director of the Moulin Rouge, asked Miss Doris to take control of the cancan in the Place Blanche. What began as a trial soon became something more. With the exception of the short interlude of *La Revue japonaise*, the Doriss Girls had come to Paris to stay. The four dancers of 1958 became twelve in 1961, and then thirty-six in 1963.

Today there are sixty-five of them who,

for seven days a week, take their turn on the stage. The girls must be at least five feet seven inches in height, and not more than five feet ten. They are recruited from all over Europe, particularly from England, and, from the age of sixteen, they are trained in the difficult school of the cancan. Some are unable to endure the torments of the splits for more than a month; the rest, of stouter stuff, duly take their place in the revue.

On three hundred evenings every year they perform their work, while several times each week, hidden in a box at the entrance to the auditorium, Doris Haug keeps her eye on the performance, linked by intercom to correct the slightest false movement. She had been the first to recognize the complexity of the choreography: 'In 1952, I had an audition as a dancer at the Moulin Rouge. When I realized the work that was involved, I turned down the offer of a job there, without any regret.'

ROLAND LÉONAR: FROM THE OPERA TO THE MOULIN ROUGE

Before becoming the managing director of the Moulin Rouge in 1977, Roland Léonar had been in turn singer, juvenile lead in comedy and operetta, music-hall comedian, song-writer, compère and even acrobatic dancer.

Born at Grenoble, his career began in 1938, on the stage of the town's municipal theatre. Firstly in the chorus, then second tenor in operetta and opera, he appeared in 1940 with Max Revol, at the Théâtre aux Armées. Two years later, as compère of a celebrated night club in Nice called the Perroquet, he was noticed by Mistinguett, who made him her partner for two years. She took him with her from the Alhambra to the Théâtre de l'Étoile, via the Casino de Paris.

He was then to be seen regularly in the company of other famous stars of the entertainment world: Edith Piaf, Frehel, Suzy Delair, Georges Milton, Charles Trenet, Fernandel and Bourvil. He was the juvenile lead in *La Bonne Hôtesse* (The Good Hostess), followed by *Ignace* (Ignatius), and he has also performed in and produced all the most famous operettas and operas.

Thus he has to his credit *The Gipsy Princess* by Kalman, *The Threepenny Opera* by Bertolt Brecht, *Bluebeard's Castle* by Béla Bartók, together with *The Bear* by Chekov, *Othello*, *Samson and Delilah*, *Il Trovatore*, *Carmen*, *Aïda*, *The Magic Flute*, *Fidelio*, *Faust* and *Bouchencoeur*, after Labiche. Very much the complete, all-round artist.

Roland Léonar and Mistinguett at the Alhambra

ANDRÉ HORNEZ: AUTHOR OF HAPPINESS

12 May 1905: Wailings of a new-born babe!

1926: Civil engineer with the Ministry of Works.

1927: After his first revues and operettas at Lille and for the school of the Ministry of Works, a decisive meeting with Saint-Granier, who took him on as his secretary.

1928: Collaboration with Saint-Granier.

1930: Saint-Granier ensures his engagement by Paramount, in place of himself. First sojourn in Hollywood: *The Big Pond*, directed by Ernst Lubitsch, with Maurice Chevalier.

1931–1939: Six visits to Hollywood, to work on fifteen films directed by Rouben Mamoulian and Ernst Lubitsch: *One hour with you, Love me tonight* and *The Merry Widow*, with Chevalier and Jeanette MacDonald. André Hornez was working alongside other of his compatriots employed in the Mecca of the cinema, including Marcel Achard, Léopold Marchand, Jacques Deval, Louis Verneuil. Later on, writing of this period, Maurice Chevalier commented: 'André Hornez – the most pleasant surprise I had in Hollywood.'
In between his visits to Hollywood, he became the friend and colleague of Paul Misraki. Jointly they provided Ray Ventura with his greatest successes. During this period André Hornez wrote the lyrics, often the scenarios and sometimes the dialogue for more than eighty films, from *Il était une gare* to *feux de joie*, and from *Retour à l'aube* to *Au son des guitares*.

1936: The liner *Normandie* made its maiden transatlantic crossing. It was also the title of a new musical comedy by Henri Decoin, André Hornez and Paul Misraki, at the Bouffes-Parisiens.

1945–1989: After his return from five years of captivity, he was to write more than one thousand songs, thirty musical comedies (*Le Chevalier Bayard* with Yves Montand and Henri Salvador, *Baratin* with Roger Nicolas, *Monsieur Nanar* with Bourvil, *Les Pieds Nickelés* with the Frères Jacques, *Mobilette* with Suzy Delair, etc), a hundred revues (at the Lido, the Folies-Begère, the Casino de Paris and the Moulin Rouge), comedies (at the Variétés, the Casino Montparnasse and the Bobino) and films (*Destins* with Tino Rossi, *Quai des Orfèvres* for Clouzot, together with *Mademoiselle s'amuse, Nons irons à Paris*, etc). He coined the word 'zazou' ('hepcat') in *Je suis swing*, by Johnny Hess, and always his songs were dominated by the universal popularity of *C'est si bon*, which was written with his friend Henri Betti, the most faithful of collaborators.

His only regret: that he never had the tragic touch, to enable him to write the sombre songs requested of him by Edith Piaf. It is undoubtedly better that way. Those who can give us so much happiness are so rare.

THE GRAND PARADE OF THE MOULIN ROUGE

The luxury of the scenes in the revues
'Frénésie' and 'Femmes, femmes,
femmes' dazzled the eyes and bewitched
the memory

179

Lisette Malidor,
the star of
'Follement'

*The great
comedian Andrex,
impersonating
Maurice Chevalier
in 'Festival'*

The French cancan and Debbie de Coudreaux (top, right), with the Belles du Moulin, the centre of attraction for audiences from all over the world

Les Belles

du Moulin

Watusi

Diane McDonald

Corrado Colabucci

Debbie
de Coudreaux

Ruth Lovick

187

An evocation of the Wild West for boys both big and small, with Elaine Thomas (top left) and Debbie de Coudreaux (top right), the queen of the saloon in 'Femmes, femmes, femmes'

NINETY YEARS OLD

Had he been able to attend the gala which celebrated the ninetieth anniversary of the Moulin Rouge, Toulouse-Lautrec would not have felt out of place. Indeed, for the occasion he would certainly have produced a poster or a canvas, which would have become immortal. Stars came from all parts of the world to commemorate the dance hall, as the great events in its history were remembered throughout the evening.

Thus, assembled with Madame Raymond Barre, the wife of the Prime Minister, and Madame Monique Pelletier, the Minister responsible for Women's Affairs, were leading figures in the cinema, the theatre, the variety stage, television, literature, painting and sport: Lino Ventura, Jacques Anquetil, Julien Clerc, Michel Sardou, Line Renaud, Sylvie Vartan, Yves Mourousi and Madame Soekarno.

These stars came to applaud other ones: singers, comedy actors and dancers who took part in a retrospective in the form of an international show. The masters of ceremony were Peter Ustinov and Jean-Claude Brialy together with, in order of their appearance: The Village People, Amanda Lear, Thierry de Luron, Nicole Croisille, Charles Aznavour, Sacha Distel, Dalida, Bernadette Lafont, in an Apache dance that Mistinguett would not have disowned, Jerry Lewis with his gags and his irresistible pantomiming and, above all, Ginger Rogers.

When the curtain rose to reveal the star in a magnificent dress of lamé and sable, she regaled an admiring audience with songs from *Mame* and *Hello Dolly*. The spectators, visibly as moved as she was herself, gave her an ovation, unaware that the surprises were not over. At the end of one of her songs, extracts from some of her films, where she danced with Fred Astaire, were shown. As the lights went up again, she reappeared – in the same costume as she had worn on the screen. A young man came on stage and reality joined forces with fiction as, in his arms, she rediscovered the rhythm of the past.

Imagine the ovation which the audience accorded her, and you will begin to form some small picture of this magic moment, from now on engraved for ever in our memories. As a souvenir of the evening, the star was presented by Sacha Distel with a straw hat which had belonged to Maurice Chevalier. Very much the appropriate symbol with which to salute the one who, as the creator of *Prosper*, possessed the secret of eternal youth.

Jean-Claude Brialy welcoming the unforgettable star Ginger Rogers

20 FEBRUARY 1988
THE CENTENARY REVUE

W ith all due deference to the birds of ill omen, Parisian life is alive and well, thank you very much, as at least nine hundred people can testify. This is the number of those who were privileged to be present at the Moulin Rouge, for the first night of *Formidable*, the centenary revue of the night club in the Place Blanche.

The backstage area and the dressing rooms have been completely renovated, but neither the auditorium nor the fashionable tradition has changed. For dinner it was necessary to lay out two thousand francs per person, which went to the Comité Français, UNICEF, the Cambridge Youth Theatre and the Children's Section of the Army Benevolent Fund, two charities which are dear to the heart of Her Majesty Queen Elizabeth.

And for good reason. The evening constituted a 'Royal Performance' in Paris. In London the latter is one of the most prestigious of British official events, attended each year by a member of the Royal Family. For the second time one has taken place in France. Five years ago it was Princess Anne who honoured with her presence the première of the previous revue, *Femmes, Femmes, Femmes*. A permanent contact between Buckingham Palace and Jean Miguel, the establishment's public relations manager, resulted in this second occasion. This time it was Prince Edward, the youngest of the family, who made the journey.

For this 'first appearance', protocol ensured that every step had been checked several weeks in advance. On the Boulevard de Clichy, where traffic was temporarily restricted to one side only, a huge jam upset a programme which had been planned to the minute. The blue Rolls-Royce of the British Ambassador carrying His Royal Highness arrived at twenty to nine, instead of the planned eight-fifteen. The crowd, which had been crammed behind barriers since six o'clock, greeted with modest applause this person whose face was not yet very familiar. Initial reactions were: 'He looks sweet' and 'Look how thin his hair is! In three years, he'll be completely bald.'

The welcome in the auditorium was much warmer. Greeted at the entrance by detachments of the Garde Républicaine and the Irish Guards presenting arms, Prince Edward was then given a standing ovation by the guests, as the Queen's Trumpeters played a fanfare, appearing on the stage in their traditional uniforms. A couple of minutes were accorded to a few of the three hundred photographers who had applied for passes, before dinner

HRH Prince Edward being welcomed by Jacki Clérico

was served. On the menu: grey pearls of the Caspian (caviar, really), *tournedos périgourdine*, and cherry dessert, all washed down with Dom Pérignon 1980. A smile at a *maître d'hôtel* would immediately bring you a bottle of water, or Bordeaux.

The Prince, who had resigned from the Marines and whose first love is the theatre, was visibly enjoying himself, even if protocol meant that he was able to converse only with his neighbours, the master of the house Jacki Clérico and Madame Clérico, together with the Minister for Foreign Affairs, Jean-Bernard Raimond and his wife, for whom it was also her first evening at the Moulin Rouge.

The other tables were thronged with Parisian Society, as well as a few 'outsiders'. The generations intermingled: Annie Cordy, Loulou Gasté (without Line Renaud, detained in Los Angeles), Alain Bernardin, Mireille Mathieu, Françoise Dorin, Henri Verneuil, Serge Craznianski, Marie-Christine Debourse, Gonzague Saint-Bris (with opera glasses, ideal for getting a closer view of the dancers), Albert Uderzo (because of a prologue to the revue in the form of an Asterix cartoon), Paul Loup Sulitzer and Alejandra (in an astonishing dress designed by Pierre Balmain), but also Anna Obregon, the rising star, with Patrice Calmette, her boyfriend, Juncal Rivero (Miss Spain and Miss Europe), Yan Erik, a Norwegian

rock musician with long green hair, Lio. and the young Vanessa Paradis (fifteen years old). Before the curtain went up she made the acquaintance of Paul-Louis Weiller (ninety-five years old), a member of the Institut and the oldest person present. At the end of a very touching conversation, the latter promised the young artist that he would listen to her new song *Manolo Manolete* that Monday morning.

Notable was the unexpected absence of the stars of the small screen. With the exception of Patrick Sabatier and William Leymergie, the television personalities were like the current activity on the channels, in other words on the decline.

The audience awarded an ovation to the ventriloquist Marc Metral and to Agathe, his white talking poodle, then exploded with laughter when a dancer playing a fortune-teller exclaimed, on catching sight of Michou and his table companion Yvette Horner: 'Monsieur, you seem to have left your wife at home.'

At the end of the finale, Prince Edward was keen to congratulate Debbie de Coudreaux, the revue's leading lady. As a souvenir he received a frame enclosing the original of a costume created in 1925 by Gesmar, whose style has influenced designers for more than fifty years. What could be more appropriate, that as the centenary approaches he should not be forgotten?

SPECIAL EVENINGS

Today's Moulin Rouge, in common with that of the past, has witnessed some great events: the ninetieth anniversary gala on 30 January 1980, together with shows by some of the greatest artists: Liza Minelli on 4 February 1982, Dean Martin on 3 July 1984, Frank Sinatra on 25 September 1984 and Mikhail Baryshnikov on 1 December 1986.

On top of these, there have been two special 'Royal Performances' in Paris – on 16 March 1983 in the presence of HRH Princess Anne, and on 20 February 1988 in the presence of HRH Prince Edward.

Frank Sinatra, with Madame and Monsieur Jacki Clérico

With Mireille Mathieu: the greatest dancer in the world, Mikhail Baryshnikov, cutting the anniversary cake

Artists and guests being presented to HRH Princess Anne

...ur and Madame Jacques Chirac
...ne Renaud and Gregory Peck

THE MOULIN ROUGE IN THE THEATRE

Some of the principal shows which have been inspired by the scenery and the history of the Moulin Rouge

DIE KEUSCHE SUSANNE

Operetta by Georg Okonkowski, after the farce *Le Fils à Papa* by Antony Mars and Maurice Desvallières. Music by Jean Gilbert. Presented on 26 February 1910 at the Wilhelm-Theater, Magdeburg.
(A light comedy, featuring the chaste Suzanne, winner of a prize for virtue, the second act taking place in the Moulin Rouge. The operetta was produced in Paris in 1913 as *La Chaste Suzanne*, in New York in 1911 as *Modest Suzanne*, and in London in 1912 (with the Moulin Rouge setting replaced) as *The Girl in the Taxi*.)

THE QUEEN OF THE MOULIN ROUGE

Musical comedy by Paul M. Potter. Lyrics by Vincent Bryan. Music by John T. Hall. Presented on 7 December 1908 at the Circle Theatre, New York.
With Flora Parker and Carter De Haven. (The show introduced the Apache dance to New York.)

A DAY IN PARIS

Ballet by Lt. Col. N. Newnham-Davis. Music composed and arranged by Cuthbert Clarke. Presented on 7 October 1908 at the Empire Theatre, London.
(The show introduced the Apache dance to London, danced by Beatrice Collier and Fred Farren.)

Programme for the ballet 'A day in Paris', which introduced the Apache Dance to London

Pierre Fresnay reincarnates Valentin de Désossé at the Théâtre Michel

LA PRINCESSE DE LA MOULIN-ROUGE (THE PRINCESS OF THE MOULIN ROUGE)

Operetta by Vincent Scotto.
Words by Codey and Denis.
Presented on 1 February 1924 at the Excelsior-Concert, Paris.

ON WITH THE DANCE

Revue by Noël Coward.
Produced by Charles B. Cochran.
Presented on 17 March 1925 at the Palace Theatre, Manchester and on 30 April 1925 at the London Pavilion.
(Included an impressionistic snapshot of the Moulin Rouge quadrille.)

VALENTIN LE DÉSOSSÉ

A play by Claude-André Puget.
Presented on 21 October 1932 at the Théâtre Michel, Paris.
With Pierre Fresnay, Hélène Perdière, Polaire and the Tabarin cancan.

WEST END SCANDALS

Revue presented on 6 August 1934 at the Garrick Theatre, London by London's Moulin Rouge.
With Anton Dolin and Jack Morrison.

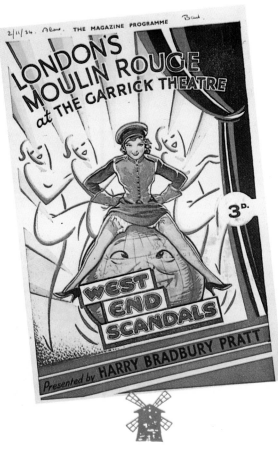

CANCAN
'THE MUSICAL'

Musical with words by Abe Burrows.
Music by Cole Porter.
Presented on 7 May 1953 at the Shubert Theater, New York.
With Lilo, Peter Cookson, Gwen Verdon.
892 performances.

The story of Môme Pistache, the proprietress of an Apache dance hall, which a magistrate of unimpeachable probity tries to close down. That is, until he falls in love with the pretty dancer, resigns his office and joins her to open the Bal du Paradis where, in an atmosphere of festivity and joyousness, they put on a show which is a great success.

Donna McKechnie, a stunning Môme Pistache, surrounded by the dancers in the last revival of 'Can-Can' at London's Strand Theatre

THE MOULIN ROUGE IN THE CINEMA

Some of the principal films inspired by the settings as well as the history of the
Moulin Rouge

LA CHASTE SUZANNE

(1938)
Produced by André Berthommier.
With Raimu,
Meg Lemonnier and Henri Garat.

A light comedy adapted from the operetta. A part of the vaudeville-like action takes place in the Moulin Rouge, between two performances of the French cancan.

MOULIN ROUGE

(1939)
A film by Yves Mirande.
With René Dary, Pierre Larquey, Maurice Escande, Simone Berriau, Marcel Vallée and Noël Roquevert.

A light comedy, embodying the black humour of Yves Mirande. Several scenes take place in a Moulin Rouge whose décor is that of the Théâtre Pigalle.

LA P'TITE FEMME DU MOULIN-ROUGE (THE LITTLE WOMAN OF THE MOULIN ROUGE)

(1950)
A film directed by Benito Perojo.
Based on *Die keusche Susanne*.
Musical arrangements by Paul Misraki.
With Tilda Thamar
and the French cancan by Margarita Walman.

DIE KEUSCHE SUSANNE

(1926)
Produced by Richard Eichberg and Hans Sturm.
With Lilian Harvey, Willy Fritsch, Albert Paulig and Ruth Wyeher.

MOULIN ROUGE

(1934)
Produced by Darryl F. Zanuck.
With Constance Bennett, Franchot Tone, Tullio Carminati and the Boswell Sisters.

FRENCH CANCAN

(1955)
A film by Jean Renoir.
Scenario, adaptation and dialogue:
André Paul Antoine and Jean Renoir.
Music by Georges Van Parys.
With Jean Gabin, Françoise Arnoul,
Maria Félix, Jean Paredes,
Philippe Clay, Michel Piccoli,
Valentine Tessier and Gabaroche.

This is a film which Jean Renoir called 'a
tapestry'. It is the story of a show business entrepreneur named Danglard, the

*The Moulin Rouge, dance hall and variety
theatre, represented in Jean Renoir's
masterpiece, 'French Cancan'. The character
played by Jean Gabin (below, right),
'Pygmalion' and lover of Françoise Arnoul,
was based on Joseph Oller*

LA CHASTE SUZANNE

(1951)
A film by César Amadori.
With Maruja Diaz, Noël Roquevert,
Armand Mestral and Duvalles.
With the voice of Mathé Althéry
and the dancers of the French cancan.

MOULIN ROUGE

(1953)
A film by John Huston.
Music by Georges Auric.
With José Ferrer, Colette Marchand,
Suzanne Flon and Zsa Zsa Gabor.

owner of the Paravent Chinois. He is about to open the Moulin Rouge, where the star is to be La Belle Abbesse, a lovely woman with a fiery temper who is a specialist in the belly-dance. One day, however, he sees Nini, the pretty laundress, as she is dancing. Instantly he has a presentiment that she could be the star of his new cabaret. An implacable rivalry between the two women is born . . .

This is the story of Toulouse-Lautrec at the Moulin Rouge, as revised and corrected by Hollywood. Sumptuous costumes, and unforgettable scenery and dancing, with La Goulue, Jane Avril, Valentin le Désossé and the rest. A classic of its kind. Of particular note was the performance of José Ferrer who, in order to ressemble the famous painter, suffered the tortures of a martyr, playing the part on his knees, with his legs strapped behind his back.

PIANO SEUL

Another version, another cinematographic masterpiece – 'Moulin Rouge' by John Huston, recounting the romanticised life of Toulouse-Lautrec, with José Ferrer, Suzanne Flon, Colette Marchand and Zsa-Zsa Gabor. La Goulue and Valentin le Désossé climbed straight out of the publicity panels and into the dance hall

CAN-CAN

(1960)
A film by Walter Lang.
Adapted by Dorothy Kingsley
and Charles Lederer.
Music by Cole Porter.
with Shirley MacLaine,
Frank Sinatra,
Maurice Chevalier, Juliet Prowse
and Louis Jourdan.

*The classic cancan pose
from Juliet Prowse. Surely
worthy of La Goulue?*

*The renowned trio of
Maurice Chevalier, Shirley
MacLaine and Frank
Sinatra in 'Can-Can'*

Some Observations on a Century at the Moulin Rouge

Charles B. Cochran's account of his first visit to the Moulin Rouge in 1891, from *Showman Looks On*.

Some early memories, some youthful impressions, are ineffaceable; they retain their vividness and colour through the years, fresh and unimpaired while more recent experiences become faint and blurred.

So it is that the excitement and interest of my first very brief visit to the Paris I was later to know so well remain unfaded, and I can recall without an effort the sights and scenes which stirred me when I first discovered the capital city in my enthusiastic youth in the year 1891. . . .

In those days all English visitors went to the Moulin Rouge, which, in spite of the Anglo-Saxon invaders, contrived to retain its Parisian tang. It was difficult to miss the sandwich-board men and the gay posters of Chéret on the kiosks of the boulevards with which Zidler, the famous director, called attention to his establishment, the name of which was renowned throughout the world. When I saw it in 1891 it was unique as a place of entertainment, and I have never seen any place like it since. Ascending the hill to the Boulevard de Clichy, one's first sight of the Red Mill, with its four enormous revolving vanes painted a brilliant red and outlined by electric lights, was anticipated by the red glow which it threw to the sky. The actual mill was on top of the entrance to the dance hall. Passing through the lobby, I recall a long corridor with posters by Chéret and Toulouse-Lautrec on the walls, which led to the great ballroom. On each side of the hall ran raised platforms from which spectators could watch the dancers. On the dance floor itself were little tables where drinks were served. Male customers were quickly invited to buy drinks by gaily dressed ladies, some of whom, it seemed to me in my twentieth year, were very charming. Certainly they were gaily dressed in many colours, and wore on their heads huge feathered and beflowered creations. The fact that it was the custom of the establishment for men to retain their headgear added something to the unconventionality of the scene, as they promenaded with the ladies, up and down in two opposite streams on each side of the long hall between the dancers, or formed a circle to watch them. Most of the Parisians were crowned with top-hats; the headgear of the foreigners was as varied as their nationalities. Even the celebrated male dancer, Valentin le Désossé, is shown in the foreground of Lautrec's Moulin Rouge poster wearing his very high hat.

To the left, as you entered the hall, was the garden, with a bandstand in the centre, around which paid dancers performed the famous Parisian *chahut*. No man took part in these dances, and it was fun to hear the shocked cries of the English matrons when the naughty ladies performed the splits, or *grand écart*, as it was called. As they held up their voluminous petticoats, despite layers of ruffles on their long drawers, there were always glimpses of pink skin to be seen. How shocked would those *petites danseuses* have been could they have seen our Phyllis Dixey!

As a diversion from dancing, the little ladies raced round the garden on little white donkeys – another excuse to display ruffles and legs. Those were innocent days!

A large papier mâché elephant stood in the garden; in the belly of the elephant many strange entertainments were given, and one in particular, indescribably gross, was hugely successful. Such laughter as greeted this performer has seldom been heard. More than one old stager will remember the performer's *affiche*:

Tous les soirs, de 8 à 9
LE PETOMANE
Le seul qui ne paie pas de droits d'AUTEUR!

The great magnet was the *Bal*, the chief attraction of which was the dancing of La Goulue, La Môme Fromage, Rayon d'Or and Jane Avril. La Goulue was generally partnered by a cadaverous-looking man in a tall – very tall – hat and tight jacket and trousers, called Valentin le Désossé. When dancing Valentin always kept his hat on, and it was a current joke that La Goulue was the only person in Paris who had ever seen Valentin with his head uncovered.

To amuse the tourists and the provincials who arrived early there was a *café-concert* from eight to nine. Naturally my young friend and I arrived even before the doors were open, and took places for the concert, at which appeared a tall skinny young woman, dressed in the traditional costume of an English nurse, with false projecting teeth, the characterstic mark of the English woman on the French comic stage of that period. The song was 'shocking,' and taking their cue from the *petit public* of Paris who, like the tourists, came early to get their money's worth, the intrepid Britishers giggled when the French roared with laughter. 'Miss Valérie,' the nurse, although prudish in the accepted British style, was not entirely deaf to the amorous proposals of those of her gentlemen patients who were disposed to be generous. It was cruel, but that it was the perfection of caricature and the work of an exceptional artiste was obvious even to the inexperienced but stage-struck youth of twenty that I was at the time. Even then Yvette Guilbert (the Nurse Valérie of the Moulin Rouge) was drawing an audience of writers, painters, and connoisseurs to Le Divan Japonais, where she appeared later in the evening with her plain dress, long black gloves, long bare neck, and red chignon immortalized in many drawings by Toulouse-Lautrec. At this time Yvette was twenty-six, and years of struggle, privation and determination had preceded her arrival at this point when, between the two places, she earned the total sum of 1,200 francs per month. The franc at this time was 25 to £1 sterling, but a Frenchwoman could buy much more with her twenty-five francs than the Englishwoman with her pound.

On the night that I saw Yvette at the Moulin Rouge a very few francs brought me a lot of fun, from dinner to a delicious breakfast of coffee and *croissants* the next morning, before I returned to my modest hotel for a bath.

Charles Castle quoting Paul Derval on the Moulin Rouge as the birthplace of striptease, from
The Folies Bergère.

The origin of striptease is said to be the *Bal des Quat'z' Arts* at midnight on 9 February 1893. A group of Paris
students had rented the Moulin Rouge for their celebrated Four Arts Ball, by tradition a night of orgiastic frenzy,
drunkenness and pandemonium. On this occasion the personal attractions of two girls were debated by their
admirers. The girls then stood on tables for their ankles to be judged. Competition extended to their legs, thighs,
hips, buttocks, breasts and shoulders. One girl ended up completely naked.

Next morning, however, Senator Béranger, a rather pompous, lugubrious fellow whose main aim was to question
the morals of the inhabitants and who had formed a League of Decency to prevent dogs from urinating in the street
(not on the grounds of sanitation so much as an example of indecent exposure), set to work to trace those
responsible for the display at the Moulin Rouge. Several weeks later, Mona and two or three of her admirers were
brought before a Paris court. The magistrates were lenient and fined them a mere 100 francs each. The Latin
Quarter, however, was not amused.

Hearing that effigies of himself (labelled 'The Father of Decency') were hanging from lamp-posts on the Boulevard
St Michel, Senator Béranger summoned the police and in the fracas that followed an innocent young man quietly
drinking Pernod at a pavement café on the Place de la Sorbonne was fatally wounded. As a result of the ensuing
riots, the Chief of Police was dismissed, and so the students decided that it was their inalienable right to enjoy the
sight of a naked woman if they so wished.

The following day the entire Latin quarter was up in arms. Gangs of students bore down on the Prefecture of Police
and laid siege to it. The youth of Paris was in open revolution. Troops were called in from the provinces; the police,
vastly outnumbered, held off the assailants as best they could; the Prefect of Police was dismissed. Order was
restored, but in championing Mona, the first 'nude' in Parisian show business, the students had proved once again
that the French capital had the democratic right to choose *liberté* – in any sense it wished.

Paul Derval (longtime director of the Folies Bergère) takes up the story:

Mona's lovely body had fired other imaginations beside those of her student audiences. Directors of music-halls
suddenly woke up to the fruitful possibilities of a new form of entertainment of which the public would never tire –
the nude. The stumbling block was, of course, the ubiquitous Senator Béranger. How was one to safeguard
oneself against the fulminations of the League of Decency?

The answer to this teasing question was forthcoming the following spring. On 13 March 1894, in a poky little
music-hall in the Rue des Martyrs boasting the exotic name of Le Divan Fayouau, a short sketch entitled *Le
Coucher d'Yvette* (Yvette Goes to Bed) was hailed with uproarious enthusiasm by an excited house.

The stratagem was a simple one. Since it was out of the question to exhibit an entirely naked woman, and since
an almost naked woman is never quite naked enough, evidently the thing to do was to rely on the spectator's
lubricous imagination by presenting him with the spectacle of an artist undressing by easy stages. Imagination
being always one jump ahead of reality, the spectator would see her as already naked when she had not yet
removed her last drapes.

Striptease was born; the vogue caught on like wildfire and soon every variety house in Paris had its own version of
Le Coucher d'Yvette and titles like *Le Bain de Maid* (The Maid Takes a Bath), *Suzanne et la Grand Chaleur* (Suzanne
in a Heatwave) and *Liane chez le Médécin* (Liane at the Doctor's) on the bills were enough to pack the house.

And on the Moulin Rouge of the 1980s:

Unlike the Folies Bergère, which is essentially a theatre, both the Lido and the Moulin Rouge present outstanding
shows which include dancing, cabaret, dinner and champagne. The cabaret performances take place twice nightly
at ten o'clock with a second show starting shortly after midnight, playing to capacity houses of some 2,000 at each
sitting. Coach-loads of tourists from all over the world, nowadays predominantly Japanese, fill the streets outside and
audiences wait in queues three deep to enjoy these magnificent shows – the sort of queues generally seen only
outside Wimbledon or a football match . . .

Nowadays, under the directorship of Roland Léonar, the Moulin Rouge opens its show with thirty-six Dorris
dancers flanked by eight statuesque nude models and four nude dancers; a far cry from the exposition of the cancan
for which the famous music-hall was renowned. The Brazilian female lead singer Watusi is the *grande vedette* of the
show, which emphasizes the current multi-racial vogue in Paris. The stage is filled with red and white befeathered
beauties of incredible sparkle and *tout d'un coup* there are seventy of them singing and performing to the 'Invitation
to the Dance' routine. The production numbers have a live orchestra, but the artists mime to backing tracks.
Speciality acts, jugglers, nude adagios and animal acts fill-in while sets are changed back-stage and the chorus put
on even more stunning costumes and feathers. But possibly the highlight of the 1982 show is the dolphin act. A
section of the stage descends into the bowels of the earth to reappear with a huge water tank containing a live
dolphin. This act involves the amusing dolphin who plays games with his trainer by removing first her bra and then her
loin-cloth, leaving her in a glittering G-string. She dives into the tank to retrieve her scanty costume from the dolphin, and
there is an under-water ballet between them as he swims about with a catch-me-if-you-can grin on his face.

Coda to the English Edition

The centenary of the Moulin Rouge was duly marked with appropriate celebrations, most immediately with a huge party attended by French cabinet ministers and cinema stars under the night sky on the terrace beneath the neon sails. For the general public, on New Year's Eve, there was a glittering television spectacular, in which the star names of the Moulin Rouge's earlier days were lovingly recreated, together with the songs they sang.

The centenary party was also chosen as the occasion for an announcement by the current owners of the Moulin Rouge, Florette Sely and Margaret Mony, the sisters who inherited it on the death of their mother in 1977. The Moulin Rouge name – surely a trade mark of rare value – was to be used to market a range of appropriate products – wine, champagne and perfume. On the labels will be a reproduction of one of the original Jules Chéret posters.

The Moulin Rouge has thus entered its second century by embarking upon yet another new phase. The famous red sails seem set to light up many a Parisian sunset yet.

ANDREW LAMB